10/31/94

To/ JOHN:

A BROTHER WESLEYAN
IN SPIRIT & BELIEF,
EXPERIENCE & LIFE.

IN HIM,

Dave

I.S. 11:1-5

The Communicator's Commentary

Isaiah 1-39

Lloyd J. Ogilvie
General Editor

The Communicator's Commentary

Isaiah 1-39

David L. McKenna

WORD BOOKS, PUBLISHER • DALLAS, TEXAS

Library of Congress Cataloging-in-Publication Data
Main entry under title:

The Communicator's Commentary
  Bibliography: p.
  Contents: OT16a. Isaiah 1–39/ by David L. McKenna
  1. Bible. O.T.—Commentaries. I. Ogilvie, Lloyd
David L. McKenna,
[(BS1151.2.C66 1986 221.7'7 86–11138)]
ISBN 0-8499-0422-6 (V. OT16a)

Printed in the United States of America

4 5 6 7 8 9 AGF 9 8 7 6 5 4 3 2 1

To

my sister Pat

With whom I share the ministry of grace

A Ph.D. in her own field
An author in her own right
A Christian in her own ministry

Contents

Editor's Preface

God has called all of His people to be communicators. Everyone who is in Christ is called into ministry. As ministers of "the manifold grace of God," all of us—clergy and laity—are commissioned with challenge to communicate our faith to individuals and groups, classes and congregations.

The Bible, God's Word , is the objective basis of the truth of His love and power that we seek to communicate. In response to urgent, unexpressed needs of pastors, teachers, Bible study leaders, church school teachers, small group enablers, and individual Christians, the Communicator's Commentary is offered as a penetrating search of the Scriptures of the Old and New Testament to enable vital personal and practical communication of the abundant life.

Many current commentaries and Bible study guides provide only some aspects of a communicator's needs. Some offer in-depth scholarship but no application to daily life. Others are so popular in approach that biblical roots are left unexplained. Few offer impelling illustrations that open windows for the reader to see the exciting application for today's struggles. And most of all, seldom have the expositors given the valuable outlines of passages so needed to help the preacher or teacher in his or her busy life to prepare for communicating the Word to congregations or classes.

This Communicator's Commentary series brings all of these elements together. The authors are scholar-preachers and teachers outstanding in their ability to make the Scriptures come alive for individuals and groups. They are noted for bringing together excellence in biblical scholarship, knowledge of the original Hebrew and Greek, sensitivity to people's needs, vivid illustrative material from biblical, classical, and contemporary sources, and lucid communication by the use of clear outlines of thought. Each has been selected to contribute to this series because of his Spirit-empowered ability to help people live in the skins of biblical characters and provide a "you-are-there" intensity to the drama of events of the Bible which have so much to say about our relationships and responsibilities today.

The design for the communicator's Commentary gives the reader an overall outline of each book of the Bible. Following the introduction, which reveals the author's approach and salient background on the book, each chapter of the commentary provides the Scripture to be exposited. The New King James Bible has been chosen for the Communicator's Commentary because it combines with integrity the beauty of language, underlying Hebrew and Greek textual basis, and thought-flow of the 1611 King James Version, while replacing obsolete verb forms and other archaisms with their everyday contemporary counterparts for greater readability. Reverence for God is preserved in the capitalization of all pronouns referring to the Father, Son, or Holy Spirit. Readers who are more comfortable with another translation can readily find the parallel passage by means of the chapter and verse reference at the end of each passage being exposited. The paragraphs of exposition combine fresh insights to the Scripture, application, rich illustrative material, and innovative ways of utilizing the vibrant truth for his or her own life and for the challenge of communicating it with vigor and vitality.

It has been gratifying to me as editor of this series to receive enthusiastic progress reports from each contributor. As they worked, all were gripped with new truths from Scripture—God-given insights into passages, previously not written in the literature of biblical explanation. A prime objective of this series is for each user to find the same awareness: that God speaks with newness through the Scriptures when we approach them with a ready mind and a willingness to communicate what He has given; that God delights to give communicators of His Word "I-never-saw-that-in-that-verse-before" intellectual insights so that our listeners and readers can have "I-never-realized-all-that-was-in-that-verse" spiritual experiences.

The thrust of the commentary series unequivocally affirms that God speaks through the Scriptures today to engender faith, enable adventuresome living of the abundant life, and establish the basis of obedient discipleship. The Bible, the unique Word of God, is unlimited as a resource for Christians in communicating our hope to others. It is our weapon in the battle for truth, the guide for ministry, and the irresistible force for introducing others to God.

A biblically rooted communication of the Gospel holds in unity and oneness what divergent movements have wrought asunder. This commentary series courageously presents personal faith, caring for individuals, and social responsibility as essential, inseparable dimensions of biblical Christianity. It seeks to present the quadrilateral Gospel in its fullness which calls us to unreserved commitment to Christ, unrestricted self-esteem in His grace, unqualified love for others in personal evangelism, and undying efforts to work for justice and righteousness in a sick and suffering world.

A growing renaissance in the church today is being led by clergy and laity who are biblically rooted, Christ-centered, and Holy Spirit-empowered. They have dared to listen to people's most urgent questions and deepest needs and then to God as He speaks throughout the Bible. Biblical preaching is the secret of growing churches. Bible study classes and small groups are equipping the laity for ministry in the world. Dynamic Christians are finding that daily study of God's Word allows the Spirit to do in them what He wishes to communicate through them to others. These days are the most exciting time since Pentecost. The Communicator's Commentary is offered to be a primary resource of new life for this renaissance.

It has been very encouraging to receive the enthusiastic responses of pastors and teachers to the twelve New Testament volumes of the Communicator's Commentary series. The letters from communicators on the firing line in pulpits, classes, study groups, and Bible fellowship clusters across the nation, as well as the reviews of scholars and publication analysts, have indicated that we have been on target meeting a need for a distinctly different kind of commentary on the Scriptures, a commentary that is primarily aimed at helping interpreters of the Bible to equip the laity for ministry.

This positive response has led the publisher to press on with an additional twenty-one volumes covering the books of the Old Testament. These new volumes rest upon the same goals and guidelines that undergird the New Testament volumes. Scholar-preachers with facility in Hebrew as well as vivid contemporary exposition have been selected as authors. The purpose throughout is to aid the preacher and teacher in the challenge and adventure of Old Testament exposition in communication. In each volume you will meet Yahweh, the "I AM" Lord who is Creator, Sustainer, and Redeemer in the unfolding drama of His call and care of Israel. He is the Lord who acts, intervenes, judges, and presses His people into the immense challenges and privileges of being a chosen people, a holy nation. And in the descriptive exposition of each passage, the implications of the ultimate revelation of Yahweh in Jesus Christ, His Son, our Lord, are carefully spelled out to maintain unity and oneness in the preaching and teaching of the Gospel.

Once again, it is my privilege to introduce the author of this volume, Dr. David McKenna. He is already familiar to may readers of the Communicator's Commentary because of his previous work on Mark and Job. These volumes, highly praised for their interpretive insight and practical wisdom, create an expectation that Dr. McKenna's study of Isaiah will be equally outstanding. Indeed, he has fulfilled this deservedly high expectation with this marvelous commentary on Isaiah.

Dr. McKenna approaches the text of Isaiah in full view of its theological, linguistic, and historical challenges. Though he has mastered the analytic discussions of the book, this commentary does far more than examine the prophecies of Isaiah in microscopic, analytic detail. Rather, it attempts to grasp the wholistic vision of God revealed to Isaiah the prophet. What Dr. McKenna undertakes as a communicator transcends the narrowly defined task of critical scholarship. If we are to see Isaiah's vision afresh, "we need to do more than just read the book of Isaiah," Dr. McKenna urges. We must prepare ourselves for an experience of the living, holy, righteous God. That is exactly what this commentary helps us to do.

Readers familiar with Dr. McKenna's work will once again appreciate his very thorough scholarship and clear exposition of the biblical text. New readers will be delighted to find him to be a very trustworthy interpreter of Scripture. As in his previous commentaries, Dr. McKenna illustrates the text of Isaiah with a wide range of materials, including personal stories, literary quotations, and trenchant applications to our contemporary culture. This commentary reflects not only careful scholarship and wise reflection but also Dr. McKenna's personal engagement with the biblical text. As he explains in the Author's Preface, Dr. McKenna heard God's voice through Isaiah at a crucial juncture in his professional life. He writes, therefore, as one who has been deeply impacted by the prophet's vision.

Since completing this commentary, David McKenna has been called by God into a new focus of ministry. After 12 years as President of Asbury Theological Seminary, he will retire in July, 1994 in order to devote more time to writing and consulting. During his tenure as president, Dr. McKenna has led Asbury onto the cutting edge of theological education. In this process, he has been recognized as a great statesman for God's Kingdom. His leadership touches not only Asbury Seminary and theological education in general but the church throughout the world. Dr. McKenna has exercised this leadership through an international speaking ministry, through more than a dozen books, and through his service to many Christian and educational organizations.

I am privileged to count Dr. McKenna as a covenant brother and a close friend. My experience of his personal faith and integrity increases my respect for this man of God and undergirds my endorsement of his commentary. I am especially grateful to David for his outstanding contributions to the Communicator's Commentary series, including this volume on Isaiah. He has helped the series reach the highest standards for excellence and usefulness to the modern communicator of God's word.

LLOYD OGILVIE

Author's Preface

Anyone who has tried to write a commentary on Isaiah knows how the prophet felt when he encountered the Lord "high and lifted up" in His holy temple. All human arrogance falls prostrate at the feet of the sovereign Lord. All human utterance fades to a whisper against the sound of "Holy, Holy, Holy" that the angels sing. All human righteousness becomes "Woe is me" in the pure light of The Holy One of Israel. All human ambition bows in shame under the prophetic privilege of seeing the vision of God and speaking the Word of God.

For the life of me, I cannot see how any student of the Word can come away from Isaiah without spiritual transformation. Never again can I enter the sanctuary of the Lord without expecting the hush of holy awe. Never again can I read the annals of human events without Isaiah's perspective of The Lord of History. Never again can I read a critical, linguistic analysis of Isaiah's text without mentally shouting, "But what's the message?" Most of all, never again can I assume that His calling to ministry is in my hands. When Isaiah asked God, "How long, O, LORD, how long?" he spoke my impatience with unproductive preaching, my frustration with people who won't listen, and especially, my desire to control my own destiny. God used Isaiah to teach me the lesson of faithfulness.

This story is very personal. While doing the research for writing this commentary on Isaiah, I confronted a career decision. After ten years as President of Asbury Theological Seminary, the logic of career planning beckoned me to consider one more executive move before retirement. The offer of a lifetime came along as a blank check for me to sign. Suddenly, a win-win choice loomed before me. I could continue as President of the Seminary or move to the presidency of another ministry with world dimensions in Christian higher education. Either presidency fulfilled my spiritual calling, but to remain at the Seminary meant continuity in role while the other position offered rare opportunities for my creative impulses.

While weighing the decision, I sought the counsel of George Brushaber, a longtime friend and colleague in the presidency. After hearing my dilemma of trying to choose between two attractive callings, George wisely answered, "When God calls us, He also releases us." In that Spirit-guided response, I realized that my dilemma was created by the lack of release from my calling to the Presidency of Asbury Theological Seminary.

Not by coincidence, my study of Isaiah had progressed to the sixth chapter of the book where the prophet is called and commissioned to speak the Word of God. Most sermons on Isaiah's calling stop with his response, "Here am I, send me." Few preachers go on to grapple with the prophet's plaintive cry, "How long, O, LORD, how long?" After learning the hard truth of the Word of judgment that he must speak, Isaiah wanted to know the time of his release from the prophetic calling. God gave him the same answer that He gave to me. To paraphrase the text, God said, "Until I release you, I call you to be faithful."

My dilemma disappeared. Without a release from my calling to the Presidency of Asbury, I declined the other offer and returned to my continuing role with an uncanny sense of peace in the decision. Less than a year later, Asbury Theological Seminary received the largest bequest given to a free-standing seminary in American history! Looking back upon that momentous event, I see the reward for faithfulness. Not that I was the indispensable agent in cultivating the gift or the worthy recipient of its grace because of my obedience. Quite to the contrary. The gift took me back into the awesome presence of the Holy God who writes human history with the impartial pen of justice and the indelible ink of mercy in order to fulfill His redemptive purpose. Before writing this commentary, I knew the joy of being obedient; after writing this commentary, I know the peace of being faithful

My partners in this project include my wife, Janet, who shared her husband with Isaiah during the sabbatical in which this commentary was written. After living for years in spacious presidential homes, we moved temporarily into a little cottage in Seattle, Washington for the sabbatical writing. Soon, we found that my level of concentration on the text of Isaiah required physical and mental space that infringed upon the daily duties of homemaking and the regular joys of phone calls, reading, shopping, and visiting that Janet enjoyed at home. Graciously, but firmly, she suggested that I repaint and refurnish a basement bedroom so that Isaiah and I could communicate without interruption. Of course, I obeyed and was reminded again how wise she is. When I surfaced after hours with Isaiah, I could leave him in the basement study and give full attention to Janet. We now laugh at the experience and thank God for giving us a preretirement lesson on living together after forty-three years of marriage.

Rob, our youngest son, partnered in the project as well. We intruded into his space in the little house in Seattle for the four months of sabbatical time. After six years of independent living during college and graduate school, it was not easy to reenter the world where mom and dad worry about your sleep and fuss about picking up your room. Yet, the bond of love between us grew even stronger as we rejoined the family table with mom's cooking and dad's latest spiritual insight from the Book of Isaiah. Those memories are permanently etched between the pages of this commentary.

Other partners in this writing to whom I am grateful include: The Board of Trustees of Asbury Theological Seminary, whose enlightened policy of presidential preservation provided me with the sabbatical opportunity; Provost Robert Mulholland, who served as chief executive officer in my absence and stayed true to our tongue-in-cheek agreement, "You don't call me and I won't call you"; Executive Assistant Sheila Lovell, whose editorial gifts for style, grammar, and footnotes relieved my dread of such details; and Presidential Secretary Carolyn Dock, who typed, typed, and retyped both volumes of the manuscript. Nor can I forget the two persons who gave me incentive to write the commentary by their honest encouragement and questionable flattery: Lloyd Ogilvie, my beloved covenant brother, and Floyd Thatcher, my mentor for every book I have ever written. For all of my partners, I praise God.

DAVID L. MCKENNA

Introduction to Isaiah

How do you communicate a vision? Recall the times when you have awakened from a vivid, multicolored dream. As you try to describe the experience, some events and images come immediately to mind with the clarity of a real-life happening. Other events defy description except as you struggle for a comparison by saying, "It was like falling off a cliff or being swept out to sea." Even while you speak, other images flash back into mind—sometimes grotesque, sometimes glamorous, and almost always disappearing before you can find words to picture them.

All of our skills of communication are put to the test when we try to describe a dream. One moment we are like a news reporter on the scene pointing out facts and details. A moment later, we are a color commentator fleshing out the facts with analogies, metaphors, and similes that bring the dream into the realm of common experience. Still another moment will test our poetic powers as we reach deep into the thesaurus of our mind to find the sounds of words that rise and fall with the rhythm of the dream.

Time, as well, becomes a blur of past, present, and future in the fleeting action of a dream. Actual happenings in history make strange connections with current events and just as quickly fade into premonitions of things to come. So history and prophecy, fact and fantasy, prose and poetry all go into the interpretation of a dream. Even then, we usually fall back in frustration as images recede into the subconscious and words fail to embrace their meaning.

With these thoughts in mind, put yourself in Isaiah's place. By his own word in the first verse of the book that bears his name, he tells us that his purpose is to communicate "the vision" he saw concerning "Judah and Jerusalem" during the "reigns of the Kings Uzziah, Ahaz, Jotham, and Hezekiah." No other claim is made. Isaiah does not purport to write a book of history, such as First and Second Kings, or a book of poetry, such as Psalms, or a book of wisdom, such as

Proverbs. He does not even profess to be writing prophecy, such as Daniel. Rather, like the final answer on a multiple choice test, Isaiah will write with "all of the above" to communicate the vision shown to him by God. Without that perspective, we cannot understand Isaiah. Scholars who insist that the unity and credibility of Isaiah depend upon conformity to the chronology of history, the discipline of logical sequence, or consistency in writing style, miss the point. Western minds, particularly those schooled in German rationalism, display an arrogance of "left brain" seeing, thinking, speaking, and writing. Presumably, unless the communication is linear, logical, sequential, and quantifiable, it cannot be correct. No wonder that Isaiah is the most controversial book of the Bible—literally the litmus test for dividing liberal and conservative scholars. By trying to prove their case for the multiple or single authorship of Isaiah by logical analysis, neither liberals nor conservatives do justice to the book.

Isaiah needs to be read and interpreted by an African, Asian, or Native American mind that still "sees things whole." African students enter a seminary in their homeland, for instance, with a learning perspective based upon creation theology. The whole is greater than the sum of the parts and over the whole is the pronouncement, "It is very good." Their first lesson, however, requires a radical reworking of that holistic perspective in order to understand a lecture by a professor schooled in Europe who dissects the whole into parts for analysis, but like Humpty-Dumpty, never puts it back together again.

Isaiah would have failed the course. When necessary, he demonstrates his ability to be logical and analytical. How often have we quoted his call to Judah in the opening chapter of the book, "Come now, and let us reason together, says the LORD" (1:18)? But to take that verse out of context and use it to justify our Western rationalism is to violate the text and tone of Isaiah's writing. What appears to be a laser beam of logic will suddenly burst into a spectrum of light with all the variations of color, tone, and intensity that we see in a skyrocket.

Isaiah, for instance, is a master of the metaphor. In his communication, he uses the metaphor as an ingenious instrument for conveying God's Word in such a way that neither kings nor commoners can mistake its meaning. His metaphors alone make a study in themeselves. What reader of Isaiah can ever forget Judah as God's "beloved vineyard" that grows only bitter grapes (5:1), Egypt as a bankrupt empire likened to "stubs of a smoking firebrand" (7:4), rebellious leaders of Judah "pulling sin like a cart" (5:18), God "shaving with a hired razor" in using Assyria as an instrument of judgment (7:20), sin that leaves a "bed too short and a covering too narrow" (28:20), or the promise of the "desert blooming as a rose" (35:1)? On and on the metaphors go, complemented by the creative use of comparisons that put sin and grace, trust and rebellion, judgment and blessing in unmistakable relief. To study Isaiah we need freedom of intellect and imagination to enter into the spirit and style of his prophecy.

Even with this perspective, we do not capture the full force of Isaiah's vision. As Oscar Wilde, the Irish literary wit, said to William Yeats, another renowned Irish countryman, "We are too poetic to be poets." The same can be said of Isaiah. He is too poetic to be a "poet," too historical to be a "historian," and too prophetic to be a "prophet." To date, no critical tool of biblical scholarship or frame of reference for theological position has closed the circle of meaning on Isaiah's vision. He remains too poetic, too historical, and too prophetic to be squeezed into the small circle of a closed mind.

But wait. Isaiah is not out of date. His critics are. In an age of television, communication is again visual—appealing to the imagination, varying in style of presentation, intermingling two or three story lines, and counting upon impact to carry the message. Almost fifty years ago, Marshall McLuhan foresaw contemporary communication when he announced, "The medium is the message."[1] Isaiah would have agreed and disagreed. With him, the message and the medium were essentially different in substance, but inseparable in communication. While the Word of God that Isaiah spoke stood alone as eternal truth, the medium of the messenger served as an amplifier for impact.

Isaiah's vision of the Lord, "high and lifted up" (6:1), proves the point. As the medium of the message, Isaiah himself had to be called, cleansed, and commissioned by God before he could speak as God would speak. For this reason alone, we need to do more than just read the book of Isaiah. To catch a glimpse of Isaiah's vision, we too must ready ourselves to read by entering the presence of the holy God, confessing the sin in ourselves, experiencing the cleansing fire upon our lips, and opening ourselves to Isaiah's message of judgment and hope. To be understood, Isaiah must be experienced.

Make no mistake. While the media for Isaiah's prophecy fire the imagination, his message is deadly serious. Eternal themes of God's sovereignty, holiness, judgment, and grace literally lace the text from beginning to end. Those who take *Isaiah* apart and leave it in pieces fail to see the single-mindedness of the prophet. Isaiah lived and died to speak the Word of God to Judah and Jerusalem as chosen vehicles for a global message to future generations. His integrity does not depend upon historical chronology or literary style, but upon consistent communication of God's *vision* in the present and to the future. Isaiah belongs to the ages, not just as a prophet, but as a communicator who speaks to us today.

Isaiah the Theologian

The prophecy of Isaiah can be read as a biography of the character of God. From beginning to end, as God speaks through the prophet He reveals the attributes that belong exclusively to the One who declares to all generations, "I, the LORD, am the first; and with the last, I am He" (41:4). From this declaration come the attributes of God that Isaiah extols as the grand theme for his prophecy.

The Holiness of God

Isaiah's favorite name for God is "The Holy One of Israel." To Isaiah, the name is more than a title of respect. At the time of his calling to be a prophet, Isaiah saw "The Holy One of Israel" on the throne of the universe and heard the angels sing,

> Holy, Holy, Holy is the LORD of hosts;
> The whole earth is full of His glory!
>
> *Isaiah 6:3*

In the presence of the Holy, Isaiah confessed his own sinfulness in order to be sanctified by fire and set apart for his own holy task.

The Justice of God

As Isaiah experienced the holiness of God in his own sanctification, he also saw the outworking of God's holiness in the cause of social justice. Out of His holiness, God speaks:

> Woe to those who decree unrighteous decrees,
> Who write misfortune . . . ,
> To rob the needy of justice
> And to take what is right from the poor of My people,
> That widows may be their prey,
> And that they may rob the fatherless.
>
> *Isaiah 10:1–2*

To Isaiah, the holiness of God is not an abstract attribute without practical application. For both God and His people, holiness is the expression of personal righteousness and social justice.

The Power of God

Isaiah saw the omnipotence of God in His plan for human history and His use of the nations of the world as the instruments for working His sovereign will. No Scripture better expresses His power than when Isaiah speaks of God's judgment against the ancient superpower of Assyria:

> This is the purpose that is purposed
>   against the whole earth,
> And this is the hand that is stretched
>   out over all nations.
> For the LORD of hosts has purposed,
> And who will annul it?
> His hand is stretched out,
> And who will turn it back?
>
> *Isaiah 14:26–27*

The Wisdom of God

Although Isaiah and Job shared the discovery that God does "as He pleases" (Job 23:13), this does not mean that His actions are whimsical or arbitrary. Wisdom, often beyond human comprehension, guides His use of power and determines the design of His redemptive plan for the whole world. Along with Job, Isaiah marvels at the mysteries of God's way and concludes,

> This also comes from the LORD of hosts,
> Who is wonderful in counsel
>   and excellent in guidance.
>
> *Isaiah 28:29*

23

The Judgment of God

As another expression of His holiness, God cannot tolerate sin, especially the sin of pride in which human arrogance contends with divine sovereignty. So, whenever human pride is encountered among either the children of Israel or the nations of the world, Isaiah sees the unrelenting judgment of God:

> The lofty looks of man shall be humbled,
> The haughtiness of men
>   shall be bowed down,
> And the LORD alone
>   shall be exalted in that day.

Isaiah 2:11

The Grace of God

With good reason, Isaiah is known as the "prophet of hope." First-time readers of his book might think that he would better be known as the "prophet of doom." Much of his writing does deal with God's wrathful judgment upon the children of Israel and the nations of the world. However, if you read the book with a view to catching the spirit of Isaiah's message, you will note that his judgment is pronounced with pain for his people, his nation, and his city. Moreover, when God calls him to his prophetic ministry, He gives him two promises of hope for his message.

One promise is the hope of a *remnant* from among the rebellious children of Israel whose faith God would honor to restore Judah and Jerusalem (6:13). The other promise is the hope of a *Savior* who will be God's suffering servant to redeem the children of Israel and all people of the world (6:13). Neither of these promises is merited by God's chosen people. Quite the contrary, Isaiah's prophecy could justifiably stop with God's wrath against a rebellious family. Grace—the unmerited favor of God—is the only explanation for the prophecies of hope. And just a tiny touch of grace is sufficient to redeem the world. So when Isaiah breaks out into song or waxes eloquent with poetry, he sings and speaks of the grace of God to let us know that even divine judgment is given for our redemption.

The Promise of God

Martin Luther King is best known for his speech, "I Have a Dream." He dreamed of equality of the races and social justice for all people. The book of Isaiah might be read as God saying, "I Have a Dream." If so, we would see that God dreamed of a future in which righteousness prevailed among the people and peace prevailed among the nations. God then went so far as to foretell how He planned to redeem the world. In the most magnificent poetry of the Old or New Testament, He foretells the coming of His servant who will bear the names, "Wonderful, Counselor, Mighty God, Everlasting Father, Prince of Peace" (9:6).

Later on, God lets Isaiah see into the mission and the ministry of the Servant of the Lord (chs. 42, 49, 50, 52, and 53). Through His Servant will come "glory for Zion" (ch. 54), "salvation for all peoples" (ch. 56), "freedom for all the oppressed" (ch. 61), "a new name for Jerusalem" (ch. 62), "new heavens and a new earth" (ch. 65), "and all nations seeing the glory of the Lord" (ch. 66). Isaiah never lived to see all of God's promises come true. The prophet's bold declaration of Judah's return from exile, and Jerusalem's restoration as a city, took place more than a century after his death. For us who still await the fulfillment of all God's promises, Isaiah is our encouragement. No promise has been proven false or been canceled by the events of history. Isaiah's posthumous hope is our assurance.

ISAIAH THE PROPHET

A prophet is easily misunderstood and often misinterpreted. If the average person were asked to define a prophet today, wild answers would come back. To some, a prophet is a hustler who gains attention by predictions that play upon the fears of people. In Korea, for instance, self-proclaimed prophets have predicted the imminent return of Christ and led their followers to the top of a mountain to await His coming. To others, a prophet is a spiritually-gifted soul to whom the Holy Spirit has given a "word of prophecy" regarding present and future events. Some charismatic televangelists will claim this gift. To still others, a prophet is an interpreter of God's word in dispensational detail that puts dates, names, and results on biblical prophecy, especially the book of Revelation. Hal Lindsey's best-selling book, *The Late Great Planet Earth*,[2] and its sequels, are examples.

Biblical prophets stand apart from other prophets. For one thing, a biblical prophet does not exploit the gift of prophecy for personal gain. As with Isaiah, no Old Testament prophets call attention to themselves except to record in detail the account of their calling and commissioning by God. For another thing, biblical prophets speak for God, not for themselves. Without exception, they certify their message with the claim, "Yahweh says. . . ." Furthermore, they speak a balanced word of judgment and salvation. Without sparing the severity of God's wrath upon sinful humanity, judgment is not an end in itself. As we will see in Isaiah's prophecy, God's ultimate purpose in judgment is to save the sinner. A prophet who speaks only gloom or hope is not biblical. Finally, we note that biblical prophets address both ethical and eschatalogical issues. Ethical issues are most often current violations of social justice that God will not tolerate. Eschatalogical issues relate to the future, and in Isaiah's prophecy, range from the downfall of the Assyrian and Babylonian empires to the return of Israel from exile, the coming of the Messiah, the re-creation of new heavens and a new earth, and the reign of peace in all creation.

Without a doubt, Isaiah is a biblical prophet. He does not call attention to himself; he speaks only for God; he balances judgment and hope; and he addresses both the ethical issues of his day and the eschatalogical issues of the future. We see all of these qualities come into focus in the prophetic cycle of his message throughout the book of Isaiah. In graphic form, the prophetic cycle is shown on the next page.

We will see this cycle written in current history when Isaiah warns Ahaz against an entangling alliance with Egypt as protection against Assyria (7:1–8:15) and in future history when he prophesies the return of the children of Israel from Babylonian captivity (40:1–11). Not that the prophetic cycle is always obvious or complete. At times Isaiah breaks into the cycle at the point of punishment or with a word of promise; at other times he cuts the cycle short and lets us assume its completion; and, still, at other times he emphasizes one phase or another in order to press his point. Nevertheless, our study of Isaiah will be enhanced if we keep the prophetic cycle in mind. While Isaiah is a free spirit in his style of communication, his message is not helter-skelter. Everything he says and does is aimed toward the redemptive promise for humankind and to the ultimate end of praise to God.

26

THE PROPHETIC CYCLE

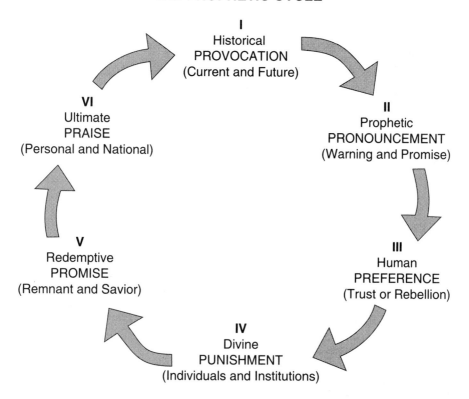

I
Historical
PROVOCATION
(Current and Future)

II
Prophetic
PRONOUNCEMENT
(Warning and Promise)

III
Human
PREFERENCE
(Trust or Rebellion)

IV
Divine
PUNISHMENT
(Individuals and Institutions)

V
Redemptive
PROMISE
(Remnant and Savior)

VI
Ultimate
PRAISE
(Personal and National)

Isaiah the Author

No one questioned the authorship of Isaiah until the advent of modern biblical scholarship. As early as the second century B.C., Ben Sira represented the Jewish perception of Isaiah when he honored the prophet with these words (Sirach 48:22b–25):

> [Isaiah was] a great man trustworthy in his vision.
> In his days the sun went backward;
> he lengthened the life of the king;
> By the power of the spirit he saw the
> last things.
> He comforted the mourners in Zion,

He revealed what was to occur to the
end of time,
And hidden things long before they
happened.[3]

A complementary record of 100 B.C. attests to the unity of the book and assumes that Isaiah authored the text. The recent archaeological discovery of the Isaiah scrolls at Qumran lends further evidence that Jewish scribes copied the text under the same assumption. Added evidence comes from Scripture itself. Jesus quoted Isaiah many times, often identifying the prophet by name. New Testament writers followed His example by quoting Isaiah freely, crediting him by name, and alluding to his writing more times than all of their references to other Old Testament prophets combined. Without question, *Isaiah* has always been included in the canon as a book intact and written by the author whose name it bears.

Of course, it can be argued that believers for centuries before and after Christ lacked the tools of critical scholarship that were used to call its unity and authorship into question. Maybe so, but the argument does not negate the fact of history: from the earliest known record until recent time, Jewish and Christian believers accepted the book of Isaiah as written by one person, unified in its text, and authorized as holy Scripture.

Modern biblical scholars are to be credited with the analysis of the book of Isaiah for its historical accuracy, literary consistency, and linguistic comparison. In the study of its historical accuracy, no one questions the fact that the prophecies of Isaiah bridge a span of time from 700 B.C. to 539 B.C., a period that extends long after the prophet's death. Nor does anyone question the problem of prophecies within the book that seem to jump back and forth among the eras of history, sometimes speaking as if the event is future and at other times inferring that the writer is presently witnessing the event. Cyrus' attack on Babylon is an oft-cited case in point (42:24–45:13). Although Isaiah has been dead for many years, the writer describes the attack as if he were an eyewitness. The episode puts to test the concept of the "prophetic present" in the vision of Isaiah. It also tests our belief in the nature of biblical revelation. Does God show Isaiah a vision of the future so real that the prophet reports it just as if he were an eyewitness?

Modern biblical scholars are equally perplexed by the variations in literary style in the book of Isaiah. Whereas chapters 1–39 touch down on verifiable points in Jewish history with prophetic responses that range from prose to poetry and song, chapters 40–66 are exclusively predictive and written as poetry with an idealistic touch. Critics also note that Isaiah does not identify himself by name in chapters 40–66. Presumably, a single author would use the same style and identification throughout his writing even though his prophecies shifted from the present to the future as they do in chapters 40–66.

Linguistic analysis takes the book of Isaiah apart word by word. Scholars have gone so far as to put the text on computer in order to compare word usage from one section to another. Using this method of study, Yehuda Radday discovered that the word variations were so great that a single author could not have written the book.[4] Rather than confirming the conclusion that the *first* Isaiah wrote chapters 1–39 and a *second* Isaiah or even a *third* Isaiah anonymously wrote chapters 40–66, his findings showed so many differences of word usage within both sections of the text that the authorship would require a school of Isaiahs to account for the variations!

Without denying the evident complexities and apparent contradictions in the book of Isaiah, the case against the unity of the book on historical, literary, and linguistic grounds can be addressed as a theological question. Basically, the question is "What do you believe about the nature and character of God?" If God is an immanent being who must work within natural forces, the credibility of the book of Isaiah will depend upon historical, literary, and linguistic analysis. But if God is a transcendent being who breaks through to human history with His own will and way, then the credibility of Isaiah rests upon a faith that overrides, but does not contradict, historical, literary, and linguistic analysis. We have a choice. If God is limited to natural forces, more than one Isaiah must be created to account for his prophecy in chapters 40–66 during the time of the Babylonian exile and after Isaiah's death. Even then, we must account for the predictions of the restoration of Israel from exile in chapters 60–66. Are they prophetic fact or fancy? If any prediction of things to come requires a new Isaiah who lives at the time of the event, we not only negate the meaning of prophecy, but demean the nature of God.

If, however, a transcendent God does break through to human history, all dimensions of the future change. The book of Isaiah becomes a God-breathed account of a vision given directly from God to man, but requiring the full range of literary and linguistic styles to convey a present and future message that is accurate to history, either during or after the lifetime of the messenger. If we take this view, the authorship of a single Isaiah is possible, but more importantly, the integrity of the message takes precedence over the analysis of the words.

The latter view is the one we take for this commentary on the book of Isaiah. Communication, in simplest terms, requires a sender, a message, and a receiver. Our purpose is to be a sender of Isaiah's message to our readers who will receive the message and become senders themselves. Therefore, without apology, we accept the inspiration and integrity of Isaiah's message for Israel in his time, after his death, and into the future for all generations to come.

NOTES

1. Marshall McLuhan, *Understanding Media: The Extensions of Man* (New York: Signet Books, 1964), 23.

2. Hal Lindsey, *The Late Great Planet Earth* (Grand Rapids: Zondervan, 1970).

3. James L. Mays, ed., *Harper's Bible Commentary* (San Francisco: Harper & Row, 1988), 542.

4. Yehuda Thomas Radday, *The Unity of Isaiah in the Light of Statistical Linguistics* (Hildesheim: H. A. Gerstenberg, 1973).

An Outline of Isaiah 1:1–39:8

Part I—The Vision Introduced 1:1–31
- I. Prologue to the Prophecy (1:1)
  - A. Who Is Isaiah?
  - B. What Is Isaiah's Message?
  - C. When Did Isaiah Prophesy?
  - D. Where Did Isaiah Prophesy?
- II. A Family in Rebellion: Judah and Jerusalem (1:2–31)
  - A. Children Turned Rebels (1:2–20)
    1. The Court of the LORD (1:2a)
    2. The Charge of Rebellion (1:2b–3)
    3. The Consequences of Corruption (1:4–9)
    4. The Offer of Clemency (1:10–17)
    5. The Appeal to Reason (1:18)
    6. The Verdict of Destiny (1:19–20)
  - B. A Daughter Turned Harlot (1:21–31)
    1. The Provocation of God (1:21–23)
    2. The Pronouncement Against Jerusalem (1:24–25)
    3. The Promise of Restoration (1:26–31)

Part II—The Vision Seen 2:1–5:30
- III. The Prophetic Cycle: Punishment and Promise (2:1–4:6)
  - A. The House of the LORD (2:1–4)
    1. God's Purpose for His House (2:1–2)
    2. The Nation's Response to the Invitation (2:3)
    3. The World's Path to Peace (2:4)
  - B. The Day of the LORD (2:5–22)
    1. A Time of Terror (2:5)
    2. The Folly of False Trust (2:6–8)
    3. The Capital Sins of Arrogance and Pride (2:9–11)
    4. The Day of Dread and Splendor (2:12–21)
    5. The Mortality of Humanity (2:22)
  - C. The Men of Zion (3:1–15)
    1. A Crisis of Resources (3:1–3)
    2. A Shortage of Leaders (3:4–7)
    3. A Heap of Ruins (3:8–12)
    4. A Betrayal of Trust (3:13–15)
  - D. The Women of Zion (3:16–4:1)
    1. Coconspirators in Corruption (3:16)
    2. Copartners in Loss (3:17–24)

PART ONE

The Vision Introduced

Isaiah 1:1–31

CHAPTER ONE

Prologue to The Prophecy

Isaiah 1:1

1 The vision of Isaiah the son of Amoz, which he
saw concerning Judah and Jerusalem in the days of
Uzziah, Jotham, Ahaz, and Hezekiah, kings of Judah.

Isaiah 1:1

Isaiah qualifies as a good journalist. In a preamble of one sentence, he answers four of the six questions that are called "The Writer's Friends"—*who, what, where,* and *when.* With this factual introduction, our appetite is whetted to read the text and find out the answers to the two remaining questions, *why,* and *how.*

WHO IS ISAIAH?

The answer to the question, *who,* is simply stated as "Isaiah, son of Amoz." Two facts come with the name. One, Isaiah means "the Lord is salvation"—the theme of his prophecy. Evidently, from his birth and christening, Isaiah bore the destiny as a prophet of God. One can imagine a scene similar to the angel's visitation of the virgin Mary when Isaiah's mother-to-be is told that her unborn son is chosen to be a prophet with the name to match his message. Or perhaps in less dramatic but equally compelling fashion, she may have been a devout woman who named her son in honor of the Lord whom she loved.

What's in a name? Paul Tournier, the celebrated Swiss psychiatrist, has written a book entitled *The Naming of Persons.*[1] Tournier's experience as a Christian counselor and therapist tells him that the name we bear directly affects our sense of self-worth and our role in life. A boy with the name of Max will react differently than a boy named Josiah. Or a girl named Crystal will see herself differently than a girl

41

named Mabel. Tournier goes so far as to say that the nicknames we bear shape our identity. A crippled child nicknamed "Limpy" will share the trauma of an obese child dubbed "Fatso." Even in these cases, Tournier says that it is better to bear a nickname of derision than to be ignored as a person without individual identity. So, while we will never know how Isaiah got his name, we do know the result. To be known by the name that means "the Lord is salvation" is to set the prophet apart as a man of destiny.

Despite the impressive meaning of his given name and his reputation as the greatest of Old Testament prophets, Isaiah entertains no grandeur for himself. After introducing himself to us by name in this opening verse, he limits further autobiographical information in the book to those encounters with God in which he lets us know that he is only an instrument for a voice that is not his own. Like Jesus, he will not speak for himself, but only as God shows him what to say.

A second autobiographical fact is found in Isaiah's family name as the "Son of Amoz." Again, our knowledge of Amoz and his family is severely limited. What we do know about Amoz, however, is essential to our study. Other sources of Old Testament history show that Amoz and his family stood in royal lineage to the kings of Judah. Again, we ask, "What's in a name?" As the son of Amoz with blue blood in his veins, Isaiah enjoyed the privilege of immediate access into the royal court and into the presence of the king. His message required this privilege. While Isaiah often spoke to the masses of people in Judah, Jerusalem, and surrounding nations, the throne room of the king served as his "bully pulpit."

The children of Israel had asked God for a king to rule over them so that they could be like the nations around them. God reluctantly obliged them with the dynasty of Saul followed by David and Solomon. From that position of power came the decisions and decrees that set not only foreign and domestic policy but the spiritual climate and the moral tone for the nation. If the king trusted God and followed after righteousness, the people followed; but if the king became arrogant and corrupt, the whole nation lapsed under his leadership. For this reason, Isaiah had to take the Word of God to the pinnacle of power. Born of royal blood, he could neither be denied entry into the presence of the king nor be dismissed summarily as a commoner. When Isaiah spoke, the king listened.

Isaiah's family name reminds us of the providences that lie dormant within us until God is ready to use them. Our youngest son, Rob, is a tennis player who seldom won a major championship in high school or college because he lacked the "killer instinct" needed to crush his opponents. After those disappointing losses, I would try to comfort him by saying, "Son, God has given you the gift of a gentle spirit. That's where you will excel." Rob would usually retaliate, "That doesn't help me now." Today, however, his competitive tennis career is behind him, but he is teaching professional tennis with unlimited opportunity because of his ability to work with people, particularly with juniors who respond to him as a model of Christian graces. God's gift of a gentle spirit has been turned from a limiting handicap to an invaluable asset. Is it any wonder that Rob has found teaching tennis a ministry?

Many college and seminary students who come to my office are trying to fit the diverse pieces of life's puzzle into a pattern for God's will. They ask such questions as, "Why did I major in art when artists are starving?" "How does an M.B.A. fit into ministry?" "Is there any way to use my short-term mission trip to Haiti?" "What do I do with my sales experience?" In response to these questions, I use Isaiah's family name. Whether his parents knew it or not, they passed on to him the heritage of a name that helped him become the prophet of God in the court of kings. Why assume less for those of us who want to serve God with the gifts we have to offer Him? As His will unfolds in our lives, it is like the glee of discovering where a stray piece of a jigsaw puzzle suddenly fits into the picture. A major in art opens up options in interior design; an M.B.A provides a base for turn-around management of the struggling organization; a mission trip gives a background for executive leadership in an international ministry; and sales experience turns into basic training for personal evangelism. Looking back, each of us can see how our hidden gifts and assumed handicaps have become invaluable assets in the plan of God.

WHAT IS ISAIAH'S MESSAGE?

The prophet announces that the content of his message will come as a "vision" from God. To make such a claim draws limits and raises expectations. By announcing his message as a vision, Isaiah disclaims any content of his own. He will speak the message of God and only the Word of God. This does not mean that Isaiah will become the kind of voice we hear on the trains between concourses in an airport—robotic sounds without feeling or understanding. God has never inspired men and women to speak or write His Word by rote memory or mechanical dictation. God's message will come through Isaiah as a vision, not a fax copy. What he sees he will say, but he will communicate the Word of God through the medium of a language that people can understand and with a style that reflects the eloquence of an inspired mind.

As a test of Isaiah's sensitivity to the promptings of God's Spirit, he had to balance the colorful and forceful language required to communicate a vision with the clarity and accuracy of divine truth. Preachers know the temptation of overbalancing the medium or the message in their sermons. Today, in particular, the television generation expects truth to come in 30-second sound bites judiciously inserted between 30-minute segments of situation comedy. To sacrifice the message of truth to the medium of entertainment is a special temptation of contemporary prophets.

Isaiah would understand this temptation. When God gave him the text for his prophetic message, He also warned him that the people of Judah and Jerusalem to whom he spoke would stop their ears, close their eyes, and harden their hearts (6:11). The lack of reception to the truth became a test of Isaiah's faithfulness to the call of God. Although at one time he went so far as to walk naked through the streets of Jerusalem for three years as a symbol of the coming Babylonian exile, the radical medium still matched the severe message. As in the fable of the little girl who cried "wolf" so often that no one responded to her scream when a real wolf appeared, the prophet of God must avoid creating a false crisis of truth or making every issue of faith a life-and-death matter. Prophets of God need to heed the advice a senior attorney gave to a law student, "If your facts are strong, hammer on the facts; but if your facts are weak, hammer on the desk." By and large, this advice should guide the prophetic announcement of divine truth. The two-edged sword of God's Word is so sharp and strong that no human embellishment is needed. Yet, in rare moments of crisis, the alarm of the human voice or a radical act must be sounded.

Isaiah's introduction also raises our expectations. A vision promises more than a recitation of the obvious. We expect a word of revelation with evidence of its supernatural origin and miraculous meaning in the natural world. By his choice of words, Isaiah declares his belief in the transcendent God who is the source of all truth. One might wonder why Isaiah does not say, "the vision of God." Are we to assume that he will claim the vision as his own? The answer is just the opposite. Isaiah's relationship with God is so close that his vision is God's vision and his word is God's Word.

This too might be considered a presumption bordering on arrogance until you read the rest of the book of Isaiah. Except for his encounter with the Lord, "high and lifted up" in the temple (ch. 6), Isaiah gives us little additional information about himself. Even in this autobiographical account, he presents himself as a worshiping, confessing, and needy creature who responds to the call of God as an obedient servant who will speak God's truth despite rejection by the people. After two or three abbreviated episodes in which he met with the kings Ahaz and Hezekiah, Isaiah himself disappears from the scene. All of his prophecies of the future exile and restoration of Israel are without the author's personal identification.

Advocates of the theory of two or three "Isaiahs" are quick to use the anonymity of chapters 40–66 as proof of multiple authorship. However, the argument can be reversed. When Isaiah records critical moments in the history of Judah or Jerusalem where he is directly involved, he does not hesitate to identify himself, albeit with modesty. But when he foresees events beyond his time, he withdraws his name because that future belongs solely to God. The crucial test, then, is not the presence or absence of Isaiah's name in the text, but whether or not he is consistent through the book in communicating the vision that he claims in the beginning as the content for his message. By this standard, Isaiah never falters. The consistent communication of the vision from the first verse to the last verse of the prophecy is one of the strongest arguments for the unity of a book written by a single author.

WHEN DID ISAIAH PROPHESY?

By now, we expect Isaiah to answer the question *when* with the same precision in which he addressed the questions *who, what,* and *where.* Although specific dates are not given, Isaiah informs us that his ministry bridged the reigns of the kings of Judah, Uzziah, Ahaz, Jotham, and Hezekiah. If Isaiah's prophecy began with the death of Uzziah, the date is about 740 B.C.; and if he continued to minister until the death of Hezekiah, the approximate date is 687 B.C. This span of seventy-one years is usually shortened by scholars who believe that Isaiah's final prophecies were given about 701 B.C. If so, the span of his ministry is reduced to fifty-nine years. On the other hand, this span can be lengthened if you assume that Isaiah prophesied before he received his call and commissioning before God in the temple (ch. 6). In any case, Isaiah's longevity as a messenger of God is noteworthy. Prophets who speak of judgment as bluntly as Isaiah did usually die young. Perhaps his royal heritage saved him from a beheading. More likely, God had reason to protect him.

When Isaiah answered God's call in the temple with those memorable words, *"Here am I! Send me,"* and heard the woeful words of judgment that he was to speak, he pled, *"Lord, how long?"* God then gave him his term of office, *"Until the cities are laid waste . . . the houses are without a man . . . the* LORD *has removed men far away"* (6:11–12). Both God and Isaiah stayed true to this charge. God preserved the prophet's life and Isaiah persevered in his ministry. A study by Mari Gonlag confirms the relationship between the call to ministry and the perseverance in ministry.[2] She found that pastors with the strongest sense of divine call were those who stayed in ministry, while those with the weakest sense of call were those who tended to drop out. The study helps us understand Isaiah's persistence in ministry despite circumstances that would discourage a person with a weak sense of calling. Isaiah's call came with the sound of angel choruses, the feeling of shaking pillars, the smell of smoking incense, and the touch of a white-hot coal. Who could ever forget such an event or doubt such a calling? Contrary to the current trial-and-error attitude toward ministry, which usually leads to drop-outs, the clarity and strength of Isaiah's call held him steady for a prophetic career that spanned fifty years or more.

Having answered the questions *who, what, where,* and *when* in the first verse of his book, Isaiah leaves the questions *why* and *how* to the unfolding story of his ministry. His vision of the Lord in chapter six will answer the question *why* and his encounters with kings will tell us *how*. With all of the suspense of a good mystery story, Isaiah uses intrigue as an invitation to read on.

WHERE DID ISAIAH PROPHESY?

By God's instructions and his words, Isaiah drew the focus for his prophecy upon the chosen nation of Judah and the holy city of Jerusalem. Several reasons may have influenced this decision. First and foremost, God called Isaiah to be his spokesperson in Judah and Jerusalem as part of His continuing plan of redemption. Isaiah's love as a son of Judah and a citizen of Jerusalem added strength to God's call. Even in his stinging indictments of the sins of Judah and Jerusalem, he speaks with the pathos of a son with a broken heart. Isaiah never forgets the kingdom of Judah represented by the people whom God had chosen to fulfill His redemptive mission on earth. The city of Jerusalem stood at the center of that kingdom as the site of the holy temple and the symbol of peace, justice, and mercy for all the world to see. Consequently, neither God nor Isaiah ever gave up on Judah or Jerusalem. With pain and sadness, Isaiah pronounces woeful judgment upon the nation and the city for their rebellion against the law of God and their betrayal of His covenant of love with them. Yet, every woe is countered by a word of hope, however small it may be, as God's promise for the redemption of Judah and the restoration of Jerusalem in order to be the seed of the Savior and the light of the world.

Isaiah's prophecies prefigure the ministry of Jesus with their common focus upon the nation of Judah and the city of Jerusalem. The intensity of that focus, however, does not limit the global influence of their message. Like ripples on a pond, both Jesus' preaching and Isaiah's prophecies reach out to surrounding nations and stretch forward to all peoples and all generations in the future. Their model is worthy of imitation. Strategies to win the world for Jesus Christ often set goals on a global scale. After an energetic thrust, however, these strategies are exhausted because they try to do too much with too little. Evangelism needs to be planned on a manageable scale to be effective. An economy of effort is not a lack of faith. Jesus and Isaiah teach us that the intensity of the impact in a limited locale may be the most effective means for a global influence.

NOTES

1. Paul Tournier, *The Naming of Persons* (New York: Harper & Row, 1975).

2. Marianna Gonlag, *Perceived Evidences of the Call to Ministry and its Experiential Affirmations* (Ed.D. dissertation, Trinity Evangelical Divinity School, 1992).

CHAPTER TWO

A Family in Rebellion: Judah and Jerusalem

Isaiah 1:2–31

True to his stated purpose, Isaiah speaks first to Judah and Jerusalem. Both the nation and the city are special objects of God's love and special instruments of His grace. Out of the seed of Judah will come the Messiah and through the glory of Jerusalem will go the light of salvation for the whole world. But alas, rather than responding to God's love and accepting their privileged role as His servants, Judah is a rebellious nation and Jerusalem is an ungrateful city. To this woeful reality, Isaiah speaks the Word of God.

CHILDREN TURNED REBELS (ISAIAH 1:2–20)

> 2 Hear, O heavens, and give ear, O earth!
> For the LORD has spoken:
> "I have nourished and brought up children,
> And they have rebelled against Me;
> 3 The ox knows its owner
> And the donkey its master's crib;
> But Israel does not know,
> My people do not consider."
> 4 Alas, sinful nation,
> A people laden with iniquity,
> A brood of evildoers,
> Children who are corrupters!
> They have forsaken the LORD,
> They have provoked to anger
> The Holy One of Israel,
> They have turned away backward.

49

5 Why should you be stricken again?
You will revolt more and more.
The whole head is sick,
And the whole heart faints.

6 From the sole of the foot even to the head,
There is no soundness in it,
But wounds and bruises and putrefying sores;
They have not been closed or bound up,
Or soothed with ointment.

7 Your country is desolate,
Your cities are burned with fire;
Strangers devour your land in your presence;
And it is desolate, as overthrown by strangers.

8 So the daughter of Zion is left as a booth in a vineyard,
As a hut in a garden of cucumbers,
As a besieged city.

9 Unless the LORD of hosts
Had left to us a very small remnant,
We would have become like Sodom,
We would have been made like Gomorrah.

10 Hear the word of the LORD,
You rulers of Sodom;
Give ear to the law of our God,
You people of Gomorrah:

11 "To what purpose is the multitude of your sacrifices to Me?"
Says the LORD.
"I have had enough of burnt offerings of rams
And the fat of fed cattle.
I do not delight in the blood of bulls,
Or of lambs or goats.

12 "When you come to appear before Me,
Who has required this from your hand,
To trample My courts?

13 Bring no more futile sacrifices;
Incense is an abomination to Me.
The New Moons, the Sabbaths, and the calling of
    assemblies—
I cannot endure iniquity and the sacred meeting.

14 Your New Moons and your appointed feasts
My soul hates;
They are a trouble to Me,
I am weary of bearing them.

15 When you spread out your hands,
    I will hide My eyes from you;
    Even though you make many prayers,
    I will not hear.
    Your hands are full of blood.
16 "Wash yourselves, make yourselves clean;
    Put away the evil of your doings from before My eyes.
    Cease to do evil,
17 Learn to do good;
    Seek justice,
    Reprove the oppressor;
    Defend the fatherless,
    Plead for the widow.
18 "Come now, and let us reason together,"
    Says the LORD,
    "Though your sins are like scarlet,
    They shall be as white as snow;
    Though they are red like crimson,
    They shall be as wool.
19 If you are willing and obedient,
    You shall eat the good of the land;
20 But if you refuse and rebel,
    You shall be devoured by the sword";
    For the mouth of the LORD has spoken.

Isaiah 1:2–20

THE COURT OF THE Lord (1:2a)

One word is all Isaiah needs to let us know that his vision is not a flight of fancy couched in esoteric language and open to a variety of interpretations. With the unmistakable sound of the sergeant-at-arms summoning a court of law into session, Isaiah snaps us to attention with the trumpeted words, *"Hear, O heavens and give ear, O earth!"*

A courtroom scene comes to mind. To a Britisher, the call would be "Oyez, oyez, oyez, her Majesty's court is now in session." To an American, the more familiar sound would be, "Hear ye, hear ye, hear ye, this court is now in session, the Honorable Judge Ewing Werlein presiding. All rise." The judge then enters the hushed hall to the flurry of a flowing black robe that symbolizes his or her authority. Arriving at the elevated bench, the judge's commanding eyes sweep the courtroom and settle for a solemn moment upon the jury before being seated as the signal for all to follow. With the rap of the gavel accompanied by the declaration, "The court will come to order," the authority of the judge is set.

"Hear, O heavens and give ear, O earth! For the LORD *has spoken"* puts Isaiah's prophecy in a cosmic courtroom with the sovereign Lord presiding. We listen as Gabriel, the archangel, summons the court into session; we see the Chief Justice of the universe take his place on the high bench, and we stand in reverent silence before His ultimate authority to await His signal to be seated and hear his announcement, "The court of the Lord is now in session." With this graphic image, Isaiah has already proven his skill as a communicator.

No human jury will decide the law in God's cosmic courtroom. Heaven and earth, the first of God's creation, are impaneled as the jury. While the physical creation is not endowed with the power of life as are the animals or the power of thinking as are humans, they represent the governance of natural law, an inviolable order upon which all creation depends. The natural law of gravity, for instance, holds the earth and its atmosphere within its orbit. The same law keeps our feet on earth and stops us from stepping off high places. A humorous story is told of a man who defied the law of gravity by jumping off a twenty-story building. As he passed each floor on his way down, he shouted, "It isn't true yet!" But each of us knows the end of the story. At ground level, the inexorable law of gravity proved to be smashingly true.

God chooses to present His case in the cosmic courtroom before a panel of jurors whose objectivity is as sure as natural law. Nothing is more fundamental than the law of nature. To obey the law is to live; to defy the law is to die. We know what happens when one of these laws is defied. Human beings who flaunt the natural order of the universe by polluting the environment upset the balance of nature. Ecology means that everything is connected to everything else. So, the deadly nuclear waste released into the air at Chernobyl will affect the whole earth for years to come; the smoke of the soft coal industry in Kentucky will bring acid rain in Canada; and even the spray can of fluorocarbons shot into the air in our backyard will contribute to the ozone hole over the South Pole.

The opposite is also true. The moral law in the Old Testament harmonized the Law of Moses with the law of nature. Eternal wisdom, for instance, dictated the "sabbatical" or seventh year when the land was to lie fallow in order to restore the nutrients needed for bearing the harvest crop. Even the dietary laws of Moses, which seem archaic to us, are confirmed again and again by scientific discovery. After the health of this generation of fast food addicts is assessed, we may find Moses' Law the diet of the future. In any case, God is willing to rest His case upon natural law with the jury of heaven and earth. He needs no other court of appeal in the case of God versus Judah.

The Charge of Rebellion (1:2b–3)

God indicts Judah for rebellion, not just against the laws of nature, but against the love of a father. George Adam Smith, in his *Expositor's Bible on Isaiah*, gives us the first glimpse into Isaiah's theme on the character of God, when he writes of this passage, "Love gets the first word."[1] Here is our hint of what to expect from the prophecy of Isaiah. Although he is commissioned for the onerous task of pronouncing God's judgment against Judah and Jerusalem for their sins, the word of love keeps breaking through.

Fathers and mothers will feel personally the pain of God's plaintive words to His children of Judah, "I reared (or nourished) children and brought them up." The truth strikes close to home. God's nourishment of His people is love, not law; and covenant—not contract. Laws and contracts are made between adversaries while love and covenants bring together relatives of blood and friends of care. In this case, the creation of humankind in the image of God sets us apart from all creation as the relatives of God in mind, spirit, and soul. We may be linked with nature in physical creation and with animals in organic creation, but we stand alone in intellectual, volitional, and spiritual creation as heirs of God. Add then the special calling of the children of Israel to be the bearers of God's truth to all nations and the seed from which the Savior will come. You can understand why God loved the children of Israel as a parent, guiding them from the Flood, through the Exodus, and into the Promised Land with the hope of a father for a child.

The thought of God nourishing His children has particular meaning for us. In an age of single parents who are most often mothers, many children are neglected rather than nourished by their birth fathers. Even in two-parent families, the father may see his role with the children as a duty to be done rather than a love to be given. Because the father's role tends to be learned, the nature of the father-child relationship may be passed on from generation to generation. Some fathers have confessed to me that they are unable to relate to their children because of their own father's distance from them.

Usually when we think about nourishment for a child, we think of the mother's milk. More than food for life is involved. With the feeding there is the tender touch of love—a hug, a kiss, a cuddle—that bonds mother and child together as one. Although the image may be feminine, it is God's choice of words to communicate the nature of His relationship with His chosen children. Both chauvinists and feminists lose their case at this point. Although God is identified as Father to us, He does not hesitate to reveal feminine characteristics in His nature. As always, when we try to create God in our own image, He shows us how small we are. As a mother's milk gives life and a mother's caress gives love, so God nourishes His children.

The image of a babe in arms being nourished by a mother now gives way to the picture of rearing a young son or daughter prior to independence and adulthood. Here again, God's love has been demonstrated in the history of the children of Israel. From the giving of the Law as a moral guide, through to the crowning of a king as a political system, and on to the building of the temple as a spiritual symbol, God has brought them up with all of the expectations of a loving and faithful parent. More than that, He promised His children an unlimited future of righteousness and peace, justice and mercy, which He sealed with the covenant of His Word. To embrace the full meaning of Isaiah's opening words we need John, the beloved, to speak for us, "Behold what manner of love the Father has bestowed on us, that we should be called the children of God!" (1 John 3:1).

How can anyone rebel against this love? Such a thought even baffles God. Calling dumb animals as silent witnesses against the children of Israel, He states the obvious, *"The ox knows its owner and the donkey its master's crib"* (v. 3). With heaven and earth in the jury box, God advances His argument to the level of natural instincts. Even dumb animals know to whom they belong and from whom they get their nourishment, God says. If only His children obeyed the promptings of their instincts, they would never rebel against their

Father or His love. Yet, like the recent landmark case in which "Gregory K." divorced his parents, the children of Israel divorced God. But note the difference between the cases. Gregory divorced his parents on the charge of neglect; Israel divorced God despite His love. Sin is always a dumb and deliberate act.

THE CONSEQUENCES OF CORRUPTION (1:4–9)

As the evidence against Israel begins to pile up, God's spokesman Isaiah cites the consequences of Israel's rebellion. Sin is neither small nor selective. Rebellion against God corrupts the whole being. In one of the most graphic pictures of the pervasiveness of sin, Isaiah asks us to see a person whose whole *head* is sick, whole *heart* is sick, and whole *body* is wounded and broken. None can doubt what he means. A rebel against God is mentally sick in the head, emotionally sick in the heart, and physically sick in the body. Sin leaves no part of our personality uncontaminated. We do not sin in parts or suffer the consequences in pieces. If our personality were likened to a house, Isaiah is saying that sin contaminates every corner of every room until the whole house is corrupted.

Throughout his prophecy, Isaiah never forgets that sin also has social dimensions. As the dreaded AIDS virus has spread among African nations until whole populations may be wiped out, so Isaiah adds the foreboding words, *"Your country is desolate."* With his genius for metaphor, he sees the daughter of Zion as *"a booth in a vineyard,"* *"a hut in a garden of cucumbers,"* and *"a besieged city"* (v. 8). Israelites would instantly understand the meaning of these scenes. What was once a flourishing vineyard, garden, or city with the security of guards in a booth, hut, or fortress, is now abandoned to haunting reminders of a glorious past.

As I write these words, we are flying at thirty-nine thousand feet over the north Atlantic ocean from Shannon, Ireland to Atlanta, Georgia. This morning we awakened on the West coast of Ireland to the sight of a crumbling Celtic tower dating back to the invasion of medieval times. Now, however, it is only a relic for tourists who try to reconstruct the glories of the past as they pore over the ruins. These hollow monuments stand in stark contrast with the historical homeplace of John Wesley at Epworth, England where the guide told us, "Even the shadows whisper." As righteousness leaves a legacy of memories that we want to recall, so sin has a way of creating an emptiness in historic places that leaves us feeling haunted and unfulfilled.

Isaiah's description of the social consequences of sin goes on to identify a corrupted nation whose spirit is lost, whose cities are wastelands, and whose culture is usurped by strangers. The analogy of a ramshackle hut in an abandoned vineyard comes into view again. Because of their rebellion, all hope for Judah and Jerusalem is gone "unless" the grace of God keeps them from the fate of Sodom and Gomorrah (v. 9).

Unless is a grace word that keeps breaking through in the prophecy of Isaiah. As we saw in the pattern of the prophetic cycle, judgment is balanced with the promise of redemption for the people of Israel. Someone once quipped, "I wanted to be a philosopher, but cheerfulness kept breaking through." Our idea of a prophet tends towards this description of a philosopher. A steely countenance, an angry voice, and a gloomy message stereotype the prophet. Isaiah proved otherwise. Without sparing the sting of truth in his pronouncements of God's judgment upon rebellious people, the promise of grace keeps breaking through. Perhaps that is the crucial test for the prophet who speaks for God. To be true to God's character, love will get the first and last word.

The Offer of Clemency (1:10–17)

With the authority of a king who can grant clemency to rebellious subjects, God offers the children of Israel redemption from their sins. His offer comes with three instructions.

First, the children of Israel must listen and stop. *"Hear the word of the Lord, you rulers of Sodom; give ear to the law of your God, you people of Gomorrah."* God lets both the rulers and the people of their corrupted nation know that He will not tolerate the mixed alloy of temple prayers and idol worship that they are offering to Him. Evidently, the children of Israel wanted the best of both spiritual worlds—sacrificing to the popular idols of the day and offering prayers to God as a holdover from the past. God's reaction to this practice comes as no surprise. If He alone is Lord of all, His first commandment is non-negotiable. "You shall have no other Gods before Me" (Exodus 20:3) does not permit "other gods along with Me." Yahweh is holy and He is jealous. Either the God of Israel or the images of idols must rule our worship. So, with a gesture that even the smallest child knows, God puts up his hand and calls, "STOP!"

God may still be saying "Listen and stop" to us today. Idols do not have to be graven images. Any God-substitute that commands our full attention and gets first order in our lives is an idol. If so, the media and the marketplace of our day may qualify. By and large, the values communicated by the media contradict biblical values and the motivation of the marketplace runs counter to the Spirit of God. If then we succumb to the wooing of these idols as the driving force for our lives while still maintaining the appearance of Godly living by the public offering of our prayers, are we not guilty of "trampling in the courts of the Lord" just as the Israelites?

Isaiah probes even deeper when he calls a halt to the *"New Moons, the Sabbaths, and the calling of assemblies"* or evil assemblies (v. 13) that have become substitutes for the Lord's day. God, the Judge on the bench, now invokes the fourth commandment. "Remember the Sabbath day to keep it holy" (Exodus 20:8) is another nonnegotiable factor of the Law that cannot be violated or compromised. All false gods require their own rituals of worship and pseudo-sabbaths for celebration. What then do we celebrate? Especially on the Lord's day? Do we have our own evil assemblies of "new moons, sabbaths and convocations" that the Lord still detests? A generation of mall shoppers, home fixers, sports goers, and media addicts may have to answer these questions again. If we only nod toward God but kneel before idols on the Sabbath day, we may hear the Judge say, "Listen and stop!"

One command follows another. "Listen and stop" leads to "cease and desist." It is not unusual for a judge to specify the charges against a defendant and order restitution. God becomes even more specific in His instructions to the people of Judah. He asks for repentance. *"Wash yourselves"* is the conscious act of purification; *"put away the evil"* is the deliberate decision to reject the past; and *"cease to do evil"* is the public evidence of changed behavior. All three steps are involved in repentance. A sinner must be open to inward cleansing, which is evidenced by a personal rejection of the past and a public demonstration of change. Augustine, after his conversion, saw a former mistress across the street who called seductively to him, "Augustine, Augustine." The newborn soul answered, "The name is the same, but the man is different."

"Cease and desist" now becomes "do and demonstrate" as God asks for the positive evidence of repentance. A fivefold agenda for a new life follows:

1. *Learn to do good*—even with inward cleansing, old habits of sin must be unlearned and new habits of righteousness must be cultivated.

2. *Seek justice*—personal repentance will inevitably lead to a renewal of social conscience.

3. *Reprove the oppressor*—those who oppress must be reproved.

4. *Defend the fatherless*—become an activist on behalf of children who are without fathers because of abandonment, divorce, or death.

5. *Plead for the widow*—become an advocate for defenseless women who are most vulnerable to schemes and scams that rob them of their sustenance.

Once again, we see how contemporary the prophecy of Isaiah is. The issues of righteousness, justice, oppression, orphans, and widows are still with us in new and aggravated forms. What we do and what we demonstrate in these areas of need is still the proof of our repentance.

THE APPEAL TO REASON (1:18)

As proof that God has not given up on the people of His choice, He invites them to dialogue with Him as intelligent and rational beings. Only God's respect for the human mind could make such an invitation possible. After judging that the head, heart, and body of the people had been wholly corrupted by sin, one might expect God to give up on His highest order of creation. But no, He appeals to the distinctive powers of reason, which only humans know, with His offer of mercy. Two facts stand out in God's invitation—"*Come now, and let us reason together.*" One is the fact that *God takes the initiative to redeem His people.* Whether it is God searching for Adam in the garden, or Christ coming "to seek and to save the lost," the initiative of love is the story of both the Old and New Testaments.

The other fact is that *God gives priority to reason over feeling or will power as the entry point to the human soul.* Although reason alone is not sufficient for salvation, people have to be convinced of the truth before they can either experience the truth or act upon it. John Wesley established the Methodist class meeting in the eighteenth century, not only for the nurture of believers, but for the participation of "inquirers" who heard the gospel but were yet to be "convinced." Today, we tend to reverse the priorities. Newcomers to the faith usually enter by an emotional experience at the altar or a volitional act of commitment on a pledge card. Intellect, then, must catch up with the experience or the decision. Sadly for some Christians, it never does. Instead of becoming inquirers who are convinced of a reasonable faith, they depend upon new emotions and repeated commitments for Christian growth and maturity. A two-legged stool, however, will not stand.

True to the character of God, the invitation to "come" naturally leads to the offer of forgiveness. As the Father who still loves His rebellious children, God promises to cleanse their sins and purify their nature. In this passage of Scripture, we foresee the parable of the prodigal son. No one would have blamed the father for letting the rebellious son suffer the full consequences for his sin, but love would not let the son go. As the father welcomed the return of the prodigal son, so God is ready to welcome home the children of His choice.

And how reasonable for rebellious children to come home! When the prodigal son "came to himself" in a pigpen, reason took over and he realized that even his father's hired servants fared better than he. With the same hope for a return to reason, God reaches out to a prodigal nation with the offer of the warmest welcome followed by the grandest of celebrations. A prodigal child coming home is an act that harmonizes with natural law, animal instinct, and human reason. The event is so natural that parables of prodigal sons are common to most cultures. But the biblical parable stands above them all. While prodigals of the other parables must work their way back into the father's good graces, the parable told by Jesus tells of the father rushing out to meet his son, embracing him with open arms, restoring his sonship, and celebrating his return. Isaiah implies the same response. The God of grace is ready to welcome His rebellious children with open arms, conditions not included.

THE VERDICT OF DESTINY (1:19–20)

As much as God wants to welcome home His prodigal family, he will not force them to return. What an insight into the character of

God! Even though He holds the power to control the physical universe and human history, He will not renege on His own creative act. When God made us "in His own image," He included the freedom of choice and took the risk of rebellion. True, God seems baffled by children who will not listen to reason and He might be tempted to do more than nudge them by the promptings of His Spirit, yet He remains true to His own character. If the prodigals are *"willing and obedient,"* they will *"eat the good of the land"* (v. 19). But if they continue to resist His Spirit and rebel against His love, they will be *"devoured by the sword"* (v. 20).

The twofold requirement, "to be willing and obedient," parallels the economic circumstances in America today. Everyone talks about the national deficit but no one does anything about it. In a word, we are unwilling to do what we know must be done. Our sin can be treated the same way. We may acknowledge our sin and talk about turning away from it, but until our will is engaged in action, nothing ever happens. Inaction, then, becomes an action. Isaiah minces no words when he tells the children of Israel that if they continue to rebel against the Law of God and refuse the offer of His love, they will be "devoured by the sword." Most of us complain that such an "either-or" choice is unfair. We want the alternative that lets us love God and hold onto our sin at the same time. Like it or not, the biblical division between saints and sinners, believers and nonbelievers, and sheep and goats, is a truth that cannot be wished away. Either we listen and stop, repent and obey, reason and return, or we put ourselves under the stroke of the devouring sword.

The court scene closes with one more word from God. As the court opened with the announcement that "the LORD has spoken," so it closes with the same words. No one can claim exemption. When God speaks, everyone must listen. Although justified in bringing swift judgment upon the rebellious children of Judah, He has shown us the love of a father and a mother in offering them forgiveness for sin and a feast off the fat of the land. Like the final appeal for a convicted criminal on death row, the children of Israel may accept His offer of grace or die by the sword. If weighed on the scales of sound reason, there is only one choice. How could the children of Israel, or any of us, reject the love of God?

A DAUGHTER TURNED HARLOT (1:21–31)

21 How the faithful city has become a harlot!
   It was full of justice;

> Righteousness lodged in it,
> But now murderers.
> 22 Your silver has become dross,
> Your wine mixed with water.
> 23 Your princes are rebellious,
> And companions of thieves;
> Everyone loves bribes,
> And follows after rewards.
> They do not defend the fatherless,
> Nor does the cause of the widow come before them.
> 24 Therefore the Lord says,
> The LORD of hosts, the Mighty One of Israel,
> "Ah, I will rid Myself of My adversaries,
> And take vengeance of My enemies.
> 25 I will turn My hand against you
> And thoroughly purge away your dross,
> And take away all your alloy.
> 26 I will restore your judges as at the first,
> And your counselors as at the beginning.
> Afterward you shall be called the city of righteousness,
>   the faithful city."
> 27 Zion shall be redeemed with justice,
> And her penitents with righteousness.
> 28 The destruction of transgressors and of sinners shall be
>   together,
> And those who forsake the LORD shall be consumed.
> 29 For they shall be ashamed of the terebinth trees
> Which you have desired;
> And you shall be embarrassed because of the gardens
> Which you have chosen.
> 30 For you shall be as a terebinth whose leaf fades,
> And as a garden that has no water.
> 31 The strong shall be as tinder,
> And the work of it as a spark;
> Both will burn together, and no one shall quench them.
>
> *Isaiah 1:21–31*

While the case of God versus Judah is still pending, God's case against Jerusalem appears to be closed. In part two of Isaiah's summary of his vision, the courtroom setting changes from a trial in process to a time of sentencing. The city of Jerusalem has been chosen by God as the symbolic center for his redemptive purpose in the world. As the site of the temple, where the tablets of the Law are preserved, and under the rule of the divinely-appointed kings, Jerusalem is expected to be the holy city, a light for peace and justice for all generations. Isaiah's metaphor for the city, the "daughter of Zion," gives unmistakable meaning to Jerusalem's chosen role in the plan of God. Like the favored daughter of a family, God has the greatest hope for His holy city. But no. With a sin that drives a stake through a father's heart, the daughter of his choice has sold herself into prostitution. Her purity of character, her purpose in life, and her promise for the future are all gone. The daughter of Zion has done worse than rebel against the father's love. She has turned that love into the shameful profession of prostitution to sell her body for the lusts of men and then be discarded when her beauty is gone. Consequently, God's response is not the appeal to reason that He made to Judah, but the pronouncement of punishment upon the convicted and criminal city.

God's responses to Judah and Jerusalem create a scenario of contrast for our study:

	Judah	**Jerusalem**
I. Relationship to God	Children	Daughter
II. Role in God's Plan	Chosen Seed	Chosen Symbol
III. Sin Against God	Rebellion	Prostitution
IV. Result of Condition	Total Contamination	Total Corruption
V. Nature of God's Test	Spiritual	Ethical
VI. Point of God's Test	Worship	Leadership
VII. Evidence of Sin	Idolatry	Injustice
VIII. Punishment	Personal Guilt	Social Destruction
IX. Promise of God	Redemption	Restoration
X. Purpose of God	Fruitfulness	Faithfulness

Just as in the case of Judah, we foresee Isaiah's prophecy concerning Jerusalem in these verses. Even though the prophetic cycle is drawn tightly, the outline of his predictions concerning the city is evident. From here on, his prophecy will be an expansion of this outline.

THE PROVOCATION OF GOD (1:21–23)

Isaiah asks us to see the saddest picture of human sin. Imagine a faithful wife who has become a harlot! The theme of Hosea's prophecy comes to mind. In the case of his adulterous wife, who is the image of Israel, Hosea writes,

> There is no truth or mercy
> Or knowledge of God in the land.
> By swearing and lying,
> Killing and stealing and committing adultery;
> They break all restraint,
> With bloodshed after bloodshed.
>
> *Hosea 4:1b–2*

Isaiah charges the daughter of Zion with similar sins, sins compounded by the memory of the days when justice and righteousness reigned in the city. The contrast is alarming. Murderers now dwell in the place of justice and righteousness, the silver splendor of the city has turned to dross, and its vibrancy symbolized by fine wine has been diluted into spiritless water (vv. 21–22).

The charge is leveled against the rulers of the city who are responsible for its decline and degradation. Instead of being led by rulers who are spiritual, honest, just, and compassionate, Jerusalem and its people are victimized by political corruption and social injustice. Once again, we are confronted with the disturbing reality that being and doing cannot be disconnected in either our personal or social life. The essential connection begins with the character of God who is at one and the same time holy in being and ethical in doing. As we saw in His case against Judah, God linked the loss of personal righteousness to religious idolatry that led to social oppression. Now, in His charge against Jerusalem, He cites leaders whose rebellion against His law and His love has led them into political corruption and social oppression of helpless people.

Leaders cannot escape the influence of their "being" and "doing." Although there are those who contend that the principles of leaders have nothing to do with the policies they enact, Isaiah thinks otherwise. Sooner or later, a leader whose integrity is flawed will compromise on principle at the expense of helpless people. Especially in the case of religious leaders, spiritual integrity will directly affect social conscience and public policy. But which comes first, being or doing? When Isaiah dealt with Judah, he told them first to "learn to do good" and then "seek justice, [and] reprove the oppressor" (v. 17). In his charge against Jerusalem, however, he cites justice first and righteousness second. He does not contradict himself. In the case of Judah, redemption is personal; in the case of Jerusalem, restoration is social. Therefore, as idolatry is the symptom of sin for the children of Israel, injustice is the evidence of betrayal for the daughter of Zion. Either one can provoke the justice of God.

THE PRONOUNCEMENT AGAINST JERUSALEM (1:24–25)

The word *therefore* is a cause and effect word informing us that God has come to a conclusion. In the startling declaration of judgment, He says that other nations who are His enemies will be instruments to relieve and avenge Him (v. 24). God Himself will become their enemy, but only for the purpose of restoring the city. Quite in contrast with His call to the children of Israel to turn from their sins in order to be redeemed, God must take action Himself to purge the city of its corruption.

Robert Bellah, in his book *The Good Society*, traces the influence of radical self-interest in our primary institutions of the home, church, and school. He describes the current condition of these institutions as "arenas for the test of character rather than being the source for the building of character."[2] When our primary institutions are in such serious trouble, it is difficult to know how to rebuild them. Certainly the moral rebuilding of the American character is a beginning point for their restoration, but is it enough? The institutions themselves may need to be purged of the values that have contributed to their corruption. Individual freedom at the expense of the common good, for instance, has undercut the institution of the family, which depends upon long-term commitment and faithfulness. Radical action, not unlike a purging, may be required to reverse the trend and restore the institution of the family. For Jerusalem, there was no alternative.

THE PROMISE OF RESTORATION (1:26–31)

Despite the gross sin of Jerusalem and its leadership, God has not given up on His chosen city. He foresees a future in which it will have a world identity as the *"city of righteousness, the faithful city"* (v. 26). The path to that end, however, will mean restoration after purging through a change of leadership. Judges and counselors—those who administer justice and those who advocate righteousness—will have to reassume leadership for the city. Then, and only then, will its divine destiny be fulfilled.

Is the city still the test of social justice for our nation? If so, we are in trouble. In the early 1960s, visionaries dreamed of renewal in our cities and proposed massive programs for a glorious future. Young mayors were elected who epitomized the dream. Then it happened: the dream was shattered by riots, ruin, and rubble. Today, our cities are like Jerusalem. The silver splendor is dross and the rich wine of spirit is dull. Los Angeles has not recovered from riots; Detroit has ghettos with the poorest children in the nation; New York awaits the collapse of its eroding infrastructure; Miami will take years to recover from natural disaster; and San Francisco quakes on the edge of an AIDS epidemic. The purging has come. But does social justice and personal righteousness prevail? Isaiah would call for leadership from judges who administer social justice and counselors who advocate personal righteousness. Here is where we fall short. Too many leaders of our cities are political opportunists who waffle on justice and waver on righteousness. Yet, there is the leaven of leadership in our cities in whom we find hope. As James Davison Hunter points out in his book *Culture Wars*, evangelical Christians, orthodox Jews, and conservative Catholics are coming together in a new coalition based upon biblical principles. This coalition may be a new force for personal righteousness and social justice in our nation. Perhaps in God's good wisdom, the path from purging to restoration for our cities will come from new coalitions of His making.[3]

God purposes to work for the restoration of Jerusalem, but the choice belongs to the people of the city. If justice is chosen, the city will be redeemed, and if the people repent, righteousness will be restored. But if rebellion continues, sin remains, and betrayal persists, the city will be broken and desolate. Shame will be the order of the day, especially for those who perpetrate idolatry and injustice. For those who choose an oak tree for the worship of Asherah rather than Yahweh, they will see withering leaves as symptomatic of a rotting core. Likewise, those who worship fertility in a garden of the gods will be disgraced by dead plants on parched ground.

Leaders who use their office to exploit their power and oppress the poor in the city of Jerusalem will be the final losers. In words reminiscent of Jesus' description of hell, the *"strong"* and their works will become the *"tinder"* and *"spark"* for eternal and unquenchable fire (v. 31). Not by coincidence, the book of Isaiah ends on the same somber note. Just as the last word of Isaiah in this introductory summary of his prophecy ends with a severe warning, so his book ends with words that are identical. For idolaters and oppressors, the message is the same, "their worm does not die, and their fire is not quenched. They shall be an abhorrence to all flesh" (66:24). If these final words were written by a second or third Isaiah, he was an unapologetic plagiarist.

NOTES

1. George Adam Smith, *The Expositor's Bible: The Book of Isaiah*, Vol. I., ed. W. Robertson Nicoll (New York: Funk & Wagnalls, 1900), 13.

2. Robert Bellah, et al., *The Good Society* (New York: Alfred A. Knopf, 1991), 6.

3. James Davison Hunter, *Culture Wars: The Struggle to Define America* (New York: Basic Books, 1991).

PART TWO

The Vision Seen

Isaiah 2:1–5:30

CHAPTER THREE

The Prophetic Cycle: Punishment and Promise

Isaiah 2:1–4:6

Isaiah advances his vision at the opening of the second chapter by stating, *"The word that Isaiah the son of Amoz saw concerning Judah and Jerusalem"* (v. 1). After a similar introduction in chapter one (1:1), he proceeded to summarize his vision concerning Judah and Jerusalem in general terms. Now he reveals the special content of the vision by detailing its major themes:

1. **The House of The Lord**: A Promise of Peace (2:1–4)
2. **The Day of The Lord**: A Time of Terror (2:5–22)
3. **The Men of Zion**: A Vacuum of Leadership (3:1–15)
4. **The Women of Zion**: An Attitude of Arrogance (3:16–4:1)
5. **The Remnant of Israel**: A Branch of Beauty (4:2–6)
6. **The God of Israel**: A Bittersweet Love Song (5:1–38)

Isaiah chooses these themes for a purpose. They represent the skeletal truth of God's Word to Judah and Jerusalem that Isaiah will speak in different modes of communication. As we study his prophecies, then, we can expect to see these themes recur in both present and future contexts. Although some scholars insist on tying them to known historical events, Isaiah has a different purpose. As part of his integrity as a prophet who speaks only God's Word, Isaiah sets a public standard of accountability for his ministry for all to judge. Of course these themes can be traced in historical events during and after Isaiah's time, but they cannot be forced into a chronology used to affirm or deny the date of the writing and the identity of the author. Rather, Isaiah puts forth these themes as prophetic propositions that will appear time and time again as he speaks God's Word in the present and to the future. Essentially, Isaiah is following the rule of thumb for good communicators, "Tell them what you are going to say, say it, and then tell them what you have said."

The House of The Lord (2:1–4)

1 The word that Isaiah the son of Amoz saw
concerning Judah and Jerusalem.
2 Now it shall come to pass in the latter days
That the mountain of the Lord's house
Shall be established on the top of the mountains,
And shall be exalted above the hills;
And all nations shall flow to it.
3 Many people shall come and say,
"Come, and let us go up to the mountain of the Lord,
To the house of the God of Jacob;
He will teach us His ways,
And we shall walk in His paths."
For out of Zion shall go forth the law,
And the word of the Lord from Jerusalem.
4 He shall judge between the nations,
And shall rebuke many people;
They shall beat their swords into plowshares,
And their spears into pruning hooks;
Nation shall not lift up sword against nation,
Neither shall they learn war anymore.

Isaiah 2:1–4

God's Purpose for His House (2:1–2)

As *love* got the first word in Isaiah's first prophecy concerning Judah and Jerusalem, so *hope* gets the first word among his specific prophecies. Isaiah's primary theme is to show God's vision for His world through the house of the Lord located on Mount Zion in His chosen city of Jerusalem. God is unapologetically an idealist as He foresees the *"latter days"* when *"all nations"* will flow like a mighty stream to the house of LORD with the recognition that it is chief among all religions of the world. God's ego is not at stake. He envisions a future in which Jerusalem, as the site of His temple, will be the model for the teaching of righteousness and the demonstration of justice. "One World Under God" is the goal of this prophecy.

Does God have this purpose for His house today? Is not the contemporary church to teach the spirit of righteousness and demonstrate justice? Arguments over spiritual being and social doing fade before this truth. The church does not have the choice between one ministry or the other. Conversion and conscience still define its primary task. As Jerusalem served as the centerpiece of Isaiah's prophecy in the ancient world, so the church serves as the agent of God's truth for the contemporary world.

THE NATIONS' RESPONSE TO THE INVITATION (2:3)

Three action verbs describe the response of the nations to this global theocracy. *"Come, and let us go up to the mountain of the LORD, to the house of the God of Jacob"* is the motivation of the nations to gather together and flow like a stream to the house of the LORD. *"He will teach us His ways"* is the reason for the nations to come to Mount Zion. They will see in His teaching the transforming spirit of righteousness and the wise law of justice to change them and their world. To sit at the feet of the Master is to sit in the world's foremost classroom. *"and we will walk in His paths"* is the outcome of their learning. To *walk* is a biblical figure of speech that embraces the conduct of the whole of life. As Paul urged the Ephesians "to have a walk worthy of the calling with which you were called" (Ephesians 4:1), he meant "to live a life" worthy of the call of God.

The motivation for coming into the house of the LORD, learning righteousness at the feet of the Master, and living a life worthy of God's calling has not changed. To *come*, to *learn*, and to *live*, is still the test of the church for public response. Each of these actions is affirmative and substantive. They embrace being and doing, spirit and law, and righteousness and justice. Churches today are spending hours, days, and weeks of time creating statements of vision and mission. Rather than relying upon visions of glamour and missions of glitter, the fundamentals of learning the ways of personal righteousness and walking in paths of social justice give every church the outlook and the ministry it needs. If churches built their future on these fundamentals, the public might once again say, "Come, and let us go up the mountain of the LORD, to the house of the God of Jacob."

THE WORLD'S PATH TO PEACE (2:4)

What would happen if the spirit and the law of God were in practice today? In the religious wars of the world, God would make judgments against aggressors and rebuke both sides for fighting in His name. He would then recommend three policies for world peace. *Economically*, the nations must turn nonproductive military spending into peaceful production in order to stimulate growth and serve the people. *Politically*, a peace pact needs to be signed that will stop the fighting. Violence breeds violence and war is not the path to peace. *Militarily*, the training for war must cease. Training for war is like a football team that is forever practicing but never playing any competition. A time comes in every training camp when frustrated players will say, "It is time to hit someone else." Training for war results in the same mental frustration. Sooner or later, the preparation for war requires the practice of war.

Isaiah's vision for the house of the LORD may not be operative yet, but his prophecy of peace confronts every nation in the world every day. At the entrance to the United Nations headquarters in New York City, a sculpture of an artisan beating a sword into a plowshare greets every world leader, diplomat, and visitor who enters the building. Under the statue is engraved the word of the LORD from Isaiah, *"They shall beat their swords into plowshares, and their spears into pruning hooks"* (v. 4). Ironically, even atheists must acknowledge this truth. When Mikhail Gorbachev led the Soviet Union and visited the United Nations, he was given a gift of golden cufflinks fashioned after the sculpture. Imagine an avowed atheist wearing the Scripture on his sleeve. If Gorbachev's praying mother saw her son's cufflinks, she would silently thank God for answering prayer.

George Adam Smith, in his commentary on Isaiah in *The Expositor's Bible*, sums up God's ideal for His house. In the last days, He sees it as the "Light of the world, school of the nations, temple of the earth, seat of judgment, throne of God, and symbol of peace."[1] All of Isaiah's prophecies and God's promises are aimed at that glorious future.

We should not be surprised to read God's gracious invitation at the end of this prophecy, *"O house of Jacob, come and let us walk in the light of the LORD."*

THE DAY OF THE LORD (ISAIAH 2:5–22)

5 O house of Jacob,
   come and let us walk
In the light of the LORD.
6 For You have forsaken Your people, the house of Jacob,
Because they are filled with eastern ways;
They are soothsayers like the Philistines,
and they are pleased with the children of foreigners.
7 Their land is also full of silver and gold,
And there is no end to their treasures;
Their land is also full of horses,
And there is no end to their chariots.
8 Their land is also full of idols;
They worship the work of their own hands,
That which their own fingers have made.
9 People bow down,
And each man humbles himself;
Therefore do not forgive them.
10 Enter into the rock,
   and hide in the dust,
From the terror of the LORD
And the glory of His majesty.
11 The lofty looks of man shall be humbled,
The haughtiness of men
   shall be bowed down,
and the LORD alone
   shall be exalted in that day.
12 For the day of the LORD of hosts
Shall come upon everything proud and lofty,
Upon everything lifted up—
And it shall be brought low—
13 Upon all the cedars of Lebanon
   that are high and lifted up,
And upon all the oaks of Bashan;
14 Upon all the high mountains,
And upon all the hills
   that are lifted up;

15 Upon every high tower,
   And upon every fortified wall;
16 Upon all the ships of Tarshish,
   And upon all the beautiful sloops.
17 The loftiness of man shall be bowed down,
   And the haughtiness of men shall be brought low;
   The LORD alone will be exalted in that day,
18 But the idols He shall utterly abolish.
19 They shall go into the holes of the rocks,
   And into the caves of the earth,
   From the terror of the LORD
   and the glory of His majesty,
   When He arises to shake the earth mightily.
20 In that day a man will cast away
       his idols of silver
   and his idols of gold,
   Which they made,
       each for himself to worship,
   To the moles and bats,
21 To go into the clefts of the rocks,
   And into the crags of the rugged rocks,
   From the terror of the LORD
   And the glory of His majesty,
   When He arises to shake the earth mightily.
22 Sever yourselves from such a man,
   Whose breath is in his nostrils;
   For of what account is he?

Isaiah 2:5–22

A TIME OF TERROR (2:5)

God's idealism for the future now becomes harsh reality for both the present and the future. His invitation, *"O house of Jacob, come and let us walk in the light of the LORD,"* extends both backwards to His hope for the house of the LORD and forwards to His wrath in the day of the LORD. While working toward the glorious future, God's purpose is frustrated by the wickedness in the house of Jacob. True to His own holy character, God cannot condone their sin or wait until the dead weight of their sin crushes them from within. Purging by divine wrath is necessary to remove the obstacles of wickedness that continue to frustrate His purpose. Thus, the day of the LORD—a time of terror characterized by both the dread and splendor of His majesty—is introduced as a major theme of Isaiah's prophecy.

In his description of the conditions in the house of Jacob that provoke the wrath of God, Isaiah foresees the destruction of Jerusalem in his time. But he also sets the stage for the prophecy to loom large over human history in an eschatological setting. The day of the LORD may be as current as the destruction of Jerusalem in 587 B.C., as continuous as the visitation of the divine wrath against human wickedness through the centuries, and as futuristic as the second coming or the final judgment. From Isaiah's prophecy to John's Revelation, "the day of the LORD" will be a concept of biblical truth that we will meet again and again. Isaiah's vision of its reality in the case of Judah and Jerusalem shows us the day of the LORD in detail.

THE FOLLY OF FALSE TRUST (2:6–8)

The vision of God for the house of the LORD on Mount Zion is obviously frustrated by the children of Israel who not only rebel against His love and flaunt His law, but put their trust in false gods of their own making. In a catalog of sins, Isaiah lists these substitutes for human trust:

- Eastern religions (v. 6)
- astrological divinations (v. 6)
- pagan alliances (v. 6)
- material wealth (v. 7)
- military might (v. 7)
- religious idols (v. 8)
- technological advancement (v. 8)

If this list of false gods seems familiar, it is because the abandonment of trust in God leads to the same substitute trusts in every generation. A contemporary example could be cited for each of these false trusts, however, one will do. We Americans have put our trust in the false god of material wealth to such an extent that any deviation from affluence is perceived as poverty. Yet, the warning is out. If the federal deficit continues to increase at run-away levels, future generations of Americans will face the shock of financial depression followed by a lowered standard of living that will come with the force of an economic holocaust. At present, the inscription on our coins, "In God We Trust" is a mockery that can be exposed only by a purging of our dependence upon material wealth. Sooner or later, we will learn the folly of this false trust.

THE CAPITAL SINS OF ARROGANCE AND PRIDE (2:9–11)

Isaiah minces no words when he identifies the *"lofty looks"* and the *"haughtiness of men"* as the sin that goes beyond rebellion against the love of God and trust in false gods. By attitude and action, the people of the house of Jacob have set themselves up as gods in their own right. Repeating the sin of Adam and Eve in the garden, they claim to be like God with all-seeing eyes and all-knowing minds (Genesis 3:4). Their pretense, however, provokes the rage of God and invokes the day of the LORD when they will be humbled and brought low while the Lord alone is exalted (v. 11). Because arrogance and pride are the major obstacles to God's redemptive purpose on earth, these twin sins become the special objects of His wrath.

Isaiah is not alone in identifying arrogance and pride as capital sins that enrage God. In the Proverbs, Wisdom speaks, "I hate pride and arrogance" (Proverbs 8:13). Jesus aligned arrogance with folly and included these sins among His listing of the grossest evils rising out of the unclean heart: "evil thoughts, adulteries, fornications, murders, thefts, covetousness, wickedness, deceit, licentiousness, an evil eye, blasphemy, pride, and foolishness" (Mark 7:21–22). Whether to make Henley's defiant declaration, "I am the captain of my fate, I am the master of my soul" or strike the pose of a person who creates false gods in his or her own image, there is the risk of the great reversal when those who exalt themselves are brought low and God alone is exalted.

THE DAY OF DREAD AND SPLENDOR (2:12–21)

Whenever the Spirit of the Lord appears in human history, people react one of two ways. Those who put their trust in God bow in praise before the splendor of His Spirit, while those who trust in the false gods of their own creation quake in dread before His holy presence. Amos shares the vision of the day of the LORD with Isaiah when he writes,

> Woe to you who desire the day of the LORD!
> For what good is the day of the LORD to you?
> It will be darkness, and not light.
> It will be as though a man fled from a lion
> and a bear met him;
> Or as though he went into the house
> leaned his hand on the wall,
> and a sepent bit him.
> Is not the day of the LORD darkness
>   and not light?
> Is it not very dark,
>   with no brightness in it?
>
> *Amos 5:18–20*

Speaking on the same theme, Isaiah informs us that those who are arrogant and proud will see all of the false gods in whom they trust crumble before their eyes. Whether the sky-piercing cedars of Lebanon or the rock-hard oaks of Bashan from which they carved their idols, the towering mountains and high hills where they erected altars in competition with Yahweh, the lofty towers from which they watched for enemies, the fortresses that guaranteed their protection, the trading ships that expanded their empire, or the stately vessels upon which they sailed in luxury to distant ports, all of these symbols of misplaced trust will fall. Out of the rubble will rise the exalted Lord, standing alone and striking dread to the wicked but showing splendor to the righteous.

The storm of God's wrath is not yet over. Ultimate humiliation awaits the arrogant and the proud. Like animals on the run from the violence of a sudden storm, Isaiah foresees the wicked fleeing to *"holes of the rocks and into caves of the earth"* after all of their false gods have fallen and disappeared. In those underground chambers, they will throw away their useless idols of silver and gold, leaving them to rats and bats, the creatures of darkness (vv. 19–21). In due time, Jerusalem would experience that prophecy come true. Before the murderous onslaught of the Babylonians in 586 B.C., the citizens of the city saw their fortress fall and sought refuge in the caves of the surrounding hills.

In due time, the prophecy will come true again. At the opening of the sixth seal of Revelation by the Lamb, the final day of the Lord will come and history will record this event:

> And the kings of the earth, the great men, the rich men, the com-
> manders, the mighty men, every slave and every free man, hid
> themselves in the caves and in the rocks of the mountains, and
> said to the mountains and rocks, "Fall on us and hide us from the
> face of Him who sits on the throne and from the wrath of the
> Lamb! For the great day of His wrath has come, and who is able
> to stand?"
>
> *Revelation 6:15–17*

THE MORTALITY OF HUMANITY (2:22)

God does not bring ultimate humiliation upon the arrogant and proud as an act of jealousy. His redemptive purpose has been frustrated, but not defeated by their sins. Like a teacher who has marshalled all of the facts, presented them patiently to the students, and drawn an irrefutable conclusion, God begs His people, "Stop trusting in man" and then proceeds to the rhetorical question their father David asked in the Psalms, "What is man?" To Isaiah, the answer is that man is a creature who depends upon God for the next breath and shrinks into insignificance before the exalted Lord. Implicit in these words is the universal question, "In whom will we put our trust?"

THE MEN OF ZION (3:1–15)

1 For behold, the Lord,
  the LORD of hosts,
  Takes away from Jerusalem
  and from Judah
  The stock and the store,
  The whole supply of bread
  and the whole supply of water;
2 The mighty man and the man of war,
  The judge and the prophet,
  And the diviner and the elder;
3 The captain of fifty

   and the honorable man,
The counselor and the skillful artisan,
And the expert enchanter.

4 "I will give children to be their princes,
And babes shall rule over them.

5 The people will be oppressed,
Every one by another and every one by his neighbor;
The child will be insolent toward the elder,
And the base toward the honorable."

6 When a man takes hold of his brother
In the house of his father, saying,
"You have clothing;
You be our ruler,
And let these ruins be under your hand,"

7 In that day he will protest, saying,
"I cannot cure your ills,
For in my house is neither food nor clothing;
Do not make me a ruler of the people."

8 For Jerusalem stumbled,
And Judah is fallen,
Because their tongue and their doings
Are against the LORD,
To provoke the eyes of His glory.

9 The look on their countenance witnesses against them,
And they declare their sin as Sodom;
They do not hide it.
Woe to their soul!
For they have brought evil upon themselves.

10 "Say to the righteous
that it shall be well with them,
For they shall eat the fruit of their doings.

11 Woe to the wicked!
It shall be ill with him,
For the reward of his hands shall be given him.

12 As for My people,
children are their oppressors,
And women rule over them.
O My people! Those who lead you cause you to err,
And destroy the way of your paths."

13 The LORD stands up to plead.
And stands to judge the people.

14 The LORD will enter into judgment

> With the elders of His people
> And His princes:
> "For you have eaten up the vineyard;
> The plunder of the poor is in your houses.
> 15 What do you mean by crushing My people
> And grinding the faces of the poor?"
> Says the Lord GOD of hosts.
>
> *Isaiah 3:1–15*

Isaiah's prophetic themes now shift from the end time visions for the house of the LORD and the day of the LORD to the more specific, current, and personal themes of the people of Judah and Jerusalem. The men of Zion, who hold responsibility for leadership in the society, are Isaiah's first subject.

A CRISIS OF RESOURCES (3:1–3)

"See now," Isaiah says, "The Lord is about to take away from Jerusalem and Judah its essential resources for survival—the quantity and quality of its food and its leadership." Some scholars argue that the reference to the food supply is a later insertion into the text because the rest of the passage deals only with the problem of leadership. They forget that the quality of leadership is always put to the critical test when there is a shortage of essential resources, such as food, money, or land, that requires wise and fair decision making. The classic case is the shortage of food that caused a dispute among the widows of Greek and Hebrew ancestry in the church shortly after Pentecost (Acts 6:1–7). In order for the twelve apostles to focus upon their spiritual tasks of teaching and preaching, seven deacons were elected as administrative leaders to make decisions, wait tables, and keep the fledgling church from fatal schism. Qualifications for election to leadership were: a good name, practical wisdom, and fullness of the Spirit (Acts 6:3). Amazing results followed this division of labor and delegation of leadership. "The Word of God spread, and the number of the disciples multiplied greatly in Jerusalem, and a great many of the priests were obedient to the faith" (Acts 6:7).

Isaiah's link between the shortage of food and the need for leadership is equally sound. He foresaw the Assyrian invasion of Judah and the siege of Jerusalem just ahead. Military tactics included more than storming the walls of the city at a high cost to the invading army. If the food and water supply to the beleaguered city were cut off, the conquest could be accomplished at minimal cost. Once the city fell, the Assyrians maintained control by deporting the leaders of the people who might incite rebellion against their conquerors. Isaiah missed no one in his list of present or potential leaders. From the "hero" of great deeds to the "enchanter" of clever words, anyone who might become a moral rallying point for the people would face the shame of exile.

A SHORTAGE OF LEADERS (3:4–7)

One of the signs of a morally bankrupt society is the dearth of qualified persons who are willing to take the risk of leadership. In our elections today, we are seeing the early warning signs of a nation in trouble when the candidates are "tissue thin" on the question of character and trust. Isaiah's description of the leadership vacuum (vv. 4–5) in Judah and Jerusalem is far more desperate. All of the symptoms of a society that is sick unto death are present in the loss of leadership:

- governance is put in the hands of inexperienced children
- oppression by man against man and neighbor against neighbor is commonplace
- civil strife pits the generations and the classes against each other.

Anarchy is the word that sums up the consequences when leadership is lost.

Isaiah adds one more step in social breakdown due to the loss of leadership. He predicts that the qualifications for leadership in the bankrupt society will be reduced to the level of the person who holds the minimal resources for survival. As an example, he cites the case of a man who has a coat while others have none. His brother grabs him and insists that he assume leadership over the people and *"let these ruins be under your hands"* (v. 6). The man demurs because he knows his leadership would be futile.

A society is in deep trouble when no one has the qualifications of a good name, practical wisdom, and spiritual maturity required for leadership; but it is in deepest trouble when no one is willing to take the risk of leadership. Warren Bennis, in his book *Why Leaders Can't Lead*, answers his own question "Where have all the leaders gone?" with this conclusion about contemporary American society,

> Precisely at the time when the trust and credibility of our alleged leaders are at an all-time low and when potential leaders feel most inhibited in exercising their gifts, America most needs leaders—because, of course, as the quality of leaders declines, the quantity of problems escalates.[2]

A HEAP OF RUINS (3:8–12)

Isaiah confirms that the quantity of problems escalates when the quality of leadership declines. Having rebelled by word and deed against God's law and defied His "glorious presence," the people carry in their faces the look of arrogant self-destruction. When my wife and I visited Bulgaria, reputed to be the most communistic of the nations in the old Soviet Union, we saw the look of oppression on the faces of the people. No one smiled at us, suspicion answered a simple request for help, and a shroud of drabness blanketed the busy streets. The younger generation, in particular, seemed bewildered with their new-found freedom. Caught between dictatorship and democracy, they were like sheep without a shepherd. One generation of leaders had died and the next generation seemed helpless to be born.

The people of Jerusalem and Judah are even more hopeless. While still carrying the look of pride in their eyes and the sneer of arrogance on their lips, they are living with self-destructive consequences of their own sin. Except for the righteous few, disaster is due.

A BETRAYAL OF TRUST (3:13–15)

Among the tales of a new America that Robert Reich tells in a book by the same title is the tale he calls, "The Rot at the Top." In this tale, he identifies the villains of our society with whom we have a love-hate relationship.[3] Political bosses, business cheats, vulgar movie stars, and spoiled athletes lead us by default. At the same time that we deny their ruinous values, we tolerate their corrupting influence. God will judge them just as He judged the elders and leaders in

Jerusalem and Judah for betraying their trust. At their feet He lays the blame for the ruin of His beloved people; they have exploited the poor and oppressed the helpless (vv. 13–15).

Leadership is a major theme in Isaiah's prophecy because God counted upon judges to administer justice and counselors to teach righteousness as the climate in which His redemptive purpose could be fulfilled. To betray that sacred trust by social injustice and personal unrighteousness is to punish the people and invite the wrath of God. Unfaithful leaders will be the first to feel the raging storm in the day of the LORD.

THE WOMEN OF ZION (3:16–4:1)

16 Moreover the LORD says:
"Because the daughters of Zion are haughty,
and walk with outstretched necks
And wanton eyes,
Walking and mincing as they go,
Making a jingling with their feet,
17 Therefore the Lord will strike with a scab
The crown of the head
of the daughters of Zion,
and the LORD will uncover
their secret parts."
18 In that day the Lord will take away the finery:
The jingling anklets,
the scarves,
and the crescents;
19 The pendants,
the bracelets,
and the veils;
20 The headdresses,
the leg ornaments,
and the headbands;
The perfume boxes,
the charms,
21 and the rings;
The nose jewels,
22 the festal apparel,
and the mantles;
The outer garments,
the purses,

> 23   and the mirrors;
> The fine linen,
>   the turbans,
>   and the robes.
> 24   And so it shall be:
> Instead of a sweet smell
>   there will be a stench;
> Instead of a sash, a rope;
> Instead of a rich robe,
>   a girding of sackcloth;
> And branding instead of beauty.
> 25   Your men shall fall by the sword,
> And your mighty in the war.
> 26   Her gates shall lament and mourn,
> And she being desolate
>   shall sit on the ground.
> 1   And in that day seven women shall
>   take hold of one man, saying
> "We will eat our own food
>   and wear our own apparel;
> Only let us be called by your name,
> To take away our reproach."
>
> *Isaiah 3:16–4:1*

Isaiah is a prophet who speaks the truth, whether in the court of kings or the marketplace of the masses. His most daring venture, however, has to be his pointed prophecy against the elitist daughters of Zion. A book was once written with the title, *How to Become a Bishop Without Being Religious*. One of the rules for pastors aspiring to be a bishop was to avoid offending the Women's Missionary Society. Obviously, Isaiah did not aspire to high ecclesiastical office or he would never have challenged the women of Zion who shared arrogance and pride with their husbands who ruled in the temple. With elaboration equal to the bracelets, bangles, and beads that symbolize their haughty spirit, the prophet indicts them along with their husbands and predicts the punishment of destitution when Jerusalem falls.

COCONSPIRATORS IN CORRUPTION (3:16)

Speaking the Word of God, Isaiah names the women of Zion as coconspirators with their husbands in the capital sins of pride and arrogance. The women, however, show their sin in a special way. With the body language of outstretched necks, flirting eyes, mincing steps, and jangling ornaments they flaunt their haughty spirit for all to see.

Because this prophecy against the women of Zion follows immediately after the prophecy against the men of Zion, especially those who are chosen to be the leaders, it implies that the haughty women are coconspirators in the oppression of the helpless and the exploitation of the poor along with their corrupt husbands. If so, it means that the luxuries they enjoy come at the expense of needy people. As their husbands have betrayed their trust, they not only know of their corruption but revel in it.

Isaiah cannot be charged with male chauvinism. God's Word does not discriminate by gender. Both the men and women of Zion stand on common footing before the scrutiny of the prophet. While the expression of their sin differs, the source is the same. Corrupt men and haughty women are equally guilty of pride, the sin that God abhors.

COPARTNERS IN LOSS (3:17–24)

Because of their sin, the haughty women of Zion will be humbled and disgraced. The humbling will come in the loss of all their finery. Isaiah's listing of the luxurious items that the women use to display their pride reads like a catalog for an ancient beauty boutique, complete with nose rings, ankle chains, and tiaras (vv. 18–23). The greater loss, however, will be the humiliation of shaved heads and running sores. A woman with a shaved head is a worldwide symbol of disgrace. During World War II, for instance, French women who sold themselves as prostitutes to the Nazi army were marched through the streets with shaved heads as the permanent symbol of their expulsion from the city. Add running sores to the shaved head, and, thus, the haughty women who had once stretched out their necks, flirted with their eyes, and walked with mincing steps would now cower in shame, hide their eyes, and shuffle their feet. All of the gaudy symbols of their pride would be traded for the symbols of shame—stench of shame rather than fragrance of perfume, ropes of poverty rather than sashes of wealth, baldness of disgrace rather than coiffured hair, sackcloth of mourning rather than threads of silk, and branding as slaves rather than beauty of skin. They are not only partners in losses with their husbands, but they bear in their bodies the evidence of corruption.

CODEFENDANTS IN JUDGMENT (3:25–4:1)

Just as the men of Zion ended up in caves with rats and bats or subsisted on the margins of human survival in their cities, so the women of Zion will suffer the ultimate reversal when Jerusalem is conquered by the Assyrian hordes. The ranks of men will be decimated by death in battle or exiled to a strange land. Their loss will leave the women of Zion sitting destitute on the ground in the posture of wailing lamentation and bitter mourning. What a contrast with their haughty looks! Worst of all, their flirting eyes, which they use to seduce men, are to no avail. The seven-to-one ratio of women to men robs them of their cherished role as wives and mothers. In desperation bordering on panic, Isaiah foresees the day when the same women of Zion who played with men will now fight over the few male survivors, who most likely are the dregs of society, and beg them for marriage even at the sacrifice of the support that Jewish law requires of husbands (Exodus 21:10–11). The fall from a haughty look to utter shame is complete. Judgment is bottomed out when the women of Zion are willing to do anything to cover their shame, so much so that those who once walked with a haughty look now cry, "Take away our reproach" (4:1).

THE REMNANT OF ISRAEL (4:2–6)

2 In that day the Branch of the LORD
   shall be beautiful and glorious;
and the fruit of the earth shall be
   excellent and appealing
For those of Israel who have escaped.
3 And it shall come to pass that he who is left in Zion and he who remains in Jerusalem will be called holy—everyone who is recorded among the living in Jerusalem.
4 When the Lord has washed away the filth of the daughters of Zion, and purged the blood of Jerusalem from her midst, by the spirit of judgment and by the spirit of burning.

5 then the LORD will create above every dwelling place of Mount Zion, and above her assemblies, a cloud and smoke by day and the shining of a flaming fire by night. For over all the glory there will be a covering.

6 And there will be a tabernacle for shade in the daytime from the heat, for a place of refuge, and for a shelter from storm and rain.

Isaiah 4:2–6

Neither God nor Isaiah can leave Judah and Jerusalem wallowing in the shameful consequences of judgment. God has not changed His redemptive purpose for the children of Israel and Isaiah has not lost this hope for his people. So, as he began this series of prophecies with God's original vision for the house of the LORD (2:2–5), he ends the series with God's vision for Judah and Jerusalem after their suffering in conquest and exile is past. In the remnant that survives, God sees a "branch of beauty" through whom His redemptive purpose will yet be accomplished.

GOD'S FAITHFULNESS (4:2)

Behind Isaiah's prophecy of a *"beautiful and glorious"* branch of the LORD that will survive the exile and see again the *"fruit of the earth"* as their pride and glory, the major theme is the faithfulness of God. Despite the sin of Israel and the judgment upon them, God will remain faithful to the promise that He gave to their father Abraham when He said,

> I will make you a great nation;
> I will bless you
> and make your name great,
> and you shall be a blessing.

Genesis 12:2

As proof of His faithfulness, God shows Isaiah how He will respond to the earlier prophecies of judgment. Having just concluded the prophecy against the daughters of Zion who lost their beauty and fell in shame, God promises a branch that will be *"beautiful and glorious."* Earlier, in the vision for Judah, God offered them the choice of obedience with the promise that they would "eat the good of the land" or, if they rebelled, they would be "devoured by the sword" (1:19–20). Because they chose to rebel, they felt the edge of the conquering sword. But we cannot forget God's message to the men of Zion. In the midst of a staggering city and a falling nation, God said to Isaiah, "*Say to the righteous that it shall be well with them, for they shall eat the fruit of their doings*" (v. 10). We should not be surprised, then, to read of God's repeated promise "*And the fruit of the earth shall be excellent and appealing for those of Israel who have escaped*" (v. 2). The faithfulness of God runs like a thread through these major themes of Isaiah's vision. God's redemptive purpose will be fulfilled because He is faithful.

GOD'S GLORY (4:3–5a)

Through conquest and exile, Isaiah sees a greater glory ahead for the house of Jacob. The remnant that returns from exile will be more than survivors, they will be a holy people, reflecting the character of God and set apart to do the will of God. Though small in number, they will be global in influence and eternal in impact. Also, through the "*spirit of judgment*" and the "*spirit of burning*," Isaiah foresees the washing of the women of Zion and the cleansing of Jerusalem so that the people and their city can fulfill their God-given purpose as the centerpiece for His redemptive plan. A holy nation and a purified city will then be ready for God's restoration of the house of the LORD on Mount Zion so that "all nations will flow to it [and] many peoples will come" (2:2–3) to learn His ways and walk in His paths. What greater destiny can be seen for Judah and Jerusalem than to glorify God as a holy nation living in a purified city and worshiping in the restored house of the LORD? What greater destiny awaits any nation, city, or church whose people are willing and obedient to learn His ways and walk in His paths?

GOD'S GUARANTEES (4:5b–6)

As added assurance of His faithfulness, God goes so far as to back up His promises with some unconditional guarantees. Bringing to mind His providence over the children of Israel during the Exodus from Egypt, the Lord promises a *"cloud and smoke by day,"* the *"shining of a flaming fire by night,"* and the *"covering"* of the Lord as *"a tabernacle for shade in the daytime from the heat, for a place of refuge, and for a shelter from storm and rain"* (vv. 5b–6). With these remembrances come two guarantees.

First, God guarantees His unfailing **presence** for His people. This is an astounding fact. Despite their sin and through their judgment, God had never left them! Sinners who return to the Lord give eloquent testimony to this truth. A son of a Christian family rebelled against his parents, left home, and disappeared into the underworld of drugs for years. When he surfaced as a cocaine-scarred prodigal, called his parents, and returned home, he said, "Although I left you and your God, He never left me." All of us need this assurance. Through our sin, our suffering, and our exile, God guarantees His unfailing presence.

Second, God guarantees His unceasing **protection**. Isaiah uses the image of a canopy over Israel that will protect from the heat of the day and the storm of the night. As people who had felt both the fire and the rain of judgment in the dreadful day of the LORD at the hand of the Babylonians in ancient times and at the hand of the Nazis in the Holocaust of modern times, the children of Israel have counted heavily upon the fulfillment of this guarantee. Of course, God's promise is given only to the branch of the LORD or those in the remnant who have been obedient to His Word and faithful to His ways.

And, of course, believers are not exempt from the fire and storm that make up the vicissitudes of life. A preacher who told his congregation that they would be protected from death because of Christ's "blood on the door post" misled a new believer. When the tragic news came of the death of a baby belonging to another couple in the congregation, the new believer immediately passed judgment upon them and claimed exemption for her children from the same fate. God's guarantee of protection does not include either natural causes or unforeseen accidents. He does guarantee that we will not suffer the "fire" of the consequences for our own sin if we are a holy people or the "storm" of His judgment if we are a forgiven people. Self-inflicted fire and God-inflicted storms are excluded from the guarantee.

Isaiah's major themes, then, are presented within the bookends of hope. On one side is God's vision for the house of the LORD as the light for the nations; on the other side is His vision for the branch of the LORD as a remnant of holy, purified, and worshiping people who are guided by His presence and protected by His grace. In between these visions of hope there are the realities of judgment upon the rebellious children of Israel and the corrupt men and haughty women of Zion. To understand these major themes is to read with understanding the prophecy of Isaiah.

NOTES

1. Smith, *Expositor's Bible*, 26.

2. Warren Bennis, *Why Leaders Can't Lead* (San Francisco: Jossey-Bass Publishers, 1990), 66.

3. Robert Reich, *Tales of a New America: The Anxious Liberal's Guide to the Future* (New York: Random House, 1988).

CHAPTER FOUR

A Bittersweet Love Song

Isaiah 5:1–30

A moral dilemma has been created by Isaiah's prophecies of judgment and redemption. Perhaps in his own mind, or in his debate with the people of Judah and Jerusalem, the question has arisen, "If God's purpose is redemptive and His promise is the assurance of restoration, how can He justify venting his wrath upon His own creation and His own chosen people?"

To answer the question, Isaiah offers "The Song of the Vineyard." In the verse he sings of God's love for His well-beloved people; in the refrain he repeats the "woes" against His rebellious people that justify His wrath. As with all parables, Isaiah has only a single point to make: If the chosen children of Israel, whom God loves, nurtures, and protects, do not produce the fruits of justice and righteousness, He will lift His protection and leave them to the consequences of their sin.

A SONG OF LOVE (5:1–7)

1 Now let me sing to my Well-beloved
  A song of my Beloved regarding His vineyard:
  My Well-beloved has a vineyard
  On a very fruitful hill.
2 He dug it up and cleared out its stones,
  And planted it with the choicest vine.
  He built a tower in its midst,
  And also made a winepress in it;
  So He expected it to bring forth good grapes,
  But it brought forth wild grapes.
3 "And now, O inhabitants of Jerusalem
    and men of Judah,

Judge, please, between Me and My vineyard.
4 What more could have been done to My vineyard
That I have not done in it?
Why then, when I expected it to bring forth good
    grapes,
Did it bring forth wild grapes?
5 And now, please let Me tell you
    what I will do to My vineyard:
I will take away its hedge,
    and it shall be burned;
And break down its wall,
    and it shall be trampled down.
6 I will lay it waste;
It shall not be pruned or dug,
But there shall come up briars and thorns.
I will also command the clouds
That they rain no rain on it."
7 For the vineyard of the LORD of hosts
    is the house of Israel,
And the men of Judah
    are His pleasant plant.
He looked for justice,
    but behold, oppression;
For righteousness, but behold, weeping.

Isaiah 5:1–7

How Much Do I Love You? (5:1–2)

The words *"Now let me sing to my Well-beloved"* are reminiscent of Elizabeth Barrett Browning's sonnet, "How do I love thee? Let me count the ways." No one can doubt the depth of love contained in these words. It is an unconditional love that is vulnerable to hurt. Not unlike the image of the Father with which Isaiah introduced us to God in the opening verse of his vision, the keeper of the vineyard expresses love in a way that everyone can understand. With elaborate detail, Isaiah walks through each step in the creation of a vineyard that has the exclusive attention of the owner. He chooses a fertile hillside, clears the stones, plants the choicest vines, builds a watchtower to protect it, and cuts a winepress in anticipation of a rich harvest of good grapes. Alas, all the work is for nought. The vineyard yields only rotten grapes whose stench repels the owner. All of love's labor is lost.

WHY DON'T YOU LOVE ME? (5:3–4)

Through this analogy in song, God reverses roles with the defendants of Judah and Jerusalem in the courtroom scene of the first chapter of Isaiah. At the risk of a "guilty" verdict, He asks the citizens of Jerusalem and the men of Judah to pass judgment upon Him and His vineyard. Throwing Himself on the mercy of the court, God asks, *"What more could have been done to My vineyard that I have not done in it?"* The question has the ring of Jesus' challenge to His accusers, "Can any of you prove me guilty of sin?" (John 8:46). When God or Jesus asks the question, the answer is rhetorical. Accusers fall silent and the burden of guilt shifts to those who refuse to believe. For the moment, at least, truth and falsehood change places. Truth takes the throne and falsehood goes to the scaffold.

WHAT CAN I DO? (5:5–7)

When the silence of the citizens of Judah and the men of Jerusalem confirms their guilt, God pronounces the sentence. He will lift His hedge of protection from the vineyard, permit animals and enemies to trample it underfoot, let it become a wild wasteland, and stop the life-giving rain upon its soil. Briars and thorns will be its bitter fruit, the biblical symbol for cursed land under threat of eternal destruction.

Usually a biblical parable has a hidden meaning that is understood only by spiritually enlightened minds. Isaiah does not take this chance with his hearers in Judah and Jerusalem. In a rare statement of the obvious, he explains the parable of the vineyard in unmistakable terms. The vineyard is the house of Israel; the men of Judah are "His pleasant plant"; and justice and righteousness are the good grapes for which He looked but found only injustice and oppression. The point of the parable is made: God did not abandon the children of Israel—they abandoned Him. Therefore, He is justified in His decision to leave them to their own devices and let them suffer the consequences of their sin as the only way to redeem them.

A CHORUS OF WOES (5:8–23)

8 Woe to those who join house to house,
   Who add field to field,
   Till there is no place
   Where they may dwell alone
        in the midst of the land!
9 In my hearing the LORD of hosts said,
   "Truly, many houses shall be desolate,
   Great and beautiful ones,
        without inhabitant,
10 For ten acres of vineyard shall yield one bath,
   And a homer of seed shall yield one ephah."
11 Woe to those who rise early in the morning,
   That they may follow intoxicating drink;
   Who continue until night,
        till wine inflames them!
12 The harp and the strings,
   The tambourine and flute,
   And wine are in their feasts;
   But they do not regard the work of the LORD,
   Nor consider the operation of His hands.
13 Therefore my people have gone into captivity,
   Because they have no knowledge;
   Their honorable men are famished,
   And their multitude dried up with thirst.
14 Therefore Sheol has enlarged itself
   And opened its mouth beyond measure;
   Their glory and their multitude and their pomp,
   And he who is jubilant,
        shall descend into it.
15 People shall be brought down.
   Each man shall be humbled,
   And the eyes of the lofty
        shall be humbled.
16 But the LORD of hosts
        shall be exalted in judgment,
   And God who is holy shall be hallowed in
        righteousness.
17 Then the lambs shall feed in their pasture,
   And in the waste places of the fat ones strangers shall
        eat.

18 Woe to those who draw iniquity
        with cords of vanity,
    And sin as if with a cart rope;
19   That say, "Let Him make speed
        and hasten His work,
    That we may see it;
    And let the counsel of the Holy One of Israel draw near
        and come,
    That we may know it."
20 Woe to those who call evil good,
        and good evil;
    Who put darkness for light,
        and light for darkness;
    Who put bitter for sweet,
        and sweet for bitter!
21 Woe to those who are wise
        in their own eyes,
    And prudent in their own sight!
22 Woe to men mighty at drinking wine,
    Woe to men valiant for mixing intoxicating drink,
23 Who justify the wicked for a bribe,
    And take away justice from the righteous man!

Isaiah 5:8–23

The song is not ended. In a repeated refrain of six woes, God speci-
fies the sins of the children of Israel that spoiled the grapes and
turned them rotten. Every civilization must deal with the same issues:

- the ownership of property (vv. 8–10)
- the use of alcohol (v. 11–17)
- the interpretation of history (vv. 18–19)
- the teaching of morals (v. 20)
- the exercise of intellect (v. 21)
- the administration of justice (vv. 22–23)

THE WOE OF GREED (5:8–10)

In each case, a decision may be made for good or evil. Judah failed
on all points. The *ownership of land* had become an exercise in greed as

persons accumulated fields, homes, mansions, and vineyards at the expense of the poor. Isaiah predicted that the day would come when their selfishness would leave them lonely, their mansions empty, and their vineyards almost worthless.

The Bluegrass region of Kentucky is a land of contrast between the mega-rich and the poorest of the poor. As a seminary student, I remember the shock of seeing mahogany-lined stables that far exceeded the hovels in which the horse handlers lived. Greed is often the driving force behind the competition to build bigger and better barns than the neighbors. The true story is told of a woman who wanted to break into the elitist social circle of horse farm owners. She spent a fortune on a grand old mansion and redecorated it in order to be "hostess with the mostest" for the extravagant parties at Kentucky Derby time. The invitations went to a highly select company, but when the night of the party came she waited alone in the midst of her splendor. No one came and the woman was so enraged that she abandoned her mansion and left the state forever. Greed has a price that not even money can buy.

THE WOE OF DRUNKENNESS (5:11–17)

The *use of alcohol* and other narcotic substances is another test of civilization that the children of Israel failed. Wine was not forbidden among the Israelites. Communal wine in religious feasts and social wine at celebrations, such as weddings, served as enhancements of spirit on those occasions. But strict taboos prohibited the abuse of alcohol because of its destructive force upon personal judgment and social morals. Isaiah's catalog of those destructive forces among drunken Israelites is as up-to-date as this morning's newspaper. He cites especially the leaders of the nation who are addicted to drink, as evidenced by their compulsion to drink early in the morning and continue until late at night. With dulled intellectual and spiritual senses, they *"do not regard the work of the LORD"* in history nor do they *"consider the operation of His hands"* in creation. At their doorstep Isaiah lays the blame for the children of Israel going into exile (v. 13), suffering famine (v. 13), and opening the jaws of hell to receive those who die from the effects of drink (v. 14).

The same "woe" might be pronounced over our society today. Substance abuse, ranging from alcohol to cocaine, has reached epidemic proportions among our people, whether young or old, rich or poor, educated or illiterate. I cochaired the local session of a national teleconference on substance abuse. The leaders of government, experts in the field, and a cross section of community members were present. After two hours of presentations and discussions on hard drugs, a high school youth spoke up. "When are we going to talk about the 'entry drug' that is the real problem in our high school? I'm referring to alcohol." Statistics on alcohol-related accidents and crime verify the student's concern. We know firsthand what Isaiah meant when he envisioned the grave enlarging its appetite and hell widening its jaws to accommodate the souls who are victims of drink. While the long-term consequences for our society are yet to be known, we can be sure that alcohol addiction contains the seeds of its own judgment.

THE WOE OF SELF-DECEIT (5:18–19)

A third "woe" is pronounced by Isaiah against those who use the *interpretation of history* to hide their sins. Using a direct quote from his critics, Isaiah scores those who challenge God to speed up His judgment as proof of the prophecies. Meanwhile, they play with sin like a pull-toy and use the timing of history as a tactic of deceit. The scene is reminiscent of the cartoon showing a white-bearded, long-robed prophet walking in the marketplace carrying a sign that reads, "The End Is Near." Those who pass by laugh at the prophet because he returns each day with the same message and nothing happens. Meanwhile, they go about their sins with a flourish.

Isaiah must have faced a similar reception in the temple of Jerusalem. Religious leaders whose responsibility included the interpretation of history for the common people, mocked Isaiah with his own words when they said, *"Let Him make speed and hasten His work that we may see it"* (v. 19). "Woe to you," Isaiah cries. "You challenge God's timing to hide your sin." Like the eccentric prophet carrying the sign in the marketplace, Isaiah would not be a welcome sight on the streets of Jerusalem or in the courts of the temple.

THE WOE OF SELF-JUSTIFICATION (5:20)

Still another "woe" is reserved for those who are responsible for *teaching morals* in Judah and Jerusalem. Rather than speaking the truth without compromise, the teachers reverse the values so that good becomes evil, evil becomes good, darkness becomes light, light becomes darkness, bitter becomes sweet, and sweet becomes bitter (v. 20). An observer of our contemporary culture illustrated this moral reversal by noting, "A thief in the night sneaked into the store and changed all of the prices on the items. The most valuable are now cheap and the cheap are now valuable."

We live with that reality. The other day, a radio preacher told about being convicted for watching movies at home and laughing at the sins for which Christ died. He sensed the same moral reversal that Isaiah condemned. To laugh at the sins for which Christ died is to cheapen the good, the light, and the sweet while inadvertently raising the value of evil, darkness, and bitterness. As Isaiah was not welcomed on the streets of Jerusalem or in the courts of the temple, so his reception might be equally cool in our homes and schools today.

THE WOE OF SOPHISTRY (5:21)

Isaiah's fifth "woe" is against those who are *"wise in their own eyes and prudent in their own sight"* in the *exercise of intellect* (v. 21). Academics who pride themselves in their own intellect will be stung by this phrase. Persons who are especially gifted with native intelligence are often responsible for the "ideas" acted out in the culture. Communism, for instance, is the idea of Lenin acted out by dictators such as Stalin and Khrushchev. Democracy, as well, is an idea acted out by Washington, Jefferson, Lincoln, and other American presidents.

Good wisdom, however, does not come automatically with high intelligence. By definition, wisdom means "to see things whole" and requires a center from which all things are seen. What then is the center from which we claim to see things whole? When Job encountered that question he likened the human search for wisdom to the genius required to mine silver and gold from a deep shaft into the center of the earth (Job 28). After all of the resources of human creativity and inventiveness were exhausted, wisdom eluded the seeker. Job then gave the answer that identified the true center, "The fear of the Lord is the beginning of wisdom."

Isaiah cries "woe" upon those who pretend to be wise with their own finite mind as the center of their seeing. History is replete with the tragic consequences of such arrogance. Whether Nietzsche's philosophy, which the Nazis practiced in the Holocaust, or Lenin's theory of Communism, which enslaved Eastern Europe for forty years, Isaiah's condemnation is justified. The prophet would also have little patience with academics today who use "political correctness" as a hammer of truth but under the guise of seeing things whole. For them, truth is the result of political pressure from minorities of race, gender, and sexual preference who want to rewrite the history books in their own favor. Although the writing of Western history may have been biased toward white, Anglo-saxon, Protestant, heterosexual males, the correction is not to rewrite the history with another politically motivated bias. At least the earlier writers of Western history used methods of scholarship that gave their work some measure of objectivity. Leaders who claim to be wise without God as the center of their reasoning are particularly dangerous because they influence the young who act out with high energy their revolutionary ideas. Revolutions and reforms that have benefited humankind invariably come from the wisdom of intellect centered in God—whether social, scientific or religious in nature.

THE WOE OF INJUSTICE (5:22–23)

Isaiah's sixth and final "woe" involves the *use of money*. Somewhat as a summary of "woes," Isaiah returns to his central theme: the loss of personal righteousness leads to social corruption and injustice. Drunken leaders who practice all of the sins of the first five "woes" bottom out in taking bribes at the expense of the poor.

One of the lasting insights from my experience as Chairman of the Governor's Select Committee to study gambling in the State of Washington came from the testimony of an expert witness on the social effects of gambling. He told us that the gambling industry depended upon political corruption to exist. With the high stakes of gambling money, payoffs to public officials are common. Whether buying politicians' votes that are favorable to gambling or influencing the police to go easy on criminal enforcement, gambling and corruption are codependents. During that same period, a long-time political reporter for a newspaper told me, "If you want to know whether a politician is honest or not, compare the balance in his checkbook before he is elected and after he leaves office."

Isaiah sees the same connection between personal sin and social corruption. Once the dominoes of personal righteousness fell among the leaders in Judah and Jerusalem, the dominoes of political corruption and social injustice followed. Long before Paul wrote to Timothy, "For the love of money is a root of all kinds of evil, for which some have strayed from the faith in their greediness and pierced themselves through with many sorrows" (1 Timothy 6:10), Isaiah pronounced "woe" upon the sin of greed.

A lifetime study of the motivation of money brought Gary S. Becker the Nobel Award in 1992. Years earlier, he advanced the idea that economic motives guided and shaped many aspects of human behavior. At first, Becker's ideas were considered farfetched. But over the years, his work has been substantiated by others' studies in economics, psychology, and sociology. While economic motives for human decisions may be made for good or evil, the power of those motives cannot be denied.

GOD'S FURY AND HIS FLAG (5:24–30)

24 Therefore, as the fire devours the stubble,
    And the flame consumes the chaff,
    So their root will be as rottenness,
    And their blossom will ascend like dust;
    Because they have rejected the law of the LORD of hosts,
    And despised the word of the Holy One of Israel.
25 Therefore the anger of the LORD is
        aroused against His people;
    He has stretched out His hand against them
    And stricken them,
    And the hills trembled.
    Their carcasses were as refuse
        in the midst of the streets.
    For all this His anger is not turned away,
    But His hand is stretched out still.
26 He will lift up a banner to the nations from afar,
    And will whistle to them from the end of the earth;
    Surely they shall come with speed, swiftly.
27 No one will be weary or stumble among them,
    No one will slumber or sleep;
    Nor will the belt on their loins be loosed,

Nor the strap of their sandals be broken;
28 Whose arrows are sharp,
    And all their bows bent;
    Their horses' hooves will seem like flint,
    And their wheels like a whirlwind.
29 Their roaring will be like a lion,
    They will roar like young lions;
    Yes, they will roar
    And lay hold of the prey;
    They will carry it away safely,
    And no one will deliver.
30 In that day they will roar against them
    Like the roaring of the sea.
    And if one looks to the land,
    Behold, darkness and sorrow;
    And the light is darkened by the clouds.

Isaiah 5:24–30

Beware. When Isaiah follows a list of "woes" with the word *"therefore,"* we can count on a conclusion that releases the wrath of God upon sin. Beware also when Isaiah invokes the formal names of God, *"the LORD of hosts"* and *"the Holy One of Israel"* (v. 24). The first name calls out God's power; the second calls out His purity. Isaiah's choice of these formal names reminds me of how our children recalled with humor the different names I used to call them on certain occasions. Our daughter, Suzanne, for instance, knew the nickname of affection "Suki" meant some generous gesture or gentle request on my part. The intensity picked up when I called her "Sue." She remembered that I usually followed that name with a specific instruction or request. If, however, she heard me bark, "SUZANNE," she knew a command or reprimand was coming. Similarly, whenever Isaiah advances the intensity from "LORD" to "the LORD of hosts" or "the Holy One of Israel," we can expect a change from the word of instruction to the word of judgment.

A DEVOURING FIRE (5:24–25)

Two metaphors describe the pending judgment upon Judah and Jerusalem. *"Fire"* is used to convey the nature of God's wrath. Like the rain that falls upon the just and the unjust, the fire of God affects both the righteous and the wicked. For the righteous, it is the source of empowering energy, for example the flaming tongues of fire at Pentecost; but for the wicked, the same fire becomes the purging flame that consumes and devours the *"rottenness"* of sin. Isaiah makes it plain that sin is self-destructive as he envisions the flame of God being fueled by the images of dead stubble, dry chaff, rotten roots, and withered flowers. As fire flares when it touches dry fuel, so the anger of God is aroused by the dead rot of sin (v. 25).

The analogy of the fire and the fuel helps us understand the meaning of Isaiah's words following another *"therefore"* (v. 25). When he says, *"He (the LORD) has stretched out His hand against them and stricken them,"* it sounds as if God's action is arbitrary and overreactive. This is not the case. Imagine the fire of God burning at all times like an eternal flame. For the righteous it does not harm but, in fact, serves as a source of warmth and energy. But when the wicked, who represent dead stubble, dry chaff, rotten roots, and withered flowers, come in contact with the same flame, the fire of God turns into a raging inferno. The truth is self-evident: sin brings judgment upon itself—a judgment so devastating that the carcasses of the children of Israel will be piled up like refuse in the middle of the street (v. 25). Such is the destruction when the fire of God is fueled by the dry rot of human sin.

AN UNFURLED BANNER (5:26–30)

Complementing the metaphor of fire is the image of an unfurled *"banner"* rising high in the sky for all nations to see. In the image of fire he answered the question *why* God's judgment would come to Judah and Jerusalem; now the meaning of the banner answers the question *how* God's judgment will come. As the fire of His anger flared when it touched the dry rot of human corruption, so the banner on the hilltop, accompanied by a whistle heard to the end of the earth, will summon the swift and deadly hordes of pagan armies to trample underfoot the promised land and march the children of Israel into shameful exile.

Again, the judgment of God is not so much His aggressive action against the sinful nation as it is His lifting the protective hedge around their borders and letting the collective forces of military power overrun them. Most of us take for granted God's protective hedge around our lives. If, however, he lifted that hedge for just a moment, we would be wasted by Satan's swift and deadly onslaught. Such a fate awaited Judah and Jerusalem in the forthcoming Assyrian invasion—a fate as destructive as a tidal wave leveling the land and wiping out so many of its inhabitants that the light of hope is almost blotted out by the dark and foreboding clouds of sorrow (v. 30). If anyone still thinks that God does not take sin seriously, Isaiah's vision of the fire and the banner should dispel that notion.

Although the wrath of God's judgment seems to be complete in the images of the fire and the banner, the purpose is still redemptive. When sin becomes so deeply ingrained in the soul of a person or a society, the purging of fire by the lifting of God's protective hedge may be the only remedy. The test is whether or not sin has corrupted the center of the soul and contaminated all parts of the individual or corporate body. God, then, will resort to radical measures to fulfill His redemptive purpose.

PART THREE

The Vision Personalized

Isaiah 6:1–13

CHAPTER FIVE

The Prophet's Calling

Isaiah 6:1–13

No controversy swirls around the date for Isaiah's encounter with God in the temple. It happened in 740 B.C., the year in which King Uzziah died. Unresolved controversy, however, does come from the question, "How does Isaiah's experience in the temple relate to the first five chapters in the book?" Is chapter six misplaced? Did Isaiah prophesy before he was called? Is his experience in the temple a confirmation of his calling? Or did he have a special reason for placing chapter six after the opening chapters?

The account of Isaiah's calling is not misplaced. To force a chronological sequence upon Isaiah is to miss the purpose of the prophet's writing. Our perspective is that he summarized his prophecies and stated his themes in the first five chapters to *show the priority of the message over the messenger*. If so, Isaiah continues to be consistent with his introduction and his writing throughout the book in which the answer to the question *what* takes precedence over the question *who*. As we have already noted, Isaiah is not a prophet on an ego trip. He mentions his own name only when it is relevant to a historical happening and omits it entirely when the vision takes him into a future of which he will not be part. Yet, we also remember that Isaiah alone among the prophets claimed to receive his prophetic authority directly from God. Logically, then, his decision to include a personal testimonial of his encounter with God when he received his vision serves as the sign and seal for his prophetic authority.

CONFRONTED BY GOD (6:1–4)

1 In the year that King Uzziah died, I saw the Lord sitting on a throne, high and lifted up, and the train of His robe filled the temple.

2 Above it stood seraphim; each one had six wings: with two he covered his face, with two he covered his feet, and with two he flew.

3 And one cried to another and said:
"Holy, holy, holy is the LORD of hosts;
The whole earth is full of His glory!"

4 And the posts of the door were shaken by the voice of him who cried out, and the house was filled with smoke.

Isaiah 6:1–4

THE SOVEREIGNTY OF GOD (6:1–2)

Every symbol in Isaiah's vision of God is significant. In the first five chapters we learn that Israel had become too complacent in its security to heed the warnings of God and too corrupted in its prosperity to escape the wrath of God. Not only that, but Uzziah, a good king for fifty-two years, had become arrogant, profaned the temple, contracted leprosy, and died in shame. All of Israel needed to be shaken by the vision of the LORD *"sitting on a throne, high and lifted up"* with the train of His robe filling the temple. Each of these symbols—the title LORD, the throne, the lofty position, and the all-encompassing robe—reinforced His sovereignty over all of the universe, over all its kings, over all of their nations, and over all peoples, including the chosen children of Israel.

The sovereignty of God is pronounced in Isaiah. Nations turn against Him, but His will prevails; kings compete with Him, but fall in shame; people turn from Him to worship idols, but their false gods crumble. Even His people refuse to trust Him, but they do not escape punishment. And, mystery of mysteries, a pagan despot becomes His instrument of judgment. But even he, Cyrus, must pay for his sins. Yet, through it all, the sovereign Lord promises to preserve a remnant through whom the Savior will come to set up an ultimate reign when swords are beaten into plowshares and the lion will lie down with the lamb. Isaiah leaves no doubt—the sovereign Lord writes the script of human history.

THE HOLINESS OF GOD (6:3)

But sovereignty is not the primary revelation of God's character in Isaiah's vision. First and foremost, it is the holiness of the Lord that Isaiah senses. Sovereignty is the powerful nature of God; holiness is the moral character of God. He is pure; He is complete; He is whole. R. C. Sproul, in his book *The Holiness of God*, notes that holiness is the only attribute of God that is presented in the Scripture in the superlative.[1] When His holiness is extolled by the seraphim in antiphonal chorus, they sing "Holy, Holy, Holy." No other attribute is so praised. Angels do not sing, "Love, Love, Love" or "Justice, Justice, Justice"—they only sing "Holy, Holy, Holy."

We understand why the seraphim used their wings to cover their feet. Even without sin, they cannot stand to have the holy God look upon their created nature. He and He alone is holy.

But the moral character of the holy God is more than a matter of "being" in His transcendence. Isaiah sees that His holiness is also a matter of "doing" in His immanence. As His transcendent holiness cannot tolerate sin among the people or the nations, wherever His immanent holiness touches down we see the ethical imprint of His character in the glorious work of God.

So the seraphim must cover their faces because they cannot gaze upon His glory. Moses had a similar experience. When he asked God to see His glory, God answered, "I will make all My goodness pass before you . . . [but] you cannot see My face . . . and live" (Exodus 33:19–20).

So, with Isaiah, in the sovereignty of the Lord we encounter the fact that His will cannot be known; in His holiness we learn of His purity that cannot tolerate sin; but in His glory we learn of His mercy that promises a remnant out of which will come a Savior who will redeem the world and all nations. No wonder Isaiah heard the song of the seraphim, *"Holy, Holy, Holy, is the LORD of Hosts. The whole earth is full of His glory!"* As the posts shook and smoke filled the temple, Isaiah entered the awesome presence of the Lord—holy in all His "being" and glorious in all His "doing."

THE WORSHIP OF GOD (6:4)

How did Isaiah respond to the presence of God—to His sovereign will, His holy character, and His glorious works? Rudolph Otto, in his book *The Idea of the Holy*, gives us a clue to Isaiah's response when he suggests that we are, at best, ambivalent. Before the *mysterium* of His holiness, we feel both *tremendum* and *fascinans*. We tremble with fear and awe, but at the same time we are fascinated by His holiness, which is attractive, desirable, promising, and compelling. Peter calls this "reverential fear" (1 Peter 1:17 NIV) when we shut our mouths, cover our feet, and close our eyes before the sovereign holiness and glory of God.

As with Isaiah, our *worship* begins in His holy and glorious presence. In his book *Reality In Worship*, J. P. Allen likens our worship to entering a planetarium from a busy, noisy street.[3] Dimming lights hush the sounds and the universe opens up over our heads. Earth becomes one of the smallest of planets and we become one of its smallest creatures. In that awesome moment, we focus upon the greatness, the goodness, and the grace of God. Our worship should be like that. It should not begin with a focus upon ourselves and our own needs, but upon the character of God; we should not proceed without the expectation of the visitation of His Spirit, but wait in His holy presence until He comes; we should not assume there is nothing new under the sun that we have not seen, but come expecting a glimpse of His glory.

In His holy and glorious presence, our *holiness* begins. Not only does the holiness of God call out the Christ who can redeem us, but it also gives us the promise that we can be imprinted with His character. "Be holy, for I am holy" (1 Peter 1:16) is not an optional command. God's desire is that we be holy as He is holy. So, we who worship in reverential fear will follow after holiness in our character (2 Corinthians 7:1) and walk circumspectly in our conduct (Hebrews 11:7). Henry Clay Morrison, founding President of Asbury Theological Seminary, spoke the truth when he said, "We are born again as God's children. Just as no honest father wants his son to be a thief, no industrious father wants his son to be a sluggard, and no upright father wants his son to be immoral, so God our heavenly Father, being holy, wants us, His children, to be holy like Himself." After entering into the awesome presence of the Holy God with Isaiah, we can only sing the prayer,

> Teach me to love Thee
> As Thine angels love,
> One holy passion,

Filling all my frame.
The baptism of the heaven-descended Dove,
My heart an altar,
And Thy love the flame.

CONVICTED OF SIN (6:5)

5 Then I said:
   "Woe is me, for I am undone!
   Because I am a man of unclean lips,
   And I dwell in the midst of a people
       of unclean lips;
   For my eyes have seen the King,
   The LORD of hosts."

Isaiah 6:5

Edgar Allen Poe wrote the short story "The Telltale Heart." As always, Poe himself is the culprit in a violent scene. An old man who lives with him has a vulture-like eye with which Poe becomes obsessed. To escape the eye, Poe decides that he must kill the old man. So, in the dark of night, he enters the old man's room, lets a crack of light out of his lantern, and sees the vulture-like eye fixed upon him. The old man's heart begins to pound, faster and louder, as Poe toys with his victim. Then, when the old man screams, Poe smothers him with a pillow and makes sure that he is dead. To cover his crime, the murderer takes up the planks of the living room floor and buries his victim. Suddenly, there is a knock at the door. The police are there to check the report of a scream coming from the house. Poe explains that he himself screamed in a nightmare and invites them in for a spot of tea. As they sit in the living room, Poe places his chair directly over the body of his victim. The policemen smile and chat as they drink their tea. What's that? Poe hears a beat, muffled at first, and then rising to a staccato sound for all to hear. Louder and louder it grows, but still the officers smile and chat. Louder, louder, and LOUDER until Poe shrieks,

Villains, dissemble no more! I admit the deed!—tear up the planks—here, here—it is the beating of his hideous heart!

Despite a story that may have risen out of a drug dream, Edgar Allan Poe comes close to a truth from which we cannot escape. As he sat in the presence of the officers, the imaginary beating of the telltale heart betrayed his guilt and exposed his sin. In the presence of the holy God, Isaiah's telltale heart also caused him to cry out, *"Woe is me, for I am undone. Because I am a man of unclean lips."* Three uncomfortable and unpopular truths confront us in this confession.

FEELING OUR ANGUISH (6:5a)

First, when we see the holy character of God, we feel anguish for our own sin. Other translations add force to Isaiah's cry when he says, "Woe is me, I am undone"(KJV). Another says, "Woe is me, I am lost" (NRSV) and still another, "Horrors, my doom is sealed." Whatever the cry, Isaiah is confessing that he is unworthy to join the seraphim in singing, "Holy, Holy, Holy."

Here is fundamental truth: whenever we see the King, the Lord of hosts, our sinfulness is exposed. Like the pounding of the telltale heart, we can only cry "woe," not upon others but only upon ourselves. Hugh Kerrand and John Mulder have written a book entitled *Conversions* in which they cite the verbatim testimonies of spiritual leaders from the Apostle Paul to Charles Colson, with such notables as Augustine, Calvin, Bunyan, Wesley, Spurgeon, Tolstoy, William Booth, Schweitzer, C. S. Lewis, and Thomas Merton in between. Using Isaiah's vision of God as the model, the authors state that in every conversion they studied, there is agony of soul:

- the stab of conscience
- the shame of inward uncleanness
- the remorse for sin
- the sensation of being lost and alone.[4]

When John Bunyan, for instance, got a glimpse of the holiness of God, he reported that he felt like a child falling into a well pit. Sprawled in the water at the bottom of the pit, he could find no handhold or foothold to lift himself out. He felt that he would die in that condition. From that memory came the allegory of the *Pilgrim's Progress*.

Soren Kierkegaard, another subject in the book, describes himself as a rower in a boat who has tried to save himself by rowing against the stream that runs toward God. Finally, in exhaustion, he drops the oars and feels himself spinning out of control toward the brink of the falls.

Why do such testimonies sound as strange and melodramatic to our ears as Isaiah's encounter with God? The answer is that our spiritual sensitivity to sin is dulled because we have lost sight of a holy God. Not unlike Isaiah and Israel, we may need to see His holiness, feel the shaking pillars, and smell the rising smoke that cause us to cry, "Woe is me, for I am undone!"

ACCEPTING OUR RESPONSIBILITY (6:5b)

Another agonizing truth comes to us from Isaiah's response. When Isaiah sees God, he accepts responsibility for his sin. "*I am a man of unclean lips*" or "I am a foul-mouthed sinner" allows for no exceptions and leaves no room for shifting the blame. Isaiah is saying that he has

- no place in the presence of God,
- no right to praise God, and
- no authority to speak for God.

Not without significance, Isaiah confesses that he is a man of "unclean lips." Jewish people saw lips as more than a specific set of sensory organs. To them, the lips spoke the motives of the heart and the decisions of the will. So, Isaiah is confessing that through his lips, his telltale heart has betrayed him. Jesus confirmed that truth when He said, "But those things which proceed out of the mouth come from the heart, and they defile a man" (Matthew 15:18).

For Isaiah, "unclean lips" had another meaning. Whether he had already been pronouncing "woes" upon the people of Israel, or would soon do so, he was called to speak for God. But, upon seeing the holiness of God and catching a glimpse of His glory, he asks, "How can I speak for God without a heart like God?" Every preacher, teacher, and witness for the Word of God must ask the same question. If there is sin in our hearts, our lips will betray us.

Hard truth comes to us again. We have failed to accept responsibility for our sin. Jacques Ellul has written a book entitled *The*

Technological Bluff.[5] In his ongoing love-hate relationship with modern technology, Ellul calls the bluff of technological progress. He says that technology promises unlimited progress and unlimited good. Therefore, whatever goes on in such fields as computer science, genetic engineering, space technology, biotechnology, or laser research will solve our problems and produce beneficial results. Our hope is that medical science will solve the problem of AIDS, superior weaponry will defeat dictators, genetic engineering will eliminate birth defects, lasers will heal cancer, star wars will assure peace, and media will bring democracy to the world. Not so, according to Ellul. All technology has its price, its problems, its harmful effects, and its unforeseen consequences.

Isaiah's woeful confession of his own sin reminds us that we may also be victims of a theological bluff. This is the contemporary ruse that makes sin a nonfatal sickness for which someone is responsible. There is the theology that objectifies our sin, the psychology that explains it, the sociology that excuses it, and the economics that pay for it. Isaiah calls the bluff. In the presence of the holy Lord, we and we alone are responsible for unclean lips that betray the sin of our telltale heart.

From Isaiah's confession, we also learn that sin has another dimension. After confessing his own sin, Isaiah goes on to say, *"I dwell in the midst of people of unclean lips."* Although sin is primarily personal, we cannot deny that sin has a social impact. So when we see the holy character of God, we also see the pervasive influence of our sin. "A people of unclean lips" symbolizes corruption at the very heart of the culture.

The pervasiveness of our sin is frightening. Statistical reports show that 70 percent to 95 percent of the perpetrators of domestic violence and sexual abuse learned the behavior as either victims or witnesses of violence and abuse. Other reports show that teenage pregnancies have increased so dramatically that the problem of teenage parents is costing billions of dollars and creating a host of other social problems. The breakdown in personal morality has a social price that we cannot count.

ADMITTING OUR INFLUENCE (6:5c)

Here is another hard fact. Isaiah accepts his responsibility as a leader for the sins of his people. He who pronounced "woes" upon leaders in Judah and Jerusalem for betraying their trust now confesses the same sin in himself. He knows firsthand the truth that, just as the sins of the father are visited upon the children, so the sins of the leader are visited upon the people. King David is a classic case. When he sinned against God by counting his armies, he confessed, "I have sinned greatly because I have done this thing; but now, I pray, take away the iniquity of Your servant, for I have done very foolishly" (1 Chronicles 21:8).

So God gave David three options: three years of famine, three months of fleeing from his enemies, or three days of plague upon the land. In response, David pled for his own skin, "Do not let me fall into the hand of man" (21:13) and God sent a plague in which seventy thousand people died. When David realized what he had done, he begged again, "I am the one who has sinned and done evil indeed; but these sheep, what have they done? Let Your hand, I pray, O LORD my God, be against me and my father's house, but not against Your people that they should be plagued" (21:17). David learned what Isaiah knew. In the presence of God, we not only see the sin in ourselves, but we also see the effects of our sin in others—our family, our congregation, our community, and our culture.

Why all of this emphasis upon sin? Why not move on quickly to the anointing of Isaiah? The answer is in the biblical qualifications for the prophetic or apostolic ministry. In the early church, two qualities served as the credentials for ordination in what is called the apostolic succession. One quality was to be blameless in character; the other was to be true to the Word of God. Later on, as the church drifted from its biblical moorings into institutional corruption, ordination became an end in itself so that even a scoundrel or a heretic could serve as an instrument for the means of grace. Corrupt popes, priests, preachers, and pastors are a blight upon the history of the church. Isaiah's encounter with God calls us back to the biblical credentials for ministry. Ordination only seals the qualifications of a person who is blameless and true to the Word. But, to be true to the Word, the person must first be blameless in character. Until Isaiah confessed his sin, he was neither ready nor worthy to be called a prophet of God.

CLEANSED BY FIRE (6:6–7)

6 Then one of the seraphim flew to me, having in his hand a live coal which he had taken with the tongs from the altar.

7 And he touched my mouth with it, and said:
   "Behold, this has touched your lips;
   Your iniquity is taken away,
   And your sin purged."

Isaiah 6:6–7

After Isaiah's confession of sin in himself and in his people, fire is the metaphor that again commmands our attention. In the image of a coal of fire upon Isaiah's lips, there is more uncomfortable truth for contemporary Christians. If our spiritual cleansing is partial, our spiritual consecration is dull, and our spiritual commitment is shaky, God has a word for us in Isaiah's vision. The word is the one that the philosopher Blaise Pascal used to describe his life-changing encounter with God in 1654. In bold, capital letters he wrote in his journal the word, "FIRE!"

THE FIRE THAT PURIFIES US (6:6)

A live coal from the altar of incense that burned in the presence of God is the only answer for the uncleanness that Isaiah saw within himself and his people after he got a glimpse of the glory of the Holy God. Any doubt about the reality and fatality of human sin is erased in this image of cleansing fire. Only the fire of God can take away our guilt and only the white heat of a live coal from His altar can atone for our sin.

We do not like to admit that our sin requires such an act of violence. An ad in a local newspaper carried the headline, "Will You Come Back to Church If We Promise Not to Throw the Book at You?" Underneath those words there was a large picture of a Bible with the explanation, "We believe in a loving and forgiving God. Come and join us this Sunday when we open up the Bible in worship." While the intentions may be good and the marketing clever, there is a sense in which the ad is false advertising. A live coal from the altar of God reminds us that behind the love that takes away our guilt and the forgiveness that atones for our sin is a Cross that extracted a cost no less than the life of the Son of God Himself. No, we do not throw the Book at sinners any more than God throws the Book at us, but we cannot deny the depth, totality, and spread of our sin that requires the violence of the cross and the purging of fire if our guilt is to be taken away and our sin is to be atoned.

Contemporary Christians are equally uncomfortable with the point of the purging fire. In Isaiah's case, his lips were touched by fire. As a prophet who would speak for God, his lips had to be clean, and if they were clean, his whole being was clean. Here is another truth from Isaiah that we cannot ignore. Each of us has a point of vulnerability that Satan attacks and God redeems. For Job, it was his righteousness; for David, it was his lust; for Peter, it was his self-confidence; and for Paul, it was his zeal. In each case, the point of personal vulnerability is the entry point for sin or cleansing.

The late Bishop Myron Boyd of the Free Methodist Church told the story of being in a prayer meeting at a national conference for evangelical Christian leaders. As he knelt next to a woman, he heard her pray, "O God, let Billy be home to help me raise our children." A long pause followed with only the sound of sobs. Then, a resolute voice prayed again, "O God, use Billy for Your glory even if I cannot have him home at all." Obviously, Bishop Boyd heard the sanctifying prayer of a woman named Ruth Graham at the point of entry to her soul. Like the touch of fire upon Isaiah's lips, her natural desire as a wife and a mother needed to be consecrated to God's will along with Billy Graham's calling to be an evangelist. We know the result. Billy's ministry and Ruth's motherhood glorify God as examples for all of us.

The Fire that Ignites Us (6:7)

Once Isaiah had been touched by the fire that purified him, he was ready to hear God speak with the fire that impassioned him. Passion is another of those missing dimensions of many contemporary Christians. Martin Marty, the church historian, says that we live in a time when the "civil have no convictions and those with convictions are not civil."[6] Only the fire of God can ignite what Marty calls "convicted civility"—the critical balance between the passion for truth and the compassion for persons.

Elton Trueblood adds another insight for our understanding in his book *The Incendiary Fellowship*. He interprets Jesus' words, "I come to bring fire upon the earth," not as His day of judgment when sinners are consumed, but as the fire of the Spirit that ignited the disciples at Pentecost. This is the welcome fire that strangely warmed the heart of Wesley; this is the contagious influence by which Augustine portrayed the spread of Christianity when "one loving heart sets another on fire." To be baptized by fire, then, means to be ignited with what William Temple called the "postive energy of righteousness, a consuming flame of purity."[8] When Isaiah answered, "Here am I! Send me," he put the poor stick of himself upon the flame of God and became part of an incendiary fellowship that would sweep the world. Or as Trueblood writes, "A good fire glorifies even its poorest fuel."[7] When we say, "Here am I; send me," we become ignited with the passionate blaze of His consuming Spirit.

Satan flees before people who give themselves as kindling to be ignited by the fire of God. In C. S. Lewis's *Screwtape Letters*, Uncle Screwtape instructs his nephew Wormwood how to handle a new convert to Christ. After the first ardors of his conversion give way to a dampening spirit, Screwtape advises,

> Make him acquiesce in the present low temperature of his spirit and gradually become content with it, persuading him that it is not so low after all. In a week or two, you will be making him doubt whether the first days of his Christianity were not, perhaps, a little excessive. Talk to him about "moderation in all things." A moderate religion is as good for us as no religion at all—and more amusing.[8]

When our lips are touched with a live coal from the altar of God, we are not only cleansed from our sin but we are set aflame to fulfill Paul's word to the Romans, "Be aglow with the Spirit" (Romans 12:11 RSV).

COMMISSIONED TO FAITHFULNESS (6:8–13)

8 Also I heard the voice of the Lord, saying:
"Whom shall I send,
And who will go for Us?"
Then I said, "Here am I! Send me."
9 And He said, "Go, and tell this people:
'Keep on hearing, but do not understand;
Keep on seeing, but do not perceive.'
10 "Make the heart of this people dull,
And their ears heavy,
And shut their eyes;
Lest they see with their eyes,

118

> And hear with their ears,
> And understand with their heart,
> And return and be healed."
> 11 Then I said, "Lord, how long?" And
> He answered:
> "Until the cities are laid waste
> and without inhabitant,
> The houses are without a man,
> The land is utterly desolate,
> 12 The LORD has removed men far away,
> And the forsaken places are many in
> the midst of the land.
> 13 But yet a tenth will be in it,
> And will return and be for consuming,
> As a terebinth tree or as an oak,
> Whose stump remains when it is cut down.
> So the holy seed shall be its stump."

Isaiah 6:8–13

Most sermons on Isaiah's vision stop with the response, "Here am I, send me." There is romance in these words, something like "Join the Navy and See the World." By stopping too soon, however, we miss the final meaning of the touch of fire. It is *the fire that refines us.* The message that Isaiah had to take to the people of Judah and the city of Jerusalem is a far cry from a recruiting slogan. God said, "Go and tell this people" the truth that will cause them to stop their ears, close their eyes, and harden their hearts. In other words, as a continuation of their rebellion, they will still refuse to hear, see, or understand so that they might be healed.

ANSWERING HIS CALL (6:8–10)

Isaiah, quite naturally, cries out in anguish, "Lord, how long?" God answers,

> . . . until My land is devastated,
> . . . until My people are in exile,
> . . . until My remnant is disciplined,
> . . . until only a holy seed remains in the stump of the once mighty oak.

The romance is gone. Only the fire of unquenchable devotion remains. As the final proof of the touch of fire upon Isaiah's lips, he is called to be faithful to the Word of God even though he will not live to see the prophecies fulfilled.

Here is where we see the refining fire of God at work. Malachi gives us the picture, "For He is like a refiner's fire. . . . He will sit as a refiner and a purifier of silver" (Malachi 3:2–3). We see a crucible of silver ore being put in a white hot furnace. As the heat is turned up, the impurities in the ore rise to the surface. With utmost care, the silversmith skims off the dross until the silver is pure. Molten silver is then poured into a cast that has the shape of an exquisite and useful vessel. After cooling, the smith hammers, chisels, and files off the rough edges before finishing the silver piece by rubbing the metal with his own bare fingers until it has the glow of perfection.

PERSISTENCE IN HIS MINISTRY (6:11–12)

Purified by fire, fashioned for use, and finished by God's personal touch—that is the process to which God is committed when He calls us. Because He is so faithful to us, we must be faithful to Him. That is why Samuel Rutherford wrote out of his life experience, "Oh, what I owe to the fire, the hammer, and the furnace of my Lord Jesus Christ." Robert Browning put the same thought in poetry,

My times are in Thy hand,
Perfect the cup as planned.

In the author's preface to this commentary I mentioned a conversation with George Brushaber, President of Bethel College and Seminary and Executive Editor of *Christianity Today*. I wondered out loud, "What do you do when the call of God to a new ministry is clear, but you still don't feel right about a move?" Dr. Brushaber answered, "When God calls us, He also releases us." What an insight! Isaiah responded to the call of God by saying, "Here am I! Send me," and received an assignment to preach a message that would neither be heard nor heeded. Naturally, Isaiah asked, "Lord, how long?" God came back with the answer, "Until I release you." So, as Isaiah watched his beloved Israel punished for its sins and purged for its unbelief until nothing was left but the smallest seed of hope, he remained faithful. The live coal from off the altar of God not only cleansed him wholly and consecrated him fully, but it burned in him with unquenchable devotion until the holy seed of hope burst forth with prophetic visions of a Savior whose name is "Wonderful, Counselor, mighty God, everlasting Father, Prince of Peace" (9:6). And because of the fire of his faithfulness, he foresaw the message of the Savior,

> The Spirit of the LORD God is upon me,
> Because the LORD has anointed me
> To preach good tidings to the poor.
> He has sent me to heal the brokenhearted,
> To proclaim liberty to the captives
> And the opening of the prison to those who are bound;
> To proclaim the acceptable year of the LORD.
> *Isaiah 61:1–2; Luke 4:18–19*

SEEING HIS PROMISE (6:13)

With the call to faithfulness, Isaiah's prophetic authority is now established. With a heart like God, he can speak for God. Now, with the question *where* answered in the fields of Judah and the streets of Jerusalem (1:2–31), the question *what* addressed in the major themes of his prophecy (2:1–5:30), and the question *who* decided in the fiery calling of the prophet (6:1–13), it is time to ask the question *when*. Isaiah answers that question by samplings of his prophetic ministry during the times of the kings Ahaz and Hezekiah (7:1–39:8).

NOTES

1. R. C. Sproule, *The Holiness of God* (Wheaton: Tyndale, 1985), 40.
2. R. Otto, *The Idea of the Holy: An Inquiry into the Non-Relational Factor in the Idea of the Divine and Its Relation to the Rational* (London: Oxford University Press, 1928), 12–35.
3. J. P. Allen, *Reality in Worship* (Nashville: Convention Press, 1965), 3–4.

4. H. T. Kerr and J. Mulder, Eds., *Conversions: The Christian Experience* (Grand Rapids: Eerdmans, 1983).

5. J. Ellul, *The Technological Bluff* (Grand Rapids: Eerdmans, 1990).

6. Quoted in J. D. Hunter, *Evangelicalism: The Coming Generation* (Chicago: University of Chicago Press, 1987), x.

7. E. Trueblood, *The Incendiary Fellowship* (New York: Harper, 1969), 106.

8. C. S. Lewis, *The Screwtape Letters* (New York: MacMillan, 1962), 43.

PART FOUR

The Vision Enacted

Isaiah 7:1–23:18

CHAPTER SIX

The Sign of the Children

Isaiah 7:1–9:7

History comes alive as Isaiah extends his autobiography from his prophetic call to his prophetic ministry. In encounters with the kings Ahaz and Hezekiah during turning points in the history of Judah and the Middle East, Isaiah becomes an active participant in decisions that ripple through time and eternity.

The historical setting begins after King Jotham's death as his son Ahaz feels the threat of conquest from Judah's neighbors, Syria and Ephraim. We can sympathize with King Ahaz because this is the first time that Judah and Jerusalem have been seriously threatened since the time of the founding of the kingdom. His distress must have been aggravated by the fact that Pekah, King of Israel or the Northern Kingdom and brother in blood, chose to align himself with the pagan King Rezin of Syria (Aram) in threatening siege against the holy city of Jerusalem. Ahaz's response and the consequences are recorded with historical precision in 2 Kings 16:1–20. Isaiah complements that account with his personalized story.

Both historians and theologians have trouble with Isaiah because he mixes the drama of revelation with the details of events. Not that Isaiah's story violates the facts of history. Quite the contrary, wherever the prophet touches down on historical events, his accuracy helps confirm the authenticity of his writing. Still, Isaiah is difficult to read and more difficult to interpret because of the "prophetic license" that he takes in the mixture of history and revelation. To approach what might be called part one (ch. 7:1–9:8) of the "historical-revelational" section of the book of Isaiah (ch. 7–39) from either the historical or revelational standpoint is an invitation to frustration. So, true to form, Isaiah helps us understand the meaning of the message by integrating history and revelation around a metaphor. The symbol of a child in five different settings is our guide.

Wherever the symbol of a child is used in Scripture, the meaning of "childlike trust in God" is inferred. Trust is the question that Isaiah poses for Judah and Jerusalem in chapters 7:1–9:8. As King Ahaz and the people of Judah are threatened with siege by Syria and Ephraim and tempted to form a costly alliance with the military might of Assyria, Isaiah poses the question, "In whom will you trust, the sovereign Lord or the human king?" Of course, he urges them to trust the Lord and offers them the images of children who represent the prophetic cycle of historical crisis, prophetic proclamation, divine judgment, redemptive promise, and a glorious future. As a guide for our study, the following simplified chart introduces the "Prophecies of the Children." Each name of a child coincides with a historical event, gives meaning to the event, and becomes the text for Isaiah's prophetic message.

PROPHECIES OF THE CHILDREN

TEXT:	NAME:	HISTORICAL EVENT	MEANING OF NAME:	ISAIAH'S MESSAGE:
7:1–10	Shear-Jashub (7:3)	Syria and Ephraim threat of invasion	"A remnant shall return" (7:3)	Trust in God (King)
7:11–25	Immanuel (7:14)	Assyria conquers Syria and Ephraim	"God with us" (7:19)	God is ever-present with us (People of Judah)
8:1–10	Maher-Shalal-Hash-Baz (8:1)	Assyria overruns Judah	"Spoil speeds, booty hastes" (8:1)	Judgment will come upon Judah (City of Jerusalem)
8:11–22	"My disciples" (8:16)	Return of the Remnant	"The Law and the testimony" (8:20)	My people will be restored (Community of faith)
9:1–7	"Wonderful Counselor Mighty God, Everlasting Father," (All future generations) Prince of Peace (9:6)	Coming of the Messiah	"Judgment and justice" (9:7)	God's promise of hope will be fulfilled (Kingdom of God)

Our choice for studying this section of Isaiah, then, is to see historical events as vehicles for the message of prophetic revelation, not as ends in themselves. Through the symbols of the children, history and revelation come together.

CHILD OF SALVATION (7:1–12)

1 Now it came to pass in the days of Ahaz the son of Jotham, the son of Uzziah, king of Judah, that Rezin king of Syria and Pekah the son of Remaliah, king of Israel, went up to Jerusalem to make war against it, but could not prevail against it.

2 And it was told to the house of David, saying, "Syria's forces are deployed in Ephraim." So his heart and the heart of his people were moved as the trees of the woods are moved with the wind.

3 Then the LORD said to Isaiah, "Go out now to meet Ahaz, you and Shear-Jashub your son, at the end of the aqueduct from the upper pool, on the highway to the Fuller's Field,

4 "and say to him: 'Take heed, and be quiet; do not fear or be fainthearted for these two stubs of smoking firebrands, for the fierce anger of Rezin and Syria, and the son of Remaliah.

5 'Because Syria, Ephraim, and the son of Remaliah have taken evil counsel against you, saying,

6 "Let us go up against Judah and trouble it, and let us make a gap in its wall for ourselves, and set a king over them, the son of Tabeel"—

7 'thus says the Lord GOD:
"It shall not stand,
Nor shall it come to pass.

8 For the head of Syria is Damascus,
And the head of Damascus is Rezin.
Within sixty-five years
   Ephraim will be broken,
So that it will not be a people.

9 The head of Ephraim is Samaria,
And the head of Samaria
   is Remaliah's son.
If you will not believe,

Surely you shall not be established." ' "
10 Moreover the LORD spoke again to
Ahaz, saying,
11 "Ask a sign for yourself from the LORD your
God; ask it either in the depth or in the height above."
12 But Ahaz said, "I will not ask, nor will I test the
LORD!"

Isaiah 7:1–12

For the first time in its history, Jerusalem is under siege. The powerful armies of Rezin, king of Syria, and Pekah, king of Ephraim, are in control of the territory around the city. Even if they have not conquered it, defeat appears to be inevitable. Facing such a prospect, Isaiah tells us that King Ahaz and his people were *"as trees of the woods . . . moved by the wind"* (v. 2).

As a signal of his desperation, King Ahaz goes out to check personally on the limited water supply in the Upper Pool to determine how long the people of Jerusalem can hold out against the enemy. Here, Ahaz meets Isaiah and his son Shear-Jashub, whose name means "a remnant shall return." As the child of salvation, Shear-Jashub symbolizes what Isaiah has to say. Utilizing one of the most graphic of his metaphors, Isaiah likens Rezin and Pekah to *"two stubs of smoking firebrands"* or, as they would say in Texas, "All hat and no cattle." Despite their pretended show of force, in reality, Syria and Ephraim are no more than the smoldering stubs of their former reputation as "firebrands."

Isaiah becomes even more bold with his declaration that no harm whatsoever will come to the city or its inhabitants. Rather, it is the dynasties of Rezin and Pekah, along with their kingdoms of Syria and Ephraim, that are doomed to destruction. The choice belongs to Ahaz. He can either exercise a childlike faith by putting his trust in God, or he can pursue the course of panic by putting his faith in a military alliance with the Assyrians. Sternly, Isaiah lays down the ultimatum, "If you do not stand firm in your faith, you will not stand at all" (v. 9).

Ahaz has good reason to quake like a leaf in the wind. As King of Judah and responsible for the safety of his people, the sight of the Syrians and Ephraim surrounding the city would cause him to explore every alternative for survival. We know that he took this responsibility seriously by conducting a personal inspection of the Upper Pool in order to gauge the time that the city could hold out before the need for water did what military power had failed to do. Leaders who carry such a weight of responsiblity are also persons with a high need for control. They are decision-makers who get things done. Imagine then how radical Isaiah's proclamation must have seemed to Ahaz. He would have been quick to respond to the command, "Don't just stand there, do something." Instead, God reversed all the systems and said, "Don't do something, just stand there."

As always, God is not insensitive to Ahaz' dilemma. Contrary to His usual prohibition against humans putting Him to the test by asking for a sign, God takes the initiative and invites Ahaz to ask for a miraculous sign that He will show in either the depths of the sea or in the heights of the heavens (v. 10). No one can ever claim that God is unfair. When He asks us to "stand firm in our faith" against the evidence of circumstances and our natural impulses, He will also give us a sign of His faithfulness.

Ahaz knows the Scriptures. Turning God's own words against Him, the king answers, *"I will not ask, nor will I test the LORD!"* His answer comes directly from Deuteronomy 6:16 where God warns, "You shall not tempt [test] the LORD your God as you tempted [tested] Him in Massah." The reference is to the time when the children of Israel set out across the desert under the command of the Lord and camped at Rephidim. When they discovered that the camp had no water, they demanded that God give them water as a sign of His continuing presence. After a bitter quarrel, Moses caved in to their demand and struck the rock with his staff. The water flowed, but Moses named the place Massah as a memorial to faith that requires a sign and thereby becomes the sin of unbelief.

Under the pretense of obeying God, Ahaz is actually trying to justify a decision he has already made. History is witness to his sin. He not only entered into an unnecessary alliance with Tiglath-Pileser, king of Assyria, but he also compromised his faith by swearing allegiance to Assyria's idols and modifying the altar in the temple at Jerusalem to accommodate pagan worship. As so often happens, a political alliance with the secular world includes a spiritual allegiance to its gods.

CHILD OF SUFFERING (7:13–25)

13 Then he said, "Hear now, O house of David! Is it a small thing for you to weary men, but will you weary my God also?

14 "Therefore the Lord Himself will give you a
sign: Behold, the virgin shall conceive and bear a Son,
and shall call His name Immanuel.

15 "Curds and honey He shall eat, that He may
know to refuse the evil and choose the good.

16 "For before the Child shall know to refuse the
evil and choose the good, the land that you dread will
be forsaken by both her kings.

17 "The LORD will bring the king of Assyria upon
you and your people and your father's house—days
that have not come since the day that Ephraim
departed from Judah."

18 And it shall come to pass in that day
    That the LORD will whistle for the fly
    That is in the farthest part of the rivers of Egypt,
    And for the bee that is in the land of Assyria.

19 They will come,
        and all of them will rest
    In the desolate valleys
        and in the clefts of the rocks,
    And on all thorns and in all pastures.

20 In the same day the Lord will shave
        with a hired razor,
    With those from beyond the River,
        with the king of Assyria,
    The head and the hair of the legs,
    And will also remove the beard.

21 It shall be in that day
    That a man will keep alive
        a young cow and two sheep;

22 So it shall be, from the abundance of milk they give,
    That he will eat curds;
    For curds and honey everyone will eat
    who is left in the land.

23 It shall happen in that day,
    That wherever there could be a thousand vines
    Worth a thousand shekels of silver,
    It will be for briers and thorns.

24 With arrows and bows men will come there,
    Because all the land will become briers and thorns.

25 And to any hill which could be dug with the hoe,
    You will not go there for fear of briers and thorns;

> But it will become a range for oxen
> And a place for sheep to roam.
>
> *Isaiah 7:13–25*

Proof of Ahaz's predetermined fate comes with Isaiah's angry retort, *"Hear now, O house of David! Is it a small thing for you to weary men, but will you weary my God also?"* (v. 13). As a rebuff to the king, he informs the people that God is still going to give them a sign—the sign of another child who will be born of a virgin and named *"Immanuel"* or "God with us."

Much ado has accompanied the debate over whether the sign of Immanuel forecasts the coming of Christ. Many scholars read the passage as a prediction of a local and current event— perhaps the birth of one of Isaiah's children. Even more heat is generated among scholars over the question of whether the word "virgin" means what it says or whether it can also be interpreted "young woman." Liberal scholars who contest the virgin birth are quick to accept the interpretation "young woman." Martin Luther, on the other hand, offered one hundred guilders to anyone who could show any other place in Scripture where the same word is translated "young woman" rather than "virgin." Whether liberal or conservative in theology, we must be true to the text and consistent in our interpretation.

If we accept the position that Isaiah's prophecies often have present and future meaning, it is possible to see the vision realized in Isaiah's time as prefiguring the birth of Christ. Matthew did not err when he quoted this verse from Isaiah almost verbatim, "Behold a virgin shall be with child and bear a Son, and they shall call his name Immanuel, which is translated, "God with us" (Matthew 1:23).

Believe it or not, the sign of Immanuel was not welcomed by Ahaz and the children of Israel. While we take great comfort in the promise "God with us," the promise of His presence is for the suffering of Israel during the forthcoming devastation at the hands of Assyria (v. 17). "Curds and honey He shall eat" is not the promise of a land flowing with "milk and honey." Rather, it is the bittersweet food of famine and plenty. Again, Isaiah has given us an image of God that brings opposite reactions from those who are faithful and those who are wicked. For the faithful, the promise of "God with us" gives assurance of His presence in plenty and in poverty, at home or in exile, and in suffering as well as in health. For the wicked, however, the same promise "God with us" brings the judgment of God—not just upon Syria and Ephraim, but upon Judah and Jerusalem from the hand of the king of Assyria.

In a vivid portrayal of the near future, Isaiah foresees the Lord putting two fingers in His mouth to whistle for flies from Egypt and bees from Assyria to swarm over the land and sting its inhabitants (v. 18). Even more vividly, Isaiah sees the Lord using Assyria as a "hired razor" to shave the last whiskers of dignity from the beard of Judah. In the Middle East, a beard is a symbol of masculine identity. No humiliation is greater than to have the beard forcefully shaven by a conquering enemy. Only the bittersweet food of "curds and honey," and the fear of "briars and thorns" in once fertile fields, will remain. Judah will be victim of the three D's of judgment: deprivation of food, depopulation of the people, and desolation of the land.[1] The price of Ahaz' sin is a cost that cannot be counted. Yet, through it all, there is the shred of promise that God will be present with those who are faithful as their comfort, and equally present with those who are wicked as their judge—all to the working of His redemptive purpose.

CHILD OF JUDGEMENT (8:1–10)

1 Moreover the LORD said to me, "Take a large scroll, and write on it with a man's pen concerning Maher-Shalal-Hash-Baz.

2 "And I will take for Myself faithful witnesses to record, Uriah the priest and Zechariah the son of Jeberechiah."

3 Then I went to the prophetess, and she conceived and bore a son. Then the LORD said to me, "Call his name Maher-Shalal-Hash-Baz;

4 "for before the child shall have knowledge to cry 'My father' and 'My mother,' the riches of Damascus and the spoil of Samaria will be taken away before the king of Assyria."

5 The LORD also spoke to me again, saying:

6 "Inasmuch as these people refused
The waters of Shiloah that flow softly,
And rejoice in Rezin
    and in Remaliah's son;

7 Now therefore, behold,
   the Lord brings up over them
The waters of the River,
   strong and mighty—
The king of Assyria and all his glory;
He will go up over all his channels
And go over all his banks.
8 He will pass through Judah,
He will overflow and pass over,
He will reach up to the neck;
And the stretching out of his wings
Will fill the breadth of Your land,
   O Immanuel.
9 "Be shattered, O you peoples,
   and be broken in pieces!
Give ear, all you from far countries.
Gird yourselves,
   but be broken in pieces;
Gird yourselves,
   but be broken in pieces.
10 Take counsel together,
   but it will come to nothing;
Speak the word, but it will not stand,
For God is with us."

Isaiah 8:1–10

Having spoken stern judgment to King Ahaz, Isaiah turns to the masses. As a master communicator, he chooses the instrument that is appropriate to his audience. Upon instruction from God, he takes a large scroll, writes upon it the name "Maher-Shalal-Hash-Baz" and has the prophecy attested by two witnesses, one of whom is the priest for the king himself. The result is a legal document that can be posted in the public square or carried through the streets for all to read. For those who scoffed at Isaiah's prophecy of God's judgment upon Judah and Jerusalem, the public decree announcing the birth of another son put Isaiah's credibility on the line.

According to plan, Isaiah went to a woman who is identified as a "prophetess," a title that most likely identified his wife, and together they bore a son. God told Isaiah to give him the name on the scroll, "Maher-Shalal-Hash-Baz," which literally means "Speed the Spoil,

Hasten the Booty." The timing of judgment now becomes the question. God informs Isaiah that His judgment will come upon Syria and Ephraim before the child can say "My father" and "My mother," or "Daddy" and "Momma." In the normal pattern of speech development, a child will speak these words within a year to eighteen months after birth. Critics of Isaiah insist that this prophecy is a symbol of exact time and therefore dispute its accuracy because Syria and Ephraim did not fall under Assyria until 722 B.C. or approximately thirteen years later. The timing also seems to conflict with Isaiah's earlier prediction that Ephraim would be broken within sixty-five years (7:8).

Scholars who are more sympathetic to Isaiah have another answer. Perhaps Isaiah is using a colloquial expression of the people when he says that the downfall of Syria and Ephraim will come by the time the child can speak "Daddy" and "Momma." Oswalt suggests that the phrase may be similar to the colloquial phrase we use to respond to the question, "When is it going to happen?" If we answer, "Before you can say Jack Robinson" we mean the event is imminent.[2] Knowing Isaiah as we do and knowing the people to whom he spoke, the explanation makes sense. As we speak of the "imminent" return of Jesus Christ without fixing a date, so Isaiah might well be speaking in the prophetic tense in which judgment upon Syria and Ephraim is "imminent" without fixing a date.

Whatever the timing, it is secondary to the totality of judgment in the meaning of Maher-Shalal-Hash-Baz's name. Speaking to Isaiah again, the Lord expands upon the meaning of "plunder" and "booty," or devastation and exile, that Assyria will wreak not only upon Syria and Ephraim but now, also, upon Judah (v. 8). With another stroke of genius as a commmunicator to the common people, Isaiah draws a comparison from the daily experience of the citizens of Jerusalem that no one can misunderstand. A gentle stream of water called Shiloah trickled through the city as a symbol of peace. In contrast, Assyria had the rushing waters of the mighty Euphrates river. For people who had never experienced the devastation of such a river at flood tide, Isaiah must have struck fear into their hearts when he used Shiloah as the symbol of the peace that they rejected when they refused to trust God and the Euphrates at flood tide flowing up to their necks as the prediction of the wrath to come.

Isaiah extends his prediction of coming judgment upon the nations of Syria, Ephraim, and Judah to all nations and all people of the world (v. 9). The contagious spirit of war will spread over the earth so that no rallying war cry, no preparation for battle, no strategy for attack, or no plan for defense will stand. All nations will be broken and feel the shattering effects of the Assyrian drive for world domination. Isaiah's prophecy has been confirmed time and time again in human history. In our twentieth century, two wars with world supremacy as the stakes have left their scars on every nation. No monument to the evil effects of warfare and world domination speaks more poignantly than the barbed wire sculpture on the marble tablet at Dachau, the Nazi concentration camp where Jews were slaughtered and burned. "Never again" are words permanently etched as a prayer in the mind of every visitor to the camp.

A haunting phrase closes both Isaiah's prophecies of judgment against Syria, Ephraim, and Judah and all nations of the world. At the end of the first prophecy, Isaiah closes with the cry, "O Immanuel" and at the end of the second prophecy he concludes with the declaration, *"For God is with us."* Immanuel, the Child of Presence and the unwanted sign from the Lord, has come back to haunt the steps of the wicked. The promise of His comforting presence for the faithful has become the promise of shattering punishment against the wicked. "God with us" can be our hope or our fear.

CHILD OF FAITH (8:11–22)

11 For the LORD spoke thus to me with a strong
hand, and instructed me that I should not walk in the
way of this people, saying:
   12 "Do not say, 'A conspiracy,'
      Concerning all that this people
         call a conspiracy,
      Nor be afraid of their threats,
         nor be troubled.
   13 The LORD of hosts,
      Him you shall hallow;
      Let Him be your fear,
      And let Him be your dread.
   14 He will be as a sanctuary,

But a stone of stumbling
   and a rock of offense
To both the houses of Israel,
As a trap and a snare to the
   inhabitants of Jerusalem.
15 And many among them shall stumble;
   They shall fall and be broken,
   Be snared and taken."
16 Bind up the testimony,
   Seal the law among my disciples,
17 And I will wait on the LORD,
   Who hides His face from the house of Jacob;
   And I will hope in Him.
18 Here am I and the children whom the LORD has
     given me!
   We are for signs and wonders in Israel
   From the LORD of hosts,
   Who dwells in Mount Zion.
19 And when they say to you, "Seek those who
are mediums and wizards, who whisper and mutter,"
should not a people seek their God? Should they seek
the dead on behalf of the living?
20 To the law and to the testimony! If they do not
speak according to this word, it is because there is no
light in them.
21 And they will pass through it hard pressed and
hungry; and it shall happen, when they are hungry,
that they will be enraged and curse their king and
their God, and look upward.
22 Then they will look to the earth, and see
trouble and darkness, gloom of anguish; and they will
be driven into darkness.

Isaiah 8:11–22

Even prophets need assurance. After Isaiah had spoken so sternly
to his own people, he must have felt the exhaustion of self-giving
and the criticism of cynics. Isaiah confesses that the Lord spoke to
him with a "strong hand" and warned him not to buckle under to
the charge of the people that he was part of a conspiracy to over-
throw the government and give Judah and Jerusalem into Assyrian
hands (vv. 11–12). To reinforce His warning and restore Isaiah's

confidence, the Lord takes the prophet back to his experience in the temple. Once again, we hear the seraphim sing, "Holy, holy, holy, is the LORD of hosts," and the pillars shake under the power of God. Out of that experience, God reminds Isaiah that he should "hallow" and "fear" only the Lord of hosts. And just as the presence of Immanuel means "comfort" for the faithful and "wrath" for the wicked, so the Lord of hosts promises to be a *"sanctuary"* for Isaiah at the same time that He is a *"stone of stumbling"* and a *"rock of offense"* to both houses of Israel, as well as a *"trap and a snare"* to his critics in Jerusalem (vv. 13–14).

God's assurance for Isaiah takes on a new dimension when He reminds the prophet that he is not alone in his faithfulness. Prefiguring the remnant of the future, the Lord has disciples in Jerusalem whom He identifies as Isaiah's "children" who represent the true community of faith in Jerusalem. For that nurturing of that community, the Lord gives three instructions (vv. 16–17):

1. Remember the testimony of the faithful.
2. Teach the law among the disciples.
3. Wait upon the Lord in prayer.

These instructions apply to the community of faith in any age. To hear the testimony of believers, teach the Word of God to disciples, and wait upon the Lord in prayer, is still the primary agenda for the church today. With all of the demands for multiple services in what Lyle Schaller calls "The Seven-Day-A-Week Church,"[3] there is the tendency to neglect the primary functions. If so, the consequences are obvious. The church may be a multiple-service agency to human need, but it may fail to be the "community of faith" in fulfilling God's purpose for its existence. We can understand Isaiah's exuberant response to this encouraging perspective given to him by God. In a note of praise, he exclaims,

> Here am I and the children whom the LORD has given me!
> We are for signs and wonders in Israel
> From the LORD of hosts,
> Who dwells in Mount Zion.
>
> *Isaiah 8:18*

137

With the strength of that voice, God tells Isaiah that those who want to consult with mediums and wizards about the future will hear only sounds like the "chirps and mutterings" of a flock of birds. "To the Law and the Testimony!" is the rallying cry of the community of faith that causes those who seek truth from any other source to flounder in frustration, resort to cursing their king and their God, and end up peering vainly into the heavens for an answer (vv. 20–21). Reality will then bring them back to earth where they will peer through the gloom of anguish at the darkness that engulfs them (v. 22). For Isaiah's children and the community of faith, the message is just the opposite: in all ages, God will preserve a remnant to fulfill His redemptive purpose.

CHILD OF HOPE (9:1–7)

1 Nevertheless the gloom will not be upon her
    who is distressed,
As when at first He lightly esteemed
The land of Zebulun
    and the land of Naphtali,
And afterward more heavily oppressed her,
By the way of the sea,
    beyond the Jordan,
In Galilee of the Gentiles.
2 The people who walked in darkness
Have seen a great light;
Those who dwelt in the land of the shadow of death,
Upon them a light has shined.
3 You have multiplied the nation
And increased its joy;
They rejoice before You
According to the joy of harvest,
As men rejoice when they divide the spoil.
4 For You have broken the yoke
    of his burden
And the staff of his shoulder,
The rod of his oppressor,
As in the day of Midian.
5 For every warrior's sandal from the noisy battle,
And garments rolled in blood,

138

Will be used for burning and fuel of fire.
6 For unto us a Child is born,
   Unto us a Son is given;
   And the government will be upon His shoulder.
   And His name will be called
   Wonderful, Counselor, Mighty God,
   Everlasting Father, Prince of Peace.
7 Of the increase of His government and peace
   There will be no end,
   Upon the throne of David
      and over His kingdom,
   To order it and establish it with
      judgment and justice
   From that time forward, even forever.
   The zeal of the LORD of hosts will perform this.

Isaiah 9:1–7

With just one word, *"Nevertheless,"* Isaiah erases all of the gloom of darkness over the earth and foresees the dawn of a *"great light,"* bringing hope even to those who live in the land of the *"shadow of death"* (v. 2). How true to the character of God! Not even the darkest gloom can keep the light of His presence from shining, even upon those who live in the land of the shadow of death.

At the 1989 World Congress on Evangelism or Lausanne II in Manila, testimonies from Christians around the world were highlighted by the witness of a Chinese believer who had been imprisoned for his faith. Demeaned as a human being and isolated from human contact, his cell was in a dark dungeon and his work assignment was to clean the sewers deep in the underground darkness. He told of standing up to his knees in human waste going about his repulsive work. But against the stench and pollution of the sewer, he began to sing,

I come to the garden alone,
While the dew is still on the roses,
And the voice I hear
Falling on my ear,
The Son of God discloses,

And He walks with me
And He talks with me
And He tells me I am His own

And the joy we share
As we tarry there,
None other has ever known.

When his captors realized that they could neither break his spirit nor put out the brightness of his song, they released him to tell his story far and wide. Needless to say, wherever he went, revival followed and village after village came to Christ.

As the capstone for Isaiah's encouragement, the Lord gives him the privilege of seeing His purpose for bringing the light of joy, the peace of nations, and the hope of salvation to every corner of the earth, including the *"Galilee of the Gentiles"* (v. 1). This is the other side of the promise of His presence as "Immanuel." In 8:9–10, Isaiah had extended the devastation of war to every nation on earth because evil flares and spreads in the anger of His presence. By the same token, the light of redemptive hope brightens and spreads to every corner of the earth from the glory of His presence.

How will this vision come to pass? God honors Isaiah's faithfulness by lifting the veil of revelation on the future and showing him the royal child of hope who is to be born. Quite in contrast with a world at war, the child will govern a world in peace where *"judgment and justice"* prevail (v. 7). One name is not enough to identify the child of the future. Rather, the Child of Five Names is introduced to us: *"Wonderful, Counselor, Mighty God, Everlasting Father, Prince of Peace"* (v. 6).

Some scholars claim that Isaiah borrowed these titles from Egyptian tombs where Pharoahs were honored with godly attributes of wisdom, power, eternal being, and peace. What empty words! The very fact that they are found in the tombs of dead pharoahs is its own witness against their validity. For the Child of Five Names, there will be no death. Instead, He will be the conqueror of death and, therefore, the great light of hope that will shine upon all humans who live in the land of darkness under the shadow of death.

This hymn of praise may be read either as eulogy looking back upon a royal personage or as eschatology looking forward to the promise of David for a kingdom with "no end" (v. 7). Only the most biased critics could contest the fact that the Child of Hope is the Messiah, the Christ, and the Son of the Living God.

NOTES

1. Smith, *Expositor's Bible*, 110ff.
2. See John Oswalt's commentary on Isaiah 8:4.
3. L. E. Schaller, *The Seven-Day-a-Week Church* (Nashville: Abingdon Press, 1982).

CHAPTER SEVEN

The Co-Signs of Judgment and Promise

Isaiah 9:8–12:6

Consistent with his style of writing, Isaiah follows the events of history with a summary of his prophecies. Having spoken with harsh judgment upon King Ahaz, the leaders, and the people of Judah and Jerusalem, Isaiah now turns to address their enemies and foresee their future. Under the common theme, "Co- Signs of Judgment and Promise," we read:

I	II	III
Oracles Against Enemies	**Oracle of the Remnant**	**Oracles for Judah**
Ephraim 9:8–10:4	10:20–34	A Savior 11:1–9
Assyria 10:5–19		A King 11:10–16
IV		
Oracle of Song 12:1–6		

Judah, despite the crucible of judgment through which it must pass because of its rebellion, is still the instrument through which God wants to work His redemptive purpose. Through this series of oracles, Isaiah puts that promise into the perspective of current and coming history with the promise of the Remnant as the turning point, and the Oracle of Song as the joyous outcome.

Ephraim the Traitor (9:8–10:4)

8 The Lord sent a word against Jacob,
And it has fallen on Israel.

9 All the people will know—
Ephraim and the inhabitant of Samaria—
Who say in pride
  and arrogance of heart:

10 "The bricks have fallen down,
But we will rebuild with hewn stones;
The sycamores are cut down,
But we will replace them with cedars."

11 Therefore the Lord shall set up
The adversaries of Rezin against him,
And spur his enemies on,

12 The Syrians before
  and the Philistines behind;
And they shall devour Israel with an open mouth.
For all this His anger is not turned away,
But His hand is stretched out still.

13 For the people do not turn to Him
  who strikes them,
Nor do they seek the Lord of hosts,

14 Therefore the Lord will cut off
  head and tail from Israel,
Palm branch and bulrush in one day.

15 The elder and honorable,
  he is the head;
The prophet who teaches lies,
  he is the tail.

16 For the leaders of this people cause
  them to err,
And those who are led by them are
  destroyed.

17 Therefore the Lord will have no joy in their young
  men,
Nor have mercy on their fatherless and widows;

> For everyone is a hypocrite
>   and an evildoer,
> And every mouth speaks folly.
> For all this His anger is not turned away,
> But His hand is stretched out still.
> 18 For wickedness burns as the fire;
>   It shall devour the briers and thorns,
>   And kindle in the thickets of the forest;
>   They shall mount up like rising smoke.
> 19 Through the wrath of the LORD of hosts
>   The land is burned up,
>   And the people shall be as fuel
>   for the fire;
>   No man shall spare his brother.
> 20 And he shall snatch on the right hand
>   And be hungry;
>   He shall devour on the left hand
>   And not be satisfied;
>   Every man shall eat the flesh of his own arm.
> 21 Manasseh shall devour Ephraim,
>   and Ephraim Manasseh,
>   And they together shall be against Judah.
>   For all this His anger is not turned away,
>   But His hand is stretched out still.
> 1 "Woe to those who decree
>   unrighteous decrees,
>   Who write misfortune,
>   Which they have prescribed
> 2 To rob the needy of justice,
>   And to take what is right from the poor of My people,
>   That widows may be their prey,
>   And that they may rob the fatherless.
> 3 What will you do in the day of punishment,
>   And in the desolation which will come from afar?
>   To whom will you flee for help?
>   And where will you leave your glory?
> 4 Without Me they shall bow down among the prisoners,
>   And they shall fall among the slain."
>   For all this His anger is not turned away,
>   But His hand is stretched out still.

Isaiah 9:8–10:4

Betrayal of a brother is a cardinal sin in human relationships. In the eyes of God, it is even more serious when spiritual relationships are involved. Pekah, the son of Remaliah, king of Israel, had violated both relationships when he entered into a military alliance with the pagan King Rezin of Syria in order to conquer Judah and take Jerusalem. His action pitted Jewish brother against brother and blurred God's vision for a united kingdom of righteousness and justice that would be a light for the world.

THE BETRAYAL OF PRIDE (9:8–12)

Four harsh judgments are spoken against Israel for betraying its brother and defying God. Each judgment is confirmed by the refrain: *"For all this His anger is not turned away, but His hand is stretched out still"* (vv. 12, 17, and 21). The first judgment is against their *"pride and arrogance of heart"* (v. 9), which is the motivation for their ambition to build a great kingdom. God announces that Israel will be crunched between the marauding armies of Syria on one side and Philistia on the other side as they try to destroy each other. Like a mouse in bed with an elephant, Israel will be crushed when Syria rolls over.

THE BETRAYAL OF IMPENITENCE (9:13–17)

The second judgment is against Israel's failure to repent of their sins, that is to *"turn to Him who strikes"* and to *"seek the LORD of hosts"* (v. 13). God will cut off the *"head"* of their current leaders who misled them and the *"tail"* of the people who followed them into destruction (vv. 14–17). Isaiah speaks a truth that cannot be ignored. While God holds elders, judges, and prophets responsible for misleading people, those who follow cannot claim innocence.

The same truth is stated in the familiar quotation, "People get the government they deserve." Evidently, there is a certain codependency between corrupt leaders and corrupted people. One cannot exist without the other. Perhaps this will help explain the continuing popularity of television evangelists who are exposed as frauds or shamed by scandal. They could not continue without the support of people whose needs are met by the exorbitant claims or charismatic presence of leaders whom they follow like a sightless herd.

Therefore, they are also guilty of arrogant ambition and calloused impenitence, which leads Isaiah to make the sweeping generalization, *"For everyone is a hypocrite and an evildoer, and every mouth speaks folly"* (v. 17).

THE BETRAYAL OF LOVE (9:18–21)

The third judgment is against Israel's betrayal of its relationship with Judah. God's wrath will be vented against them when the same spirit of betrayal is turned inward and against each other. It is one thing to see the resources of the land burned up in judgment; it is quite another thing to see the relationships of blood relatives become the fuel for the fire. When the bonds of heredity and love that hold these relationships together are destroyed, civilization itself breaks down. Civil war leads to anarchy and anarchy bottoms out in cannibalism. Brother against brother, tribe against tribe, and nation against nation; the betrayal that began as an alliance with Syria has extracted the ultimate cost of fratricide and cannibalism. Israel will fall lower than the animals.

THE BETRAYAL OF INJUSTICE (10:1–4)

In Isaiah's fourth and final judgment against the Northern Kingdom of Israel, the charge is against corrupt judges who write *"unrighteous decrees"* of social injustice. In a Bill of Particulars against those who are expected to be models of righteousness and guardians of justice, the judges themselves are indicted for robbing the needy of justice; taking what is right away from the poor; making widows their prey; and robbing the fatherless of their rights (v. 2). Isaiah challenges them with the question they cannot answer, *"What will you do in the day of punishment?"* (v. 3). A plaintive answer is heard in the words, *"Without Me they shall bow down among the prisoners, and they shall fall among the slain"* (v. 4).

Their doom is sealed. When the Assyrians scorch the land, they will be the first to march into exile with shaved heads and faces as the mark of their humiliation. But the more important message is that the cause of their shame will be the emptiness of their soul, which is without the indwelling presence of the Lord. They will have no

146

protection against desolation of spirit, no refuge for help against the advancing hordes, and no place or position of honor to which they can leave their glory. Along with the people of Israel whose betrayal turned against them, the corrupt judges will become victims of their own injustice. The oracle concludes on the ominous refrain, *"For all this His anger is not turned away, but His hand is stretched out still"* (v. 4).

ASSYRIA THE UNGODLY (10:5–19)

5 "Woe to Assyria, the rod of My anger
And the staff in whose hand is My indignation.
6 I will send him against an ungodly nation,
And against the people of My wrath
I will give him charge,
To seize the spoil, to take the prey,
And to tread them down like the mire of the streets.
7 Yet he does not mean so,
Nor does his heart think so;
But it is in his heart to destroy,
And cut off not a few nations.
8 For he says,
'Are not my princes altogether kings?
9 Is not Calno like Carchemish?
Is not Hamath like Arped?
Is not Samaria like Damascus?
10 As my hand has found the kingdoms of the idols,
Whose carved images excelled those of Jerusalem and
Samaria,
11 As I have done to Samaria and her idols,
Shall I not do also to Jerusalem
and her idols?"
12 Therefore it shall come to pass, when the LORD has performed all His work on Mount Zion and on Jerusalem, that He will say, "I will punish the fruit of the arrogant heart of the king of Assyria, and the glory of his haughty looks."
13 For he says:
"By the strength of my hand
I have done it,
And by my wisdom, for I am prudent;
Also I have removed the boundaries of the people,

And have robbed their treasuries;
So I have put down the inhabitants like a valiant man.
14 My hand has found like a nest the riches of the people,
And as one gathers eggs that are left,
I have gathered all the earth;
And there was no one
    who moved his wing,
Nor opened his mouth
    with even a peep."
15 Shall the ax boast itself against
    him who chops with it?
Or shall the saw magnify itself against
    him who saws with it?
As if a rod could wield itself against
    those who lift it up,
Or as if a staff could lift up,
    as if it were not wood!
16 Therefore the Lord,
    the Lord of hosts,
Will send leanness among his fat ones;
And under his glory
He will kindle a burning
Like the burning of a fire.
17 So the Light of Israel will be for a fire,
And his Holy One for a flame;
It will burn and devour
His thorns and his briers in one day.
18 And it will consume the glory of his forest and of his
    fruitful field,
Both soul and body;
And they will be as when a sick man wastes away.
19 Then the rest of the trees of his forest
Will be so few in number
That a child may write them.

Isaiah 10:5–19

Why should God pronounce "woe" upon Assyria whom He chose as the "rod" of His anger and the "staff" of His wrath against Judah and Jerusalem? Our human understanding is stretched to the limit as we probe for the answer. Isaiah tells us that God gave Assyria the charge to attack His people, seize their wealth, march them into exile, and trample through their streets (vv. 15–16). As total as the destruction was to be, the charge was still limited to Judah and within the sovereignty of God.

Our human understanding is stretched by these stipulations because we cannot comprehend God's part in such violence, His choice of a heathen nation as His instrument of judgment, or His expectation that the insatiable appetite of violence can be kept under control. For the answer to these questions, we will have to await the perspective of eternity. We can understand, however, the specific charges that God brought against Assyria as an outgrowth of its attack upon Judah and Jerusalem.

THE SIN OF SEEKING WORLD DOMINATION (10:5–8)

Sargon is the king of Assyria against whom the first charge is leveled. God will judge him for violating the limits of God's charge and seeking world domination. Isaiah tells us, "*it is in his heart to destroy, and cut off not a few nations.*" Throughout human history, dictators have been driven by the desire to rule the world. Their evil ambition runs counter to the sovereignty of God who alone has domination over all nations. Wars are fought for many reasons, with limited resources, competing religions, and ethnic hatred leading the way. While no war can be fully justified, least justification can be given for sending troops to die on behalf of a leader's exaggerated ego. God will tolerate no pretenders to His throne, and when Sargon's motives for world domination were exposed, judgment was inevitable.

THE SIN OF PLAYING GOD (10:9–10)

Not by surprise, Sargon's ambitions for world domination were matched by his boasting that he himself began playing god. "*Are not my princes altogether kings?*" is a rhetorical question he would answer by bragging, "Of course, and if my princes are kings, then I the king am God!" As presumptuous as Sargon may seem, he has a contemporary in Saddam Hussein. Before his defeat in Desert Storm, Hussein claimed succession to Nebuchadnezzar II, the Old Testament character who imagined himself equal with God. As symbols of his arrogance, Saddam Hussein restored Babylon and its hanging gardens to their original glory, minted coins with Nebuchadnezzar's visage on one side and his own profile on the other, and under his own image inscribed the title, "Nebuchadnezzar III."

Saddam should have read the fourth chapter of Daniel before claiming this heritage. Nebuchadnezzar II lost his sanity and fed on the grass of the field like an animal until he praised, exalted, and glorified the King of Heaven, confessing, "All of [His] works are truth and His ways justice" (Daniel 4:37). Although Sargon (722–705 B.C.) preceded Nebuchadnezzar (605–562 B.C.) in Old Testament history, he faced judgment for the same sin.

THE SIN OF DEMEANING GOD (10:11)

Sargon made another fatal mistake in his role as the "rod" and "staff" of God's judgment upon Judah and Jerusalem. He assumed that the God of Jerusalem was just another god. In a colossal show of arrogance, Sargon lumped the holy city of Jerusalem in the category of the other cities and lands that he had conquered—Calno, Carchemish, Hamath, Arpad, Samaria, and Damascus. Each had its local gods and domestic idols, and he had destroyed and replaced them without bringing divine judgment down on his head. With the same cavalier attitude, he bragged, *"As I have done to Samaria and her idols, Shall I not do also to Jerusalem and her idols?"* (v. 11).

World domination, playing God, and treating the Holy One of Israel as a common god are attitudes tied together by the extreme of human arrogance. Isaiah's verbatim quotations of Sargon highlight the fact that the Assyrian king flaunted his power and presumed upon the limited authority that God had given to him. Yet, dictators are not alone in this. The temptation comes to all persons whom God chooses for a special task. Scholars can use the biblical text to advance their own prejudice; preachers can exploit the power of the pulpit to manipulate their congregation; counselors can play upon vulnerable persons to seduce them; and teachers can use their authority to pontificate on any subject they choose. We who are in the academic community tell a standing joke about new teachers who have just received their Ph.D. degree and become instant experts on any subject in the classroom. They are victims of the disease called "Ph. Deity"—cured only by a dose of humility.

The Timing of Judgment (10:12–14)

"Therefore" (v. 12) is the word that Isaiah uses to introduce the timing, the reason, and the consequences of judgment upon King Sargon and the nation of Assyria. The timing for judgment will come after the Lord has finished His work of purging on Mount Zion and Jerusalem; the reason for judgment is the arrogant heart and the haughty looks of the king of Assyria; and the consequences of judgment will fall upon the fruit of the king and the glory of his looks (v. 12). Before bringing down the curtain of judgment upon Sargon and Assyria, God reclaims His rightful position as the One who is all powerful in human history—moving the boundaries of nations, plundering their treasures, and subduing their kings—without "a flap of the wings" or "a peep from the mouth" of anyone on earth. With surgical precision, God lets Sargon know that He, and He alone, has the power to dominate the earth.

The Reason for Judgment (10:15)

God also restates His claim as the sovereign Lord whose role cannot be played by mortal kings. Four inanimate instruments with the power for good or evil are used to illustrate the point: (1) an ax that chops; (2) a saw that cuts; (3) a rod that punishes; (4) and a staff that lifts. Humor is evident in the ludicrous questions, *"Shall the ax boast itself against him who chops with it? Or shall the saw magnify itself against him who saws with it?"* (v. 15). How stupid, Isaiah says. Imagine a powerless rod swinging at the person who picks it up or a lifeless club lifting itself up and flaying in the air. Sargon's arrogance is exposed as sheer stupidity. To pose the power of God, claim the sovereignty of God, and deny the uniqueness of God is the peak of human folly.

The Effects of Judgment (10:16–19)

Another *"therefore"* (v. 16), brings us to God's punishment upon Sargon and Assyria. Sargon must have prided himself in the fruitful fields and the glorious forests of his nation (v. 18). However, Isaiah prophesies *"leanness"* for the fields and *"burning"* for the forests. With fruitfulness gone and glory charred, Sargon and his nation will waste away—body and soul—until nothing is left but a few scrub trees that even a child can count (vv. 18–19). Judah is thus assured that even its most formidable foe will come to judgment without the trace of a remnant.

Promise for the Remnant (10:20–34)

20 And it shall come to pass in that day
    that the remnant of Israel,
And such as have escaped of the house of Jacob,
Will never again depend on him who defeated them,
But will depend on the Lord,
    the Holy One of Israel, in truth.
21 The remnant will return,
    the remnant of Jacob,
To the Mighty God.
22 For though your people, O Israel,
    be as the sand of the sea,
Yet a remnant of them will return;
The destruction decreed shall overflow with righteousness.
23 For the Lord God of hosts
Will make a determined end
In the midst of all the land.
24 Therefore thus says the Lord God of hosts: "O My people, who dwell in Zion, do not be afraid of the Assyrian. He shall strike you with a rod and lift up his staff against you, in the manner of Egypt.
25 "For yet a very little while and the indignation will cease, as will My anger in their destruction."
26 And the Lord of hosts will stir up a scourge for him like the slaughter of Midian at the rock of Oreb; as His rod was on the sea, so will He lift it up in the manner of Egypt.
27 It shall come to pass in that day
That his burden will be taken away from
    your shoulder,
And his yoke from your neck,
And the yoke will be destroyed because of the
    anointing oil.

28 He has come to Aiath,
   He has passed Migron;
   At Michmash he has attended to his equipment.
29 They have gone along the ridge,
   They have taken up lodging at Geba.
   Ramah is afraid,
   Gibeah of Saul has fled.
30 Lift up your voice,
   O daughter of Gallim!
   Cause it to be heard as far as Laish—
   O poor Anathoth!
31 Madmenah has fled,
   The inhabitants of Gebim seek refuge.
32 As yet he will remain at Nob that day;
   He will shake his fist at the mount of the daughter
      of Zion,
   The hill of Jerusalem.
33 Behold, the Lord,
   The LORD of hosts,
   Will lop off the bough with terror;
   Those of high stature
      will be hewn down,
   And the haughty will be humbled.
34 He will cut down the thickets of the forest with iron,
   And Lebanon will fall by the Mighty One.

Isaiah 10:20–34

FAITH WILL BE REWARDED (10:20–23)

For both Judah and Israel, the promise of a remnant is the word that makes the present tolerable and the future hopeful. As much as Isaiah may have wished to see the day of restoration in his lifetime, and be part of a crowd of faithful believers in the temple, he must speak the truth. Destruction *"overflow[ing] with righteousness"* has already been decreed, he says, and after the purging of exile, only a handful of the faithful will make up the remnant for the return. Later history confirms Isaiah's prophecy. Judah and Jerusalem were overwhelmed by Babylon in 586 B.C. and subjected to the humility of two forced marches into Babylonian exile. Leaders were taken first in order to strip the nation of its memory, its ideas, and its morals. An army of commoners followed as slave laborers for constructing the Babylonian buildings. All that Isaiah predicted about a denuded land and culture came to pass.

Forty-eight or more years later, and for the first time in the history of an exiled nation, the Jews were given the option of returning home. Those who had come as leaders had ingeniously worked their way into the culture as merchants of commerce, and those who came for slave labor lacked the incentive to return, so natural attrition reduced the remnant to a handful.

God works best with minorities. Through church history, whenever believers have come into the majority position, they lose the edge of faith and succumb to political power. Arrogance is not reserved just for dictators like Sargon. Once utter dependence on God begins to wane and the intoxication of political power takes over, even people of faith are capable of making pronouncements and judgments that sound like the voice of God but lack the humility and grace of human wisdom. Minorities can be equally obnoxious, particularly if they develop the paranoia that makes them feel persecuted without cause. But as Jesus watched the masses go away when He preached the truth until only the twelve disciples remained, He asked the eternal question of them and of us, "Will you also go away?" Faithfulness, that creates a small company of faithful who dare to take the risk of return from exile in order to do the will of God is a rare virtue indeed.

JUDGMENT WILL BE TRANSFERRED (10:24–34)

Building upon His promise of the remnant, Isaiah utilizes another *"therefore,"* his favorite word of conclusion and consequence, to assure God's people that His anger will soon be turned from them to the destruction of Assyria (v. 25). Reaching back into their memory of deliverance from Egypt, God promises to whip the Assyrians soundly as He did the Midians at Oreb, to part the waters of the Red Sea to provide a route of escape, and to lift the yoke of oppression from their necks as He did with their foreparents in the land of the Pharoahs (vv. 26–27). In further support of His promise, God traces the path of the Assyrians on the way to their destruction. Their march will be halted at Nob and they will shake their fists in frustrated defiance at the unconquerable Jerusalem (v. 32). With that gesture, the tall and stately trees, which symbolize the fruit and glory of King Sargon's arrogant heart and haughty looks, are trimmed and felled like the mighty oaks of Lebanon (vv. 33–34).

PROMISE FOR JUDAH (11:1–16)

1 There shall come forth a Rod
from the stem of Jesse,
And a Branch shall grow
out of his roots.
2 The Spirit of the LORD
shall rest upon Him,
The Spirit of wisdom
and understanding,
The Spirit of counsel and might,
The Spirit of knowledge
and of the fear of the LORD.
3 His delight is in the fear of the LORD,
and He shall not judge by the sight of
His eyes,
Nor decide by the hearing of His ears;
4 But with righteousness He shall judge
the poor,
and decide with equity for the meek of
the earth;
He shall strike the earth with the rod
of His mouth,
and with the breath of His lips He
shall slay the wicked.
5 Righteousness shall be the belt of His
loins,
And faithfulness the belt of His waist.
6 "The wolf also shall dwell
with the lamb,
The leopard shall lie down
with the young goat,
The calf and the young lion
and the fatling together;
And a little child shall lead them.
7 The cow and the bear shall graze;

Their young ones shall lie down together;
And the lion shall eat straw like the ox.

8 The nursing child shall play
    by the cobra's hole,
and the weaned child shall put his hand in the
    viper's den.

9 They shall not hurt nor destroy in all My
    holy mountain,
For the earth shall be full of the knowledge of the LORD
As the waters cover the sea.

10 "And in that day there shall be a Root of Jesse,
Who shall stand as a banner to the people;
For the Gentiles shall seek Him,
And His resting place shall be glorious."

11 It shall come to pass in that day
That the LORD shall set His hand again the second time
To recover the remnant of His people who are left,
From Assyria and Egypt,
From Patros and Cush,
From Elam and Shinar,
From Hamath and the islands of the sea.

12 He will set up a banner for the nations,
And will assemble the outcasts of Israel,
And gather together the dispersed of Judah
From the four corners of the earth.

13 Also the envy of Ephraim shall depart,
And the adversaries of Judah shall be cut off;
Ephraim shall not envy Judah,
And Judah shall not harass Ephraim.

14 But they shall fly down upon the
    shoulder of the Philistines toward the west;
Together they shall plunder the people of the east;
They shall lay their hand on Edom and Moab;
and the people of Ammon shall obey them.

15 The LORD will utterly destroy the tongue of the
    Sea of Egypt;
With His mighty wind He will shake His fist over
    the River,
And strike it in the seven streams,
And make men cross over dryshod.

16 There will be a highway for the remnant of His people
Who will be left from Assyria,

As it was for Israel
In the day that he came up
    from the land of Egypt.

Isaiah 11:1–16

THE SEED OF THE SAVIOR (11:1)

Out of the same promise of the remnant, Isaiah develops the metaphor of the "holy seed" from the "stem in the land" that God showed in his vision in the temple (6:13). The "holy seed" has now grown into a shoot from the *"stem of Jesse"* and a fruitful branch from the root of Jesse (v. 1). God lets the children of Judah know that, despite their sin and punishment, they are still the chosen people for bringing the redemptive hope of new life to the deadness of a world rotted by sin and felled by divine wrath.

Only the most calloused critic would try to deny that this oracle announces the coming of Jesus Christ as the Messiah. In an earlier passage, we were introduced to Him as the Prince of Five Names (9:6) with an emphasis upon His attributes of wisdom, power, love, and peace. Now, Isaiah extends those virtues into the promises for His character (11:2–3), His governance (11:3–5), and His kingdom (11:10–16). What more can we ask? To foresee the promises of God for the coming of the Christ is to break out into song. As his final oracle for Judah, Isaiah gives us the song to sing in that day when God's promises are fulfilled (12:1–6).

THE SPIRIT OF THE SAVIOR (11:2–3)

The Spirit of the Lord is inseparable from the character of the Christ. Whenever God calls a person to the divine mission or a holy task, He endows His chosen candidate with the indwelling presence of His Holy Spirit. Moses (Numbers 11:17) and David (1 Samuel 16:13), for example, were recipients of the Spirit. From this endowment come six qualities that characterize the servant of the Lord: wisdom, understanding, counsel, power, knowledge, and fear of the Lord. Roman Catholics add "delight in the fear of the Lord" to make the "seven gifts of the Holy Spirit" in their tradition.

Whether the number of gifts is six or seven, they stand as qualities that Isaiah found missing in the leaders of Judah and Jerusalem. Still fresh in our mind is the "woe" that Isaiah pronounced against those "who are wise in their own eyes and prudent in their own sight" (5:21). We also remember Isaiah warning the children of Judah against consulting with "mediums and wizards who whisper and mutter" rather than seeking the counsel of their God (8:19). Christ, however, will be guilty of neither of these sins. With the Spirit of the Lord resting upon Him, He will be His own counsel.

The gifts of the Spirit that Isaiah identifies, then, represent the endowment for leadership that Christ will bring to His Messianic role. In evident contrast with the leadership whom Isaiah has scored time and time again for personal unrighteousness and social injustice, Christ will come with wisdom (seeing things whole), understanding (sensitivity to relationships between issues), counsel (willingness to listen and advise), power (ability to influence by example), knowledge (knowing the facts), and fear of the Lord (centering upon the will of God).

Leadership theory has come full circle in recent days. When serious study of leadership began, effectiveness was identified with the charismatic personality of the leader. As the field developed, however, personal characteristics of leadership got lost in a maze of "situational" theories that emphasized *how* the leader functioned rather than *who* the leader was. But now, the deeper the studies go, the closer they come to the fact that the character of the leader makes the difference.

American politics reflects the change. Watergate is the turning point. Before Watergate, the character of candidates for presidential leadership did not come into question. Today, however, character and trust are questions that take precedence over such critical issues as economics, health care, and education. Isaiah drew that same conclusion centuries ago. Leadership is not a haphazard role in any setting or situation. Special responsibility is *given to* a leader by God and special accountability is *required of* a leader to God. Without the Spirit of the Lord resting upon the person who is called to lead, there is the danger of leaders becoming "wise in their own eyes and prudent in their own sight." Christ is the example for all to follow.

The Governance of the Savior (11:4–5)

Character is directly reflected in the governance of a leader. To assume that a scoundrel can govern with justice would cause Isaiah to gasp in disbelief. To him, unless the leader is a person of righteousness, justice will go begging because the leader has no objective standard for judgment. Without this standard, the judge will have to rely upon the evidence of what is seen and heard (v. 3) for decision-making.

Anyone who has witnessed a courtroom scene knows how faulty the eyes and ears of witnesses can be. Different persons see and hear different, and even contradictory, things. Defendants who can afford to hire a clever attorney have a clear advantage over those whose poverty permits them only the counsel of a public defender. In such cases, the poor can be victims of oppression rather than recipients of justice. The judge must possess the integrity of character and the objectivity of truth to guarantee their inalienable rights.

Christ stands out among all leaders of the earth in the excellence of His governance. With righteousness as His belt and faithfulness as His sash, He will do what is right in His judgments and what is fair in His decisions. While assuring justice for the needy and the poor, He will also bring down the *"rod"* of justice upon the wicked and scorch them with the *"breath of His lips"* (vv. 4–5). Judges can do that. When the judge convicted Jeffrey Dahmer of murder that included counts of sexual mutilation, dismemberment, and cannibalism, his voice must have been hard as steel as he said, "You deserve death because you have violated one of the most fundamental laws of humankind." Christ, the judge, will speak with the same intensity in the final judgment when He announces it to those who have been leaders of the faith. Because they lack the inner standard of righteousness and the long-term evidence of faithfulness, He will say, "I never knew you. Depart from Me, you who practice lawlessness" (Matthew 7:23).

THE PEACE OF THE SAVIOR (11:6–9)

To illustrate how the character and governance of Christ will influence the earth, Isaiah resorts to the image of Eden restored. Wolves, leopards, lions, bears, and cobras are all deadly enemies of such defenseless creatures as lambs, goats, calves, cows, and infant children. Yet, in the reign of Christ, God promises not only righteous judgment for the needy in society but also peace for the helpless in creation. Such a radical reversal will come about when the earth is full of the *"knowledge of the LORD"* (v. 9). In other words, the sin of Adam and

Eve, by which they wanted to be as wise as God, will be forgiven and all the earth will know that He, and He alone, is God. The promise is far-reaching and anticipates the new heavens and the new earth that Isaiah foresees at the end of his prophecy (65:17–25).

THE SIGNS OF THE SAVIOR (11:10–16)

Isaiah is always looking into the distant future when he employs the phrase, *"In that day"* to introduce a prophecy. We stand with him on the peak of prophetic vision as he peers forward to the day when the root of Jesse *"shall stand as a banner"* for the rallying of all peoples and all nations (v. 10). Like the mountain climbers who scaled Mount Everest and planted their national flag at the highest point on earth, we can envision the day when the banner bearing the name of Christ will be unfurled at the top of the world. That day has not yet come. For while no one on earth can ignore the name of Christ in human history, all peoples and all nations are not yet rallying to Him. Many efforts are underway to "win the world for Christ" by the turn of the century when we enter a new millennium. Such visions are consistent with the prophecy of Isaiah and the great commission of Jesus Christ. We do not know how and when the banner of Christ will be raised over all the world, but we do know that it will come to pass. Therefore, we must be part of the effort to prepare the way for the day when the *"[nations] shall seek Him, and His resting place shall be glorious"* (v. 10).

Another sign *"in that day"* will be the Lord reaching out His hand a *"second time to recover the remnant of His people who are left"* from every nation in the world. History records the diaspora or *dispersal* of the Jews through the Babylonian exile to the four corners of the earth. History also records the first return of the Jews from Babylonian exile in 538 B.C.

Modern prophets are quick to see the second return of the Jews in the Zionist movement, which is bringing Jewish people back to Israel from across the world. Of course, the same prophets read this sign as evidence that the second coming of Christ is imminent.

Isaiah would not dispute their claim, although he might well contest their penchant for putting precise dates on the prophecy. Isaiah himself, while claiming to speak for God, does not give a date other than to say, "In that day." With him, we are better to anticipate the day with righteousness and faithfulness than to expend our energy on the date of which Jesus Himself said, "It is not for you to know the times or seasons which the Father has put in His own authority. But you shall receive power when the Holy Spirit comes upon you; and you shall be witnesses to Me in Jerusalem, and in all Judea and Samaria, and to the end of the earth" (Acts 1:7–8). No one can confuse these instructions. We must not worry about the date, but we must be ready recipients of the power of the Holy Spirit in order to be His witnesses, beginning at home and spreading through the nations to the ends of the earth.

In that day Christ will not only be the banner for the nations of the world and the rallying point for the second return of the remnant but He will heal the hostility between Judah and Israel to create a united kingdom; he will conquer the nations that are enemies of Israel; and he will prepare the way for the return of the remnant by miraculous deeds not unlike the parting of the Red Sea and the building of a highway as He did for the Exodus from Egypt (vv. 12–16).

Isaiah is criticized for his show of militancy and triumphalism in this prophecy. The vision of the United Kingdom of Judah and Israel swooping down upon Philistia, plundering the people of the East, conquering Edom and Moab, and making slaves of the Ammonites seems to contradict the reign of the Prince of Peace (11:6–9). We must remember Isaiah's consistent contention that the same holy fire that heals also burns. Also, he had forewarned us that "with the breath of His lips" Christ would slay the wicked (11:15). Reality informs us that there are enemy nations whose evil designs will frustrate the redemptive purpose of God. As we found out with Russia in the Cuban missile crisis, those nations only understand the language of military force. At the same time, we cannot use this passage to justify the naked aggression of Israel against neighboring Arab nations when righteousness and justice are the motives or the outcomes of the military action. Only the Spirit of the Lord resting upon the leadership can draw the critical distinction.

PROMISE OF A SONG (12:1–6)

1 And in that day you will say:
   "O LORD, I will praise You;
   Though You were angry with me,
   Your anger is turned away,
      and You comfort me.

> 2 Behold, God is my salvation,
>   I will trust and not be afraid;
>   'For YAH, the LORD,
>   is my strength and my song;
>   He also has become my salvation.'"
> 3 Therefore with joy you will draw water
>   From the wells of salvation.
> 4 And in that day you will say:
>   "Praise the LORD, call upon His name;
>   Declare His deeds among the peoples;
>   Make mention that His name is exalted.
> 5 Sing to the LORD,
>   For He has done excellent things;
>   This is known in all the earth.
> 6 Cry out and shout,
>   O inhabitant of Zion,
>   For great is the Holy One of Israel in your midst!"
>
> *Isaiah 12:1–6*

Isaiah has already shown us his mastery as a communicator of prose and poetry. Now, he reveals himself as a composer of magnificent song. Like a composer of a symphony who creates varying movements leading to a climactic ending, Isaiah's oracles have been building to the grand finale of a song that begins on the note, *"O LORD I will praise you,"* (v. 1) and swells to the full chorus, *"Cry out and shout"* (v. 6).

THE PATTERN OF PRAISE (12:1–2)

Two verses make up the oracle of song. Each verse begins with the introduction, *"In that day"* and ties the song into the oracles for Judah that promise the coming of the Christ out of the root of Jesse. Before this oracle, Isaiah had little about which to sing. But when God shows him the character, governance, and kingdom of the Christ, the prophet bursts forth with a hymn of praise. "In that day," he sings, God's anger will be past and His comfort will be given. In response, the children of Israel will once again put their trust in Him and lose their fear of the forces of evil that surround them. With one voice, they will extol the Lord as their strength, their song, and their salvation (v. 2). Best of all, they will again know the *"joy"* that comes from the life-giving water that is drawn from the *"wells of salvation"* (v. 3).

The pattern of praise has not changed. We sing of God's forgiveness and His comfort; we sing of trust in Him and the freedom from fear; we sing of Him as our strength, our song, and our salvation. All hymns of praise should be measured by this pattern. If the focus of our singing is upon ourselves and our needs, we miss the value of praise when God is extolled as our strength, our song, and our salvation. Classic hymns, which last for generations, meet this standard. Bill Moyers, the television producer, did a show entitled "Amazing Grace" in an effort to dicover why the hymn persists through the generations and across cultures. Isn't the answer in the pattern of praise given to us by Isaiah?

> Amazing grace, how sweet the sound
> That saved a wretch like me.
> I once was lost, but now am found,
> Was blind but now I see.
>
> When we've been there ten thousand years,
> Bright shining as the sun,
> We've no less days to sing God's praise
> Then when we've first begun.

THE PURPOSE OF PRAISE (12:3–4)

The second verse is also introduced with the words, *"In that day."* Having foreseen the return to total trust in God on the part of the children of Israel, Isaiah now envisions the recovery of their divine destiny as God's chosen people. It is thanksgiving as the people sing the fourfold theme:

1. Give thanks to the Lord
2. Call on His name
3. Make known among the nations what he has done
4. Proclaim that His name is exalted.

People who are fulfilling God's purpose for their lives have good reason to sing. God chose Israel to be the instrument to proclaim His name and show His way among the nations. Sin temporarily aborted that grand purpose, but Isaiah foresees the day when through the joy of song, they will *"sing to the* LORD, *for He has done excellent things; this is known in all the earth"* (v. 5). Music has been called the universal language. No other means of communication is so effective. During a recent trip to Bulgaria, within months after it gained its independence from the Soviet Union and Communism, we felt the confusion of the people as they struggled with their new-found freedom. Three grace notes broke through the gloom: the sound of a violin concerto, the harmony of a symphonic orchestra, and the joyful hymns of the church. We left Bulgaria realizing that they were still balancing on a razor's edge between democracy and dictatorship, but we also felt the joyous spirit of music that welled from the source of their hope.

THE POWER OF PRAISE (12:5–6)

The contemporary church cannot sacrifice its songs of praise in proclaiming Christ to the world. As President of Asbury Theological Seminary, I emphasize and reemphasize the importance of the music in worship and evangelism for the ministers of tomorrow. Special emphasis is placed upon the chapel services where the music of the Seminary organist, the chapel choir, and the singing congregation draw capacity crowds. In their first worship of orientation and in their service at commencement, the students sing together what I call "The Asbury Anthem":

> And can it be that I should gain
> An interest in the Savior's blood.
> Died He for me who caused His pain,
> For me who Him to death pursued
> Amazing love, how can it be
> That Thou my God should'st die for me.

As renewed trust in the God of salvation is the theme of Isaiah's first verse of song, so a renewed proclamation of His glorious deeds is the theme of the second verse. Israel had a large repertoire of songs growing out of the Exodus and extolling the Lord for His deliverance. Now, Isaiah says that Israel will sing again new songs of deliverance that proclaim His glorious deeds to the whole world. The song of God's greatness and His glory is still the song of the people of God that the world will hear. At the risk of criticism, our song of joy might even warrant the loud shout that Isaiah heard when Israel began to sing again.

CHAPTER EIGHT

Prophecy Against Babylon

Isaiah 13:1–14:23

We enter now what scholars of Isaiah call a "jungle of prophecy." Patient and prayerful study is required to enter the mind of Isaiah to understand his reason for writing these prophecies against the nations of the world in both current and future history. Of course we are not without help from the prophet himself. His opening words sound familiar when he introduces the section with the subscript, "The burden against Babylon which Isaiah the son of Amoz saw" (v. 1).

Twice before, we read similar subscripts—in the opening verse of his prophecy (1:1) when he writes a synopsis of his vision and in his introduction to the major themes of his theophanies (2:1). Now, with the same words, Isaiah helps us anticipate another set of prophecies that have a different perspective from the previous "Oracles of Promise," which he spoke on behalf of Israel. From the springboard of the "Oracle of Song," which sets the tone for praising God "in that day" when His banner was unfurled on Mount Zion to rally all nations to the kingdom of righteousness and judgment, Isaiah stops, backs up, and retraces the path of judgment upon the nations of the world that brings them to the doorstep of Jerusalem—not in siege, but in respect.

Burden is synonymous with *oracle* or *load*. In this case, "burden" is the most appropriate translation because of the weight of doom that Isaiah foresees upon the nations that have opposed Israel and defied God. Pride and arrogance are not sins peculiar to Judah and Jerusalem. They are endemic to human nature. So, when God uses surrounding nations to punish Judah and Jerusalem for their sins, and those nations flaunt that power by assuming that they are sovereign in the universe, God brings down upon them judgment that is even more severe than His wrath upon Israel. At least His judgment upon Israel leads to the promise of the remnant through which God's redemptive purpose will be realized. In the case of the nations of the world, their prospect for the future rests not upon a special calling as God's instruments of hope, but upon Israel's return and the Messiah's coming.

Because each of the oracles in this section touches upon some event in imminent or distant history, our study is further complicated. Isaiah does not follow a chronological sequence by which we can walk step by step with him through events that are as immediate as Ahaz' alliance with Assyria in 734 B.C. and lead to Babylon's destruction by the Medes in 539 B.C. His movement is outward from the surrounding nations of Edom, Moab, and Arabia (ch. 15 and 21) to the conquering nations of Assyria and Damascus (ch. 14 and 17), and on to the massive empires of Babylon on the north (ch. 21) and Egypt on the south (ch. 18–20) before stretching out to the world seaport of Tyre (ch. 23) as the thoroughfare to the ends of the earth itself (ch. 24).

Even in this sequence, historical time and physical space give way to spiritual symbol. The oracles begin, for instance, with the "burden" of Isaiah concerning Babylon—definitely a threat of the future long after the prophet's death. Yet, Babylon epitomizes the spirit of pride and arrogance that usurps the power of God and sets itself upon His sovereign throne. Isaiah's message, then, remains the same. He pronounces judgment upon all people and nations that fail to trust in God because of pride and arrogance. To the end of time, and to the ends of the earth, no generation or civilization is exempt.

As a guide for studying these "Oracles of Doom," the following questions can be asked of each nation or empire included in the prophecies:

1. When does the historical event take place?
2. What is the point of pride against which the prophecy speaks?
3. How does God punish the sin of the nation?
4. What is the prospect of that nation for the future?

Fair warning is given that Isaiah's oracles never fit a neat package. The questions, however, are consistent with the prophetic cycle of historical events that comprise the parts of Isaiah's vision: (a) prophetic proclamation, (b) punishment for sin, and (c) promise for the future .

A HOLY WAR (13:1–22)

1 The burden against Babylon which Isaiah the son of
   Amoz saw.
2 "Lift up a banner on the high mountain,
   Raise your voice to them;
   Wave your hand, that they may enter the gates of the
       nobles.
3 I have commanded My sanctified ones;
   I have also called My mighty ones for My anger—
   Those who rejoice in My exaltation."
4 The noise of a multitude in the mountains,
   Like that of many people!
   A tumultuous noise of the kingdoms of nations gath-
       ered together!
   The LORD of hosts musters
   The army for battle.
5 They come from a far country,
   From the end of heaven,
   Even the LORD and His weapons of indignation,
   To destroy the whole land.
6 Wail, for the day of the LORD is at hand!
   It will come as destruction from the Almighty.
7 Therefore all hands will be limp,
   Every man's heart will melt,
8 And they will be afraid,
   Pangs and sorrows
       will take hold of them;
   They will be in pain
       as a woman in childbirth;
   They will be amazed at one another;
   Their faces will be like flames.
9 Behold, the day of the LORD comes,
   Cruel, with both wrath and fierce anger,
   To lay the land desolate;
   And He will destroy its sinners from it.
10 For the stars of heaven and their constellations
   Will not give their light;

The sun will be darkened in its going forth,
And the moon will not cause its light to shine.
11 "I will punish the world for its evil,
And the wicked for their iniquity;
I will halt the arrogance of the proud,
And will lay low the haughtiness of the terrible.
12 I will make a mortal more rare than fine gold,
A man more than the golden wedge of Ophir.
13 Therefore I will shake the heavens,
And the earth will move out of her place,
In the wrath of the Lord of hosts
And in the day of His fierce anger.
14 It shall be as the hunted gazelle,
And as a sheep that no man takes up;
Every man will turn to his own people,
And everyone will flee to his own land.
15 Everyone who is found
    will be thrust through,
And everyone who is captured
    will fall by the sword.
16 Their children also will be dashed
    to pieces before their eyes;
Their houses will be plundered
And their wives ravished,
17 "Behold, I will stir up the Medes against them,
Who will not regard silver;
And as for gold,
    they will not delight in it.
18 Also their bows will dash
    the young men to pieces,
And they will have no pity
    on the fruit of the womb;
Their eye will not spare children.
19 And Babylon, the glory of kingdoms,
The beauty of the Chaldeans' pride,
Will be as when God overthrew Sodom and
    Gomorrah.
20 It will never be inhabited,
Nor will it be settled
    from generation to generation;
Nor will the Arabian pitch tents there,
Nor will the shepherds make their sheepfolds there.

21 But wild beasts of the desert will lie there,
     And their houses will be full of owls;
     Ostriches will dwell there,
     And wild goats will caper there.
22 The hyenas will howl in their citadels,
     And jackals in their pleasant palaces.
     Her time is near to come,
     And her days will not be prolonged."

Isaiah 13:1–22

THE MOTHER OF ALL BATTLES (13:1–5)

As already noted, Babylon symbolizes evil as the major antagonist of God. Prophecies against the spirit of Babylon range from David's Psalm, "O Daughter of Babylon, who are to be destroyed" (Psalm 137:8) to its fulfillment in the book of Revelation, "Babylon the great is fallen, is fallen, and has become a habitation of demons, a prison for every foul spirit" (Revelation 18:2). In between are the many prophecies of Isaiah (13:19; 14:22; 21:9; 43:14; 47:1; and 48:14) and Jeremiah (25:12; 50:1–13; and 51:1) who speak with equal rancor against the empire that personifies evil. Perhaps this is the reason why Isaiah put this oracle first. Babylon is not just another nation marching across the Middle East with world domination in mind; it is the symbol of the holy war that is being waged between the forces of God and Satan in the events of human history.

A Spirit-guided balance is needed to keep in proper perspective the idea of God and His people waging a "holy war" between the forces of good and evil. The temptation is to go from one extreme to the other. Violence in the name of God is not unknown in Christian history, as we remember in the Children's Crusades to take the Holy City from the Turks or as we see in the religious civil war of Protestants against Catholics in Ireland. Belligerence is also justified among some theologians who believe that a secular democracy is an enemy that should be replaced by a theocracy of Christian leaders. Still other believers fall prey to a paranoia that sees demons behind every historical event or personal act as the explanation for evil in the world.

At the other extreme there is a passivity among complacent Christians that allows them to let down their guard as secular influences contaminate the culture. In its most extreme form, this passiveness becomes active in a "civil religion" that equates democracy with

Christianity. Only a Spirit-guided watchfulness can keep alert to the reality of the "holy war" between God and Satan that is still raging without falling victim to a paranoia that leads to grandiose schemes and potential violence.

THE DAY OF THE LORD (13:6–10)

Readers of the oracle have to wait until verse 17 to find the historical event to which Isaiah speaks. Although Babylon has been used as the "rod" of God's wrath against Judah and Jerusalem, now the tables are turned. In 539 B.C., almost two hundred years after Isaiah's time, the Medes marched against the proud empire of Babylon and completely devastated the land under the leadership of Cyrus, the Persian king.

Without a doubt, the fall of Babylon is one of the pivotal events in biblical history upon which God's redemptive purpose turns. Why then does Isaiah place the identification of the Medes as the conquering army so late in his oracle (v. 17)? George Adam Smith answers that question by noting that Isaiah's primary purpose is "moral impressiveness" rather than "historical connectiveness."[1] From this perspective we gain insight into this first oracle of doom that might otherwise escape us. Babylon, throughout Scripture, symbolizes the essence of the evil that is at the root of all sin. So, after Isaiah foresees the day when the Lord's name will be exalted among all peoples (12:4) and the glory of His excellent works will be known in all the earth (12:5), he comes back to the reality that evil still exists in the world and must be utterly destroyed before ultimate victory can be assured. Babylon represents the core of depravity brought on by the Fall that pervades all humanity, all cultures, and all creation. Consequently, it is the moral magnitude, not the historical consequence, of Babylon's fall that dominates Isaiah's message. The prophecy might well be entitled the "Oracle of Apocalypse" because Isaiah foresees the downfall of Babylon as a coming event in history whose meaning can be projected to the end times when *the day of the LORD is at hand* (v. 6).

THE "SANCTIFIED" PAGAN ARMY (13:11–18)

By now, we are well acquainted with God's choice of pagan nations as the instruments of His judgment. In the opening overview of his vision, Isaiah prophesied that the Lord would lift up a banner to be seen by distant nations and would whistle them to His command for swift and sharp strokes of judgment against sinful nations—including Judah, the land of His own chosen people (5:26–30). In speaking his burden against Babylon, Isaiah sees the same banner lifted, the same rallying call sounded, and the same command given to the army that God musters for judgment upon Babylon (vv. 2–3). Here, however, the two prophecies part. In the oracle against Babylon, the LORD of hosts is now preparing for a holy war between good and evil in which one force or the other will be vanquished. The moral escalation of this warfare is evident when God calls the pagan armies under His command *"My sanctified ones," "My mighty ones,"* and *"those who rejoice in My exaltation"* (v. 3). These massed armies of the world then become the corporate counterpart to Cyrus, pagan king of the Medes, who led the armies against Babylon with the Lord's commendation as "My shepherd" (45:28).

Mystery of mysteries! With our limited human perspective, we cannot comprehend how the Lord commands a pagan army as His "sanctified ones" and calls a pagan king His "shepherd." Isaiah would not be as troubled as we are. His vision in the temple gave him a large perspective of God's will for the world that meant full confidence for God's ways in the world. Isaiah's viewpoint can be likened to the topside of a quilt in which an exquisite pattern appears. The bottom side of the quilt, however, appears as a tangle of disconnected knots that make no sense at all. Our human perspective on God's will and ways in the world is a bottom-side view. A "sanctified" pagan army and a "shepherd" pagan king appear as confusing, even contradictory, to us. In modern terms, it would take a major paradigm shift in the way we view the world for us to see these historical happenings from the topside of God's perspective. As a finite human being, Isaiah had the same problem. After all, he was prophesying events he would never see come to pass. Yet, with only a glimpse of the holy character and the glorious purpose of God that he received in the temple, Isaiah saw these happenings through the eyes of God. Where the vision blurred beyond his lifetime, he trusted where he could not see.

THE ULTIMATE VICTORY (13:19–22)

Not a word of hope is given for the future of Babylon. The keynote for understanding the apocalyptic oracle against Babylon is God's personal word: *"I will punish the world for its evil, | and the wicked for their iniquity, | I will halt the arrogance of the proud | and will lay low the haughtiness of the terrible"* (v. 11).

Arrogance and pride have been targets for Isaiah's barbed arrows of judgment in each of his prophecies. "Evil" and "iniquity" are new to his language and reinforce the fact that his prophecy against Babylon has escalated the level of God's judgment to the finality of the end time. The destruction of evil and iniquity requires more than limited military action or temporary conquest with some hope of future recovery. Isaiah's picture of God's *"wrath and fierce anger"* (v. 9) is utter destruction for total victory.

Evil and iniquity are not easily destroyed. Isaiah tells us that a terror will strike the hearts of evil humanity with such fear that the results will be physical paralysis, heart failure, psychological trauma, and hypertension never known before (vv. 7–8). Added to that will be eclipses of the sun and moon that will plunge the universe into utter darkness (v. 10) followed by earthquakes that will literally shake the earth off its orbit (v. 13). As the battle on earth heightens, people who have been slaves of the Babylonian conquest will flee the city like *"the hunted gazelle"* and will become refugees returning to their homeland (v. 14). Those who remain will be obliterated by a slaughter that will leave Babylon forever uninhabited and unsettled (v. 20). Instead of the sounds of people celebrating the glory of the city, Isaiah leaves us with the picture of a place of desolation where only the hyenas howl in abandoned citadels and the jackals play in haunted palaces (v. 22). In a word, Babylon will be no more.

History bears out Isaiah's prophecy. In 539 B.C. Babylon was sacked and devastated by the Medean army under the command of Cyrus. The city never recovered and remains until this day only a hollow shell of its former self. Saddam Hussein, imagining himself as the twentieth-century successor to Nebuchadnezzar, king of Babylon at the time of its fall, tried to restore its Hanging Gardens as one of the seven wonders of the world. Shortly after a concocted celebration intended to reclaim the glory of Babylon, Desert Storm broke and shattered Saddam's futile dream. Once again, the hyenas are howling in its citadels and the jackals are playing in its palaces. Whether Hussein knows it or not, Babylon in its desolation is a monument to God's conquest over evil and iniquity through the death and resurrection of His Son Jesus Christ. In that monument we also foresee the final battle in the holy war between good and evil:

> The kingdoms of this world
> have become the kingdoms
> of our Lord and of His Christ,
> And He shall reign for ever and ever!
>
> *Revelation 11:15*

THE POSTWAR ERA (14:1–23)

1 For the LORD will have mercy on Jacob, and will still choose Israel, and settle them in their own land. The strangers will be joined with them, and they will cling to the house of Jacob.

2 The people will take them and bring them to their place, and the house of Israel will possess them for servants and maids in the land of the LORD; they will take them captive whose captives they were, and rule over their oppressors.

3 It shall come to pass in the day the LORD gives you rest from your sorrow, and from your fear and the hard bondage in which you were made to serve,

4 that you will take up this proverb against the king of Babylon, and say:
> "How the oppressor has ceased,
> The golden city ceased!
5 The LORD has broken the staff
>   of the wicked,
> The scepter of the rulers;
6 He who struck the people in wrath
>   with a continual stroke,
> He who ruled the nations in anger,
> Is persecuted and not one hinders.
7 The whole earth is at rest and quiet;
> They break forth into singing.
8 Indeed the cypress trees rejoice over you,
> And the cedars of Lebanon,
> Saying, 'Since you were cut down,
> No woodsman has come up against us.'

9 "Hell from beneath is excited about you,
   To meet you at your coming;
   It stirs up the dead for you,
   All the chief ones of the earth;
   It has raised up from their thrones
   All the kings of the nations.
10 They all shall speak and say to you:
   'Have you also become as weak as we?
   Have you become like us?
11 Your pomp is brought down to Sheol,
   and the sound of your stringed instruments;
   The maggot is spread under you,
   And worms cover you.'
12 "How you are fallen from heaven,
   O Lucifer, son of the morning!
   How you are cut down to the ground,
   You who weakened the nations!
13 For you have said in your heart:
   'I will ascend into heaven,
   I will exalt my throne above the stars of God;
   I will also sit on the mount of the congregation
   On the farthest sides of the north;
14 I will ascend above the heights of the clouds,
   I will be like the Most High.'
15 Yet you shall be brought down to Sheol,
   To the lowest depths of the Pit.
16 "Those who see you will gaze at you,
   And consider you, saying:
   'Is this the man who made the earth tremble,
   Who shook kingdoms,
17 Who made the world as a wilderness
   And destroyed its cities,
   Who did not open the house of his prisoners?"
18 "All the kings of the nations,
   All of them, sleep in glory,
   Everyone in his own house;
19 But you are cast out of your grave
   Like an abominable branch,
   Like the garment of those who are slain,
   Thrust through with a sword,
   Who go down to the stones of the pit,
   Like a corpse trodden under foot.

20 You will not be joined with them in burial,
   Because you have destroyed your land
   And slain your people.
   The brood of evildoers shall never be named.
21 Prepare slaughter for his children
   Because of the iniquity of their fathers,
   Lest they rise up and possess the land,
   And fill the face of the world with cities."
22 "For I will rise up against them,"
   says the LORD of hosts,
   "And cut off from Babylon
      the name and remnant,
   And offspring and posterity,"
      says the LORD.
23 "I will also make it a possession
      for the porcupine,
   And marshes of muddy water;
   I will sweep it with the broom of destruction," says the
   LORD of hosts.

Isaiah 14:1–23

MERCY FOR JACOB (14:1–2)

Off the grand design of God's ultimate victory over evil, Isaiah returns to the local scene to assure the children of Israel of their return from Babylonian exile and their special role in the divine plan. Neither the forthcoming defeat of the evil empire of Babylon in human history, nor its ultimate conquest as the essence of evil in moral history, is without its redemptive purpose. By assuring the house of Jacob that the defeat of Babylon in human history will lead to their return from exile and their restoration as God's choice instrument for the proclamation of His Word, Isaiah is preparing the way for the prophetic announcement that the ultimate victory over evil will lead to the reign of righteousness, justice, and peace through the Messiah that God has also promised (ch. 11).

God's unfailing love for His people and His unswerving dedication to His redemptive purpose motivate Him to have *"mercy on Jacob"* and *"still choose Israel"* (v. 1). Evidence of His love and purpose will be shown in the fulfillment of four special promises. First, the children of Israel will be settled in their own land (v. 1). Although

176

stated as a matter of fact, we remember that no other exiled people had ever returned to their homeland. A miracle of God equal to the Exodus from Egypt is implied in this promise.

Second, Gentiles will join with the house of Jacob and become one with them in the house of the LORD. No one who has visited modern Israel and the surrounding Arab nation will doubt that Isaiah is predicting another event of miraculous proportions. Ancient hatreds run so deep in the rift between Jews and Arabs that only divine intervention could bring them together. At home, we have the National Conference on Christians and Jews, which is dedicated to bringing the two faiths together in a cooperative and working relationship. Yet, when I gave an invocation at a local Rotary Club and ended my prayer, "in Jesus' name," a leader of the Jewish community and an officer of the National Conference on Christians and Jews brought formal protest against my prayer. The rift still runs deep and only a miracle can make the difference.

Third, nations of the world will look to Israel as the model of righteousness, justice, and peace and come to the land in order to learn the ways of the Lord (v. 2). What a contrast! From exile to exaltation, Israel will rise from the depths of shame to the heights of glory in another demonstration of God's miraculous grace.

Fourth, the children of Israel will be conquerors rather than the conquered, victors rather than the vanquished, and rulers rather than the ruled (v. 2). To understand this miraculous turnabout, Israel's place among the nations of the Middle East in Isaiah's time must be understood. Against the size, wealth, armies, and cities of Assyria, Egypt, Babylon, and Phoenicia, Israel was an impoverished, rural, and weak dwarf. Least among nations, it is almost inconceivable to think of Israel as the possessor of nations that once possessed them, the captor of the people that once captured them, and the ruler of kings who once ruled over them. God promises that a complete turnabout of power will be added to prestige for Israel in the time to come. Our natural reaction is to be repulsed by the thought that God plays in the power game among nations. We must remember, however, that the exercise of power is not evil in itself. When power is tempered by personal righteousness and social justice under the Spirit of the Lord (11:2–3), Israel can possess nations, hold captives, and rule governments without sin.

OBLITERATION FOR BABYLON (14:3–11)

The holy war between the forces of good and evil is not a moral abstraction. As the city of Babylon represents the evil opponent of the holy city of Jerusalem, so the king of Babylon personifies Satan, the evil antagonist against God. Again, Isaiah's prophecy has current and endtime implications. On the day in history when Babylon will be utterly ruined and the house of Jacob will be restored, the Jews will sing a song taunting the King of Babylon as he falls into disgrace and loses his place in human history (v. 3).

In the apocalyptic context, a similar fate awaits Satan when he, his name, and his influence over humanity are utterly broken by the conquest of Jesus Christ. Whether in the historical or the apocalyptic context, Isaiah prophesies that the results will be the same for the king of Babylon or Satan. Utter disgrace and absolute destruction await the person of evil when Isaiah declares, *"How the oppressor has ceased!"* (v. 4). Earlier oracles of doom spoke of destruction, but not with the totality and the permanence of the prophecies against Babylon and its king.

Isaiah also foresees that *"the LORD has broken the staff of the wicked and the scepter of the rulers"* (v. 5). The metaphor of the "staff" and the "scepter" representing the Lord's judgment against the nations is now used to symbolize the ultimacy of the holy war between good and evil. In the "staff," power meets power and in the "scepter" authority confronts authority. Furthermore, in this "mother of all battles" the anger of the Lord is vented against the anger of Satan and the fury of the Lord rages against the fury of Satan. Needless to say, Isaiah has set before us the image of an ultimate battle of white-hot intensity in which the stakes are eternal.

ANNIHILATION FOR LUCIFER (14:12–23)

As Babylon faced obliteration, so the king of Babylon faced annihilation. Resulting from the triumph of the Lord of hosts, all creation breaks into singing. Nations who cowered under the threat of the evil king are now at peace (v. 7) and even the forests that feared his careless cutting are rejoicing at his downfall (v. 8). Beneath the earth in Sheol, the spirits of the dead eagerly await the arrival of the arrogant king whose mortal weakness has been exposed by death itself (v. 10).

Heaven does its own rejoicing over the downfall of the king of Babylon. Lucifer is now identified as the person of evil and iniquity whom the king of Babylon symbolizes and the protagonist of God in the final battle of the ages. *"How you are fallen from heaven, O Lucifer, son of the morning!"* (v. 12) may be duly interpreted as a realistic insight into Satan's original fall from heaven and as a symbolic representation of the heights from which the king of Babylon fell. Both Lucifer and the king of Babylon had said in their hearts,

> I will ascend into heaven,
> I will exalt my throne above the stars of God;
> I will also sit on the mount of the congregation
> On the farthest sides of the north;
> I will ascend above the heights of the clouds,
> I will be like the Most High.
>
> *Isaiah 14:12–14*

As pretenders to the loftiest throne of God and as usurpers of His exalted nature, Lucifer and the king of Babylon are in for a fall. From the highest heights of the heaven to the lowest depths of the pit of hell they will plunge.

Isaiah uses direct quotes of Lucifer and the king of Babylon to reveal the evidence of their supreme egotism. Five times they speak, "I will, I will, I will, I will, I will." Setting themselves up in competition with God, they have committed the cardinal sin of assuming that they are sovereign above the stars, worthy of being worshiped, and rulers of the universe.

Psychiatrists report that persons of national visibility and power frequently dream of falling off a cliff. While basking in the glory of their fame, their greatest fear is that they will fall. If they do, the distance from the heights of fame to the depths of shame is far greater than it is for the average person who fails. Richard Nixon, for instance, lied about his involvement in Watergate to protect his presidency. When he failed, he was like Humpty-Dumpty who had a "great fall." Once the fragile shell of his public trust was broken, neither "all of the king's horses" nor "all of the king's men, could put Humpty-Dumpty back together again." Lucifer and the king of Babylon's downfall is even more irredeemable. Nixon has made a partial comeback as an adviser in foreign affairs and undoubtedly history will balance his contributions as well as his betrayal. But for Lucifer and the king of Babylon there is no partial recovery. Once Lucifer is brought to his knees, he will be no more; once the king of Babylon is defeated, he will cease to exist.

Isaiah traces their downfall through a series of demeaning steps. From the heights of self-proclaimed glory, Lucifer and the king of Babylon become the laughingstock of the world as they are ridiculed, *"Is this the man who made the earth tremble?"* (v. 16). Shame is then heaped upon shame when they are denied a decent burial in contrast with the regal mourning and monumental tombs reserved for the kings of the earth (vv. 18–19). Instead, they will die as the most despised of criminals and will be responsible for the slaughter of their own children (vv. 20–21). Finally, in a plunge to the bottom of the pit, their name, their remnant, their offspring, and their posterity will disappear from the face of the earth and the annals of eternity (v. 22). In a most fitting analogy, God has used a stiff broom for a clean sweep of evil and iniquity (v. 23).

Kings and rulers have not changed. They accept criticism but cannot stand to be made a laughingstock. Dan Quayle, Vice President of the United States under George Bush, countered effectively against the jabs of his critics, but he never fully recovered from the jibes of comics who refused to take him seriously. Kings and rulers are also extremely sensitive to their place in history. As with John F. Kennedy, they want to be remembered for standing firm against Russia in the Cuban missile crisis rather than the Bay of Pigs; or as with Jimmy Carter, they want to remembered for the Camp David accord that brought peace between Israel and Egypt rather than the speech that pointed out our national malaise. Then, when kings and rulers die, they envision a nation in mourning as their casket is carried on a horse-drawn carriage to the sound of muffled drums and the salute of twenty-one cannons. To be denied a grave, even in a potter's field, would be shame above shames.

But most of all, kings and rulers want their names to be on the lips of future generations, as American school children speak the names of Washington and Lincoln. If they are kings, they want their dynasty to continue; if they are presidents, they want their children to be honored. As they cannot stand being laughed at in life, so they cannot handle the thought of being forgotten in death.

In Isaiah's vision, the downfall of Lucifer and the king of Babylon takes on eternal dimensions. From the heights of self-glory in competition with God they will fall to the depths of nameless nonexistence without even a footnote in history or a thread of hope for the future. The "broom of destruction" in the hands of the Lord of hosts will make a clean sweep of evil for time and eternity.

NOTES

1. Smith, *Expositor's Bible*, 403.

CHAPTER NINE

Book of Woes

Isaiah 14:24–19:25

God is no respecter of persons or nations. As He pronounced judgment upon Babylon, the proud image of evil, so He swears on His power as Lord of hosts that He will act with equal justice in punishing the nations of the world. "Woe" is the word that signals the burden of judgment that he bears. Beginning with the "burden" against Philistia "in the year that King Ahaz died" (14:28), similar woes are spoken against Moab (15:1–16:14); Damascus (17:1–11); the world (17:12–14); Ethiopia (18:1–7); and Egypt (19:1–17) before Isaiah draws a summary with a promise of peace for Israel and its surrounding nations (19:18–24). Each "burden" or "woe" that Isaiah speaks to these nations is unique to the role of that nation in relationship to Judah.

Whether in warning, punishment, or promise, God responds individually and personally to the nature of the nations. Egyptian, Roman, and Greek civilizations all fell from the internal weight of their strength becoming their weakness. Egypt fell from the weight of idolatrous worship; Rome fell from the burden of political corruption; and Greece fell under the lodestone of intellectual cynicism. We in Western civilization should be duly warned. The strength of our democratic government, our economic prosperity, or our technological advancement can turn against us and become the weakness upon which we can fall. As individuals, too, we should be duly warned. More often than not, if our strengths get out of hand as a source of arrogance and pride, they will become our weaknesses and the cause of our downfall.

THE OATH OF GOD (14:24–27)

24 The LORD of hosts has sworn, saying,
    "Surely, as I have thought,
        so it shall come to pass,
    and as I have purposed,
        so it shall stand:
25 That I will break the Assyrian in My land,
    And on My mountains tread him under foot.
    Then his yoke shall be removed from them,
    And his burden removed from their shoulders.
26 This is the purpose that is purposed against the
        whole earth,
    And this is the hand that is stretched out over
        all the nations.
27 For the LORD of hosts has purposed,
    And who will annul it?
    His hand is stretched out.
    And who will turn it back?"

Isaiah 14:24–27

I SWEAR FOR YOUR SAKE (14:24–25)

In a very short prophecy, Isaiah turns from the symbolic to the specific in order to assure the children of Israel that God is not so absorbed with the future that He forgets the present. Assyria, not Babylon, is the immediate threat upon the minds of the people when Isaiah writes these words. One can imagine the person on the street listening to Isaiah's prophecy of the future about Babylon and saying, "All well and good, but what about the Assyrians who are on our doorstep?" This is a natural question that neither God nor Isaiah feels to be unfair. So, in a strong passage of Scripture, God swears an oath, *"Surely, as I have thought, so it shall come to pass, and as I have purposed, so it shall stand"* (v. 24).

I SWEAR ON MY HONOR (14:26–27)

God is not in the business of saying, "read my lips," and then justifying actions contrary to His promise. Instead, He swears an oath upon His own character and His own deeds, which can be tested by history, as assurance to the children of Israel that He will do just as He says He will do. Behind this oath is the implicit assumption that the children of Israel can trust God, not Egypt or any other human power, for their protection and their future.

Sworn and *purposed* are the key words in this oracle. After the Lord of hosts is willing to take an oath on His promise, the word "purposed" is used three times to attest the faithfulness of His actions against Assyria, against the nations, and *"against the whole earth"* (vv. 26–27). By such a sworn oath, God is putting Himself on the line and, in effect, saying to the people, "Put Me to the test. If I have not done what I said I was going to do or if I do not do what I said I am going to do, do not believe in Me. But if I have done what I said I was going to do, and if I do what I promise to do, trust Me." The case in point is Assyria. Even though its armies are in Judah and on the threshold of Jerusalem, God promises to break the yoke of conquest that threatens the children of Israel (v. 25). With the swearing of an oath, God assures His people that He will be faithful, whether in protecting them or punishing their enemies. Moreover, the promise He makes for them will coincide with His purpose for *"all the nations"* and the *"whole earth"* (v. 26).

WOE TO PHILISTIA (14:28–32)

28 This is the burden which came in the
year that King Ahaz died.
29 "Do not rejoice, all you of Philistia,
Because the rod that struck you is broken;
For out of the serpent's roots
    will come forth a viper,
And its offspring will be
a fiery flying serpent.
30 The firstborn of the poor will feed,
And the needy will lie down in safety;
I will kill your roots with famine,
And it will slay your remnant.
31 Wail, O gate! Cry, O city!
All you of Philistia are dissolved;
For smoke will come from the north,
And no one will be alone in his appointed times."
32 What will one then answer the
messengers of the nation?

That the LORD has founded Zion,
And the poor of His people shall take refuge in it.

Isaiah 14:28–32

THE LAND OF THE VIPER'S STING (14:28–31)

Isaiah's burden against Philistia came *"in the year that King Ahaz died"* (v. 28). Although the date is uncertain, Ahaz' death is estimated on or about 715 B.C. Therefore, the Assyrian kings who might be the *"rod,"* *"viper,"* and *"fiery flying serpent"* to which Isaiah refers might be Tiglath-Pileser (died 727 B.C.), Shalmaneser V (died 722 B.C.), or Sargon II (died 705 B.C.). The most likely historical connector between this oracle and the Judean-Philistine relationship is the invitation for Judah to join with the Philistines in revolt against Assyria at the time of the death of one of the Assyrian kings. If so, Isaiah warns Judah against such an entangling alliance because the next Assyrian king will be even more vicious in his vengeance upon Philistia. Famine will kill the sustaining roots of the culture and Assyrian slaughter will annihilate the civilization (v. 30). The "smoke from the north" is a direct reference to the Assyrian invaders who attacked and punished Philistia time after time as Assyrian kings marched in succession through the land.

THE ANSWER TO THE NATIONS (14:32)

Isaiah's warning is crystal clear. When Philistia sends its ambassadors to Judah with the invitation to join in rebellion against Assyria, the answer is, "the LORD has founded Zion, and the poor of His people shall take refuge in it" (v. 32). Judah is to reject the Philistine's offer without hesitation and put its trust in the Lord. For emphasis, Isaiah adds the fact that even the poorest and most helpless of the people of Judah will find refuge in the Lord when they put their trust in Him (v. 32).

The alternative is grim. If Judah joins in a foolish alliance with Philistia, even the children of Israel will feel the sting of the viper and the bite of the fiery, flying serpent. In the most graphic terms, Isaiah has again posed the question for Judah, "In whom will you trust, the Lord of hosts or a human power?"

WOE TO MOAB (15:1–16:13)

1 The burden against Moab.

Because in the night
  Ar of Moab is laid waste
And destroyed,
Because in the night
  Kir of Moab is laid waste
And destroyed,
2 He has gone up to the temple and Dibon,
To the high places to weep.
Moab will wail over Nebo
  and over Medeba;
On all their heads will be baldness,
And every beard cut off.
3 In their streets they will clothe
  themselves with sackcloth;
On the tops of their houses
And in their streets
Everyone will wail, weeping bitterly.
4 Heshbon and Elealeh will cry out,
  Their voice shall be heard as far as Jahaz;
Therefore the armed soldiers of Moab will
    cry out;
His life will be burdensome to him.
5 "My heart will cry out for Moab;
His fugitives shall flee to Zoar,
Like a three-year-old heifer.
For by the ascent of Luhith
They will go up with weeping;
For in the way of Horonaim
They will raise up a cry of destruction,
6 For the waters of Nimrim
  will be desolate,
For the green grass has withered away;
The grass fails, there is nothing green.
7 Therefore the abundance they have gained,
And what they have laid up,
They will carry away to the Brook of the Willows.
8 For the cry has gone all around the borders of Moab,
Its wailing to Eglaim
And its wailing to Beer Elim.
9 For the waters of Dimon
  will be full of blood;
because I will bring more upon Dimon,

Lions upon him who escapes from Moab,
And on the remnant of the land."

1 Send the lamb to the ruler of the land,
From Sela to the wilderness,
To the mount of the daughter of Zion.

2 For it shall be as a wandering bird
thrown out of the nest;
So shall be the daughters of Moab at
the fords of the Arnon.

3 "Take counsel, execute judgment;
Make your shadow like the night in the middle
of the day;
Hide the outcasts,
Do not betray him who escapes.

4 Let My outcasts dwell with you, O Moab;
Be a shelter to them from the face of the spoiler.
For the extortioner is at an end,
Devastation ceases,
The oppressors are consumed
out of the land.

5 In mercy the throne will be established;
And One will sit on it in truth,
in the tabernacle of David,
Judging and seeking justice
and hastening righteousness."

6 We have heard of the pride of Moab—
He is very proud—
Of his haughtiness and his pride
and his wrath;
But his lies shall not be so.

7 Therefore Moab shall wail for Moab;
Everyone shall wail.
For the foundations of Kir Hareseth
you shall mourn;
Surely they are stricken.

8 For the fields of Heshbon languish,
And the vine of Sibmah;
The lords of the nations have broken down its choice
plants,
Which have reached to Jazer
And wandered through the wilderness.
Her branches are stretched out,

187

> They are gone over the sea.
> 9 Therefore I will bewail the vine of Sibmah,
>   with the weeping of Jazer;
>   I will drench you with my tears,
>   O Heshbon and Elealeh;
>   For battle cries have fallen
>   Over your summer fruits
>   and your harvest.
> 10 Gladness is taken away,
>   And joy from the plentiful field;
>   In the vineyards there will be no singing,
>   Nor will there be shouting;
>   No treaders will tread out wine
>   in their presses;
>   I have made their shouting cease.
> 11 Therefore my heart shall resound like a harp for Moab,
>   And my inner being for Kir Heres.
> 12 And it shall come to pass,
>   When it is seen that Moab is weary on the high place,
>   That he will come to his sanctuary to pray;
>   But he will not prevail.
> 13 This is the word which the Lord has spoken
> concerning Moab since that time.
>
> *Isaiah 15:1–16:13*

As the prophetic vision of Isaiah turns toward the east and across the Dead Sea, the nation of Moab comes into view. The land and the people have a special place in God's heart because when Lot's oldest daughter was impregnated by her father, she bore a son and named him Moab (Genesis 19:37). Lot, the nephew of Abraham, had accompanied the father of Israel in his journey by faith from Ur of the Chaldees as far as Sodom and Gomorrah (Genesis 13). Tragedy followed when God threatened to wipe out the cities because of their sin. Abraham interceded and Lot fled the city only to fall into the sin of incest with his daughters. Moab, the son of his illicit relationship with his oldest daughter, became the father of the Moabites on the southeast side of the Dead Sea after he settled from his wanderings. Despite Lot's sin and Moab's shame, God never forgot the relationship between Israel and Moab. Moses, for instance, was buried in an unknown grave somewhere in Moab (Deuteronomy 34:6). With this background, we can understand why the "burden" against Moab differs from the other oracles of judgment against the nations surrounding Judah. The oracle is more a lament for judgment than a declaration of judgment. In no other oracle do we read the words of the Lord, *"My heart will cry out for Moab"* (16:5), *"I will drench you with My tears"* (v. 9), and *"My heart shall resound like a harp for Moab,"* (16:11). Of all the prophecies against foreign nations, Moab is closest to the heart of God.

In 2 Kings 24:2 we read that the Moabites joined the Babylonian armies of King Nebuchadnezzar in a raid to destroy Judah. Along with the other instruments of judgment that God used to punish His people for their sins, Moab placed itself under judgment for sin.

THE LAND OF THE BALD AND BEARDLESS (15:1–4)

When Amos prophesies against the nations for their sin, Moab is singled out for "three sins . . . even four" from which God will not turn back His wrath (Amos 2:1–3). The act of burning the bones of Edom's king is cited as their special sin. Cremation itself is not directly condemned in Scripture; however, to cremate a king as an idolatrous act is a point of condemnation. What are the other three sins? Isaiah may give us the answer when he charges Moab with the same sins as other nations—pride, conceit, and insolence (16:6 NIV). More specifically, pride is the sin of exalting oneself to compete with God, conceit is the sin of assuming to be wise in one's own mind, and insolence is the sin of rebelling against the love of God and refusing to trust Him.

THE FLIGHT OF THE FUGITIVE (15:5–9)

Because of its four sins, Moab must suffer the consequences of returning to the homeless wandering of its father Moab. The people will become a nation of refugees fleeing in shame with shaven heads and beardless faces before the onslaught of the enemy (vv. 2 and 5). Two metaphors vividly describe their plight. They will be like a three-year-old heifer running in panic and like a *"wandering bird thrown out of the nest"* (16:2).

Millions of refugees are still wandering over the earth. They flee from floods in Bangladesh, from famine in Somalia, from civil war in

Yugoslavia, and from dictatorship in Iran. Their growing numbers will not stop as we move into the twenty-first century. Whether from natural disaster, religious hatred, ancient hostility, or political oppression, refugees will continue to haunt us as we see their hollow faces and bloated bellies on our television screens. Whatever the cause for their flight, we weep for the innocent victims, especially mothers and children.

A memory from years ago comes back to my mind as if the event had just happened. While visiting in a Cambodian refugee camp located in Thailand within artillery range of communist guns, my wife and I toured a mud hut hospital where raised mats and board walks kept the patients from lying in the monsoon rivers that flowed beneath their feet. As our guide told us about a shocking mortality rate among the victims due to disease and malnutrition, I felt two arms wrap around my leg. Looking down, I peered into the dulled eyes of a little girl with a body crippled and dwarfed by tropical disease. As she hugged me, the doctor explained that she was a refugee of unknown identity who could not be relocated in Thailand or sent back to Cambodia. She was a child without a name and without a future. I wept as I picked her up in my arms and felt her head snuggle into the nape of my neck.

The experience helps me understand why God's heart cries out for the refugees of Moab, why His tears flow, and why the strings of His heart resound with the plaintive sound of a harp. Even though Moab is only "shirttail relation" to the children of Israel, they tug upon the love of God and cause Him to weep.

THE ASYLUM FOR THE HOMELESS (16:1–10)

Out of His tears, God appeals to Moab to be the refuge for the children of Israel who are also in flight. More than refuge is needed, however. Counsel needs to be taken and judgment executed to protect the wandering people. With the spirit of open arms, God asks Moab to *"Make your shadow like the night in the middle of the day"* (v. 3).

The beauty of these words matches the motto of America on the Statue of Liberty at the entrance to New York harbor, "Give me your tired, your poor." When the Haitian boat people were turned back from our shores and faced either death at sea or execution in their homeland, many people questioned whether we still meant those words. Only Native Americans are the natural citizens of our nation.

All the rest of us are beneficiaries of the spirit and laws that welcomed our forefathers and mothers as immigrants. God goes a step further. As an expression of His compassion for the refugee, He proposes that people of Moab hide the outcasts and protect those who escape from the clutches of the oppressor. Images of the underground railway for slaves during the Civil War and the little attic in Amsterdam where Anne Frank was hidden all come to mind. Where refugees are concerned, God even makes provision for nonviolent civil disobedience on their behalf.

Isaiah's vision from God includes intimate knowledge of the land of Moab and its cities. Through a succession of names of regions, cities, and rivers, the flight of the refugees is traced (15:5–9 and 16:6–9). Furthermore, God is sensitive to the culture of the people of Moab. As harvesters of grapes and treaders of the winepress, they are a glad people who celebrate the making of the wine. A boat trip on the Rhone or the Rhine rivers through the grape country in France and Germany at harvest time is a series of celebrations. Each village has its own vintage wine and festivals of joyous singing and dancing to celebrate the harvest. Moab must have known similar days, but now under the judgment of God their songs are silenced, their shouts are stilled, and their gladness is taken away (v. 10). Their tears will mingle with the Lord's.

THE HARP STRINGS OF GOD (16:11–13)

A footnote follows the oracle against Moab. Isaiah reports an update on the timing of Moab's punishment. *"Within three years, as the years of a hired man,"* he says, *"the glory of Moab will be despised with all that great multitude, and the remnant will be very small and feeble"* (v. 14). Assuming that Isaiah's first prophecy came at the death of Ahaz in 715 B.C., he might be referring to the episode in 711 B.C. when Moab came under threat from Sargon II's army or perhaps in 704 B.C. when Sennacherib threatened invasion. While history is not exact on this timing, Isaiah's message is exact. Moab's glory will be despised and only the smallest and weakest of remnants will remain. At least, Moab will have a shred of hope. Babylon and Assyria are fated for utter destruction and total devastation without a shred of hope for the future. For Moab, the strings in God's heart can still be plucked like a harp with the plaintive sound of weeping in his *"inner being"* (v. 11).

191

WOE TO DAMASCUS (17:1–11)

1 The burden against Damascus.
"Behold, Damascus will cease from being a city,
And it will be a ruinous heap.
2 The cities of Aroer are forsaken;
They will be for flocks
Which lie down,
    and no one will make them afraid.
3 The fortress also will cease from Ephraim,
The kingdom from Damascus,
And the remnant of Syria;
They will be as the glory of the children of Israel,"
Says the Lord of hosts.
4 "In that day it shall come to pass
That the glory of Jacob will wane,
And the fatness of his flesh grow lean.
5 It shall be as when the harvester gathers the
    grain,
And reaps the heads with his arm;
It shall be as he who gathers heads of grain
In the Valley of Rephaim.
6 Yet gleaning grapes will be left in it,
Like the shaking of an olive tree,
Two or three olives at the top of the
    uppermost bough,
Four or five in its most fruitful branches,"
Says the Lord God of Israel.
7 In that day a man will look to his Maker,
And his eyes will have respect
    for the Holy One of Israel.
8 He will not look to the altars,
The work of his hands;
He will not respect what his fingers have made,
Nor the wooden images
    nor the incense altars.
9 In that day his strong cities
    will be as a forsaken bough
And an uppermost branch,
Which they left because of
    the children of Israel;
And there will be desolation.

10 Because you have forgotten
        the God of your salvation,
    And have not been mindful of the
        Rock of your stronghold,
    Therefore you will plant pleasant plants
    And set out foreign seedlings;
11 In the day you will make
        your plant to grow,
    And in the morning you will make
        your seed to flourish;
    But the harvest will be a heap of ruins
    In the day of grief and desperate sorrow.

                                        Isaiah 17:1–11

Geography is guiding the prophecies of Isaiah concerning the nations surrounding Judah. Having covered the immediate southern borders with oracles against Philistia and Moab, Isaiah turns to the north and focuses upon Damascus, the crossroads city where the caravan trails run north and south, east and west. Although Syria and Israel are the target nations for the prophecy, the focal point of Damascus gives meaning to Isaiah's "burden" for all the nations of the north.

The Land of Ruined Heaps (17:1–3)

In Isaiah's earlier prophecies during the Syro-Phoenician crisis, he warned Syria and Israel that their sins would bring down the wrath of Assyria on their heads (7:4 and 8:1–4). As he predicted, they suffered terrible, but not total, devastation. The burden is still not lifted. Damascus stands as a symbol of human wealth, power, and self-glory. In the future, Isaiah foresees further judgment that will be even more devastating. And so it came to be. About 732 B.C., the Assyrians attacked Damascus, sacked the city, executed the king, and divided up the territory into four fiefdoms as a protection against rebuilding the empire. As Isaiah predicted, Damascus became a *"ruinous heap,"* other cities were forsaken, fortresses were torn down, kingdoms taken away, and only a pitiful remnant was left (vv. 1–3).

The Forsaken Bough (17:4–6)

Isaiah employs the common words, *"In that day"* to point out the sin of Damascus and prescribe its punishment. Four sins are named or inferred following those introductory words. Damascus stood condemned: first for the sin of self-glory (v. 4); second, for the sin of idol worship (v. 7); third, for the sin of forgetting God (v. 10); and fourth, for the sin of taking prosperity for granted (v. 11).

Although Damascus may be the geographical focus for this prophecy, the Northern Kingdom of Israel is the historical center for the judgment. When Isaiah, for instance, refers to the sin of self-glory, he refers to the waning glory of Jacob (v. 4). When he condemns idol worship, he reminds them of the day when they revered only the Holy One of Israel (v. 7). And when Isaiah speaks of the devastation of their cities, he reminds Israel of the desolation of the cities that they inherited from the heathen in the promised land. The same fate awaits them because they have forgotten the God of their salvation (v. 10).

Solemn warnings for those of us who are Gentiles reverberate through this oracle of judgment. Just as Isaiah reminded the Israelites that they inherited their land by the providence of God, so the apostle Paul reminds us that we are like branches grafted into the trunk of an olive tree and sustained by its roots (Romans 11:17–19).

> You will say then, "Branches were broken off that I
> might be grafted in." Well said. Because of unbelief
> they were broken off, and you stand by faith. Do not
> be haughty, but fear. For if God did not spare the
> natural branches, He may not spare you either.
>
> *Romans 11:19–21*

Isaiah's case is clear. For both Jews and Gentiles, faith is the common element that brings and sustains the blessing of God. Without continuing trust in God, neither occupied cities in the promised land nor grafted branches on the tree of life will be spared.

THE FOREIGN FRUIT (17:7–11)

Each of the four sins has its punishment. For the sin of *self-glory*, Isaiah predicts leanness for the harvests of grain, grapes, and olives (vv. 4–6). Israel gloried in these crops and counted upon an abundant harvest to sustain its agricultural affluence. *"In that day,"* however, Isaiah foresees only a pittance of the expected harvest. Olive trees, for instance, should yield thousands of ripened fruit. Imagine the harvester coming to the tree, seeing no fruit and shaking its branches until two or three olives from the topmost boughs, and four or five from the most fruitful branches dribble to the ground. Figuratively, the image also applies to the leanness of soul that the sin of self-glory will bring to the Northern Kingdom of Israel.

Idol worship is the second sin of Damascus in which Israel also indulged. "In that day," Isaiah says, Israel will realize that all the altars, artifacts, graven images, and incense that are part and parcel of idolatry cannot save them. Instead of looking to their idol with respect, they will look again to their *"Maker"* and respect the *"Holy One of Israel"* (v. 7).

Punishment for the third sin of *forgetting God* will be the devastation of the cities in the Promised Land given to Israel as its inheritance. Like the olive tree that is shaken to yield only a few olives, Israel will be reduced to a remnant of the faithful (v. 9).

Finally, for the sin of *taking God's blessings for granted*, Israel is in for a surprise. Following all of the rules of proper planting for an abundant harvest, including some *"foreign seedlings,"* which most likely symbolize entangling alliances, the nation will reap only a *"heap of ruins"* (vv. 10–11). Whether the reference is to famine or conquest, the result is the same—grief and desperate sorrow await Israel.

Despite all of their sins, however, God does not forget His people. In the image of the olive tree, there are a few fruits that remain in the topmost and fullest branches. As sparse as the evidence may be, God is true to His promise of a remnant. Even more encouraging is the prophecy that Israel will turn from the futility of idol worship and once again will look to the Maker and worship the Holy One of Israel. Not even the forthcoming devastation of their cities and the grief of widespread famine can override the promises of God.

WOE TO THE WORLD—A SUMMARY (17:12–14)

12 Woe to the multitude of many people
    Who make a noise like the roar of the seas,
    And to the rushing of nations
    That make a rushing like the rushing of mighty waters!
13 The nations will rush like the rushing of many waters;
    But God will rebuke them
        and they will flee far away,

And be chased like the chaff of the mountains before
   the wind,
Like a rolling thing before the whirlwind.
14 Then behold, at eventide, trouble!
And before the morning, he is no more.
This is the portion of those who plunder us,
And the lot of those who rob us.

Isaiah 17:12–14

Summaries are common to the prophetic style of writing. After Isaiah has had a word for Judah's neighbors, south, east, and north, his vision opens up to the whole world. With a word of *"woe"* he makes sure that his prophecies forewarn any aggressor nation against threatening Judah and Jerusalem. Whether by words of threat that he likens to the *"roar of the seas"* or by armies of might that he compares to the *"rushing of many waters"* Isaiah warns the nations of the world that they are in for the same fate as those who have threatened or invaded Judah and Jerusalem (vv. 12–13a). Although they may come in with the sound and the fury of mighty waters, they will leave under God's judgment like the chaff scattered by the wind or like a tumbleweed bouncing across the desert (v. 13). With these images in mind, Isaiah drives home his point in the unmistakable warning, *"This is the portion of those who plunder us, and the lot of those who rob us"* (v. 14). All nations, beware. God may punish His own for their sins, but He will not tolerate anyone else taking that punishment into their own hands.

WOE TO ETHIOPIA (18:1–7)

1 Woe to the land shadowed with buzzing wings,
Which is beyond the rivers of Ethiopia,
2 Which sends ambassadors by sea,
Even in vessels of reed on the waters, saying,
"Go, swift messengers,
   to a nation tall and smooth of skin,
To a people terrible
   from their beginning onward,
A nation powerful and treading down,
Whose land the rivers divide.
3 All inhabitants of the world and dwellers on the earth:

196

When he lifts up a banner on the mountains, you see it;
And when he blows a trumpet, you hear it.
4 For so the LORD said to me,
"I will take My rest,
And I will look from My dwelling place
Like clear heat in sunshine,
Like a cloud of dew in the heat of harvest."
5 For before the harvest,
    when the bud is perfect
And the sour grape is ripening
    in the flower,
He will both cut off the sprigs with pruning hooks
And take away and cut down the branches.
6 They will be left together for the mountain birds of prey
And for the beasts of the earth;
The birds of prey will summer on them,
And all the beasts of the earth will winter on them.
7 In that time a present will be brought to the
    LORD of hosts
From a people tall and smooth of skin,
And from a people terrible from their beginning
    onward,
A nation powerful and treading down,
Whose land the rivers divide—
To the place of the name of the LORD of hosts,
    to Mount Zion.

Isaiah 18:1–7

THE LAND OF BUZZING WINGS (18:1–3)

In keeping with the pattern of Isaiah's prophecies, he moves from a "woe" upon all nations of the world to a specific "woe" upon Ethiopia, the biblical land of Cush. The historical event that triggered this prophecy is the delegation of ambassadors from Egypt who came to Judah to persuade Hezekiah to join in a mutual pact against the threat of Assyrian vengeance. Accordingly, Isaiah's "woe" against Ethiopia rather than Egypt is explained.

In 716 B.C., the king of Ethiopia took Egypt captive and ruled over the land during the revolt in 714 B.C. against the Assyrians. Descriptive imagery identifies a *"land shadowed with buzzing wings"* with *"vessels of reed"* as a special means of transportation. The "buzzing wings" may refer to the land of locusts that swarm across the sky to shadow the sun. "Vessels of reed" undoubtedly refers to the papyrus boats that sailed the Nile and along the Mediterranean coast.

As we know, Isaiah sternly opposed any alliance with a foreign nation but especially with Egypt because he foresaw a "paper tiger" in its posturing of power. To frighten Judah into the alliance, however, they pictured the people of Assyria as giants *tall and smooth of skin* with a history of atrocity and a power that could not be turned back by any one nation alone (v. 2). Isaiah counters these scare tactics with a repetition of the prophecy that the LORD of hosts will lift a banner and blow a trumpet that will signal His triumph over all the nations of the earth, including the Assyrian hordes (v. 3). God will do this, however, in His own time. For the present, He will rest and delay His judgment while retaining control of human history and choosing the time for the pruning of the harvest in order to fulfill His good purpose (vv. 5–6).

A TIME FOR PRUNING (18:4–6)

Isaiah knew what it meant to wait upon the resting Lord. In the temple, he had cried, "How long, O LORD, how long?" The response came as a call for patience and faithfulness. God said, "Until the cities lie ruined . . . until the houses are left deserted . . . until the LORD has sent everyone far away . . ." (6:11–12). For those of us who carry the burden of impatience, it is not easy to accept the word *until* from the resting Lord. Honesty, however, leads to the confession that whenever we take the will of God into our hands and act ahead of His timing, we fail miserably. We must also confess that when we exercise patience and trust in the Lord, we invariably look back upon the results to confess, "Forgive me, Lord. Your timing is best." If only we would wait.

A GIFT FOR GOD (18:7)

God's good timing for Judah and Jerusalem carries the promise of the day when *a present will be brought to the LORD of hosts* from the same tall, smooth-skinned, terrible, powerful, and dreaded Assyrians before whom Judah quaked in fear (v. 7a). Who said that Isaiah had no sense of humor? In this prophecy he shows how ludicrous it is for

Judah to fear the Assyrians and trust in a foolish alliance with Ethiopia for their protection. With a laugh, he foresees the time when Assyria will join the nations of the world streaming to Mount Zion where they will worship the LORD of hosts, honor His name, and learn of His ways (compare 18:7b with 2:2–4).

With such great hope, one would think that the people of Judah would have heard Isaiah's message and put their trust in the Lord. Unfortunately, the sad story is that King Hezekiah entered into the alliance with Ethiopia and brought down God's wrath upon his people. Once again, Isaiah learned what God meant when He told him that His children would fail to understand or accept his message because of calloused hearts, dull ears, and blind eyes (6:10).

WOE TO EGYPT (19:1–25)

1 The burden against Egypt.
  Behold, the LORD rides
      on a swift cloud,
  And will come into Egypt;
  The idols of Egypt will totter
      at His presence,
  And the heart of Egypt
      will melt in its midst.
2 "I will set Egyptians against Egyptians;
  Everyone will fight against his brother,
  And everyone against his neighbor,
  City against city,
      kingdom against kingdom.
3 The spirit of Egypt will fail in its midst;
  I will destroy their counsel,
  And they will consult the idols
      and the charmers,
  The mediums and the sorcerers.
4 And the Egyptians I will give
  Into the hand of a cruel master,
  And a fierce king will rule over them,"
  Says the Lord, the LORD of hosts.
5 The waters will fail from the sea,
  And the river will be wasted
      and dried up.

6 The rivers will turn foul,
    And the brooks of defense will be emptied and dried
        up;
    The reeds and rushes will wither.
7 The papyrus reeds by the River,
        by the mouth of the River,
    And everything sown by the River,
    Will wither, be driven away, and be no more.
8 The fishermen also will mourn;
    All those will lament who cast hooks into the River,
    and they will languish who spread nets on the waters.
9 Moreover those who work in fine flax
    And those who weave fine fabric will be ashamed;
10 And its foundations will be broken.
    All who make wages will be troubled of soul.
11 Surely the princes of Zoan are fools;
    Pharaoh's wise counselors give foolish counsel.
    How do you say to Pharaoh,
        "I am the son of the wise,
    The son of ancient kings?"
12 Where are they?
    Where are your wise men?
    Let them tell you now,
    And let them know what the Lord of hosts has pur-
        posed against Egypt.
13 The princes of Zoan have become fools;
    The princes of Noph are deceived;
    They have also deluded Egypt,
    Those who are the mainstay of its tribes.
14 The Lord has mingled
        a perverse spirit in her midst;
    And they have caused Egypt
        to err in all her work,
    As a drunken man staggers
        in his vomit.
15 Neither will there be any work
        for Egypt,
    Which the head or tail,
    Palm branch or bulrush, may do.
16 In that day Egypt will be like women, and will
be afraid and fear because of the waving of the hand
of the Lord of hosts, which He waves over it.

17 And the land of Judah will be a terror to Egypt; everyone who makes mention of it will be afraid in himself, because of the counsel of the LORD of hosts which He has determined against it.

18 In that day five cities in the land of Egypt will speak the language of Canaan and swear by the LORD of hosts; one will be called the City of Destruction.

19 In that day there will be an altar to the LORD in the midst of the land of Egypt, and a pillar to the LORD at its border.

20 And it will be for a sign and for a witness to the LORD of hosts in the land of Egypt; for they will cry to the LORD because of the oppressors, and He will send them a Savior and a Mighty One, and He will deliver them.

21 Then the LORD will be known to Egypt, and the Egyptians will know the LORD in that day, and will make sacrifice and offering; yes, they will make a vow to the LORD and perform it.

22 And the LORD will strike Egypt, He will strike and heal it; they will return to the LORD, and He will be entreated by them and heal them.

23 In that day there will be a highway from Egypt to Assyria, and the Assyrian will come into Egypt and the Egyptian into Assyria, and the Egyptians will serve with the Assyrians.

24 In that day Israel will be one of three with Egypt and Assyria, even a blessing in the midst of the land,

25 whom the LORD of hosts shall bless, saying, "Blessed is Egypt My people, and Assyria the work of My hands, and Israel My inheritance."

Isaiah 19:1–25

THE LAND OF TOTTERING IDOLS (19:1–2)

From the specific prophecy against Ethiopia with the stern warning to Judah against entering into the alliance of revolt against Assyria, Isaiah's vision broadens in scope again. Egypt represents a counterforce of arrogance and pride against the sovereignty of God. In other pagan nations, idol worship tended to be polytheistic, but in

Egypt the sun god Ra had been exalted to a monotheistic position indirectly in competition with Yahweh, the God of the Jews. Moreover, the Pharoahs of Egypt claimed direct ancestry with divinity and demanded worship from the people of Egypt. We understand, then, why Isaiah introduces his "burden" against Egypt with the image of the Lord riding on a swift cloud into the sunny land of Ra with judgment that topples idols and strikes fear into the hearts of the people. Both the idolatrous system and the blasphemous spirit will feel the wrath of the LORD of hosts (v. 1).

No specific event in the history of relationships between Judah and Egypt is cited in this oracle. Rather, we know that kings Ahaz and Hezekiah sought alliances with Egypt at different times. These are the entangling alliances based upon trust in human might that God will judge.

Alliances between Christians and nonbelievers for political and moral purposes are still popular. A few years ago, Francis Shaeffer urged Christians to enter into alliances with groups he called "cobelligerents" to fight against moral issues, such as abortion. Later on, evangelical Christians became closely identified with the political right wing of the Republican Party to advance an agenda of opposition to family breakdown, pornography, feminism, homosexuality, pro-choice activists, and military weakness. Still later, a coalition made up of former adversaries—evangelical Christians, orthodox Jews, and conservative Roman Catholics—formed around their common belief in God and His revelation of moral absolutes as the basis for their opposition to such issues as abortion, homosexuality, and sexual promiscuity. While the motives may be good, one wonders how long such alliances can last before conflicts arise over other nonnegotiables of belief. By and large, God's warning against entangling alliances applies to political coalitions and moral crusades as well as to Judah and Egypt.

The Spirit of Failing Pride (19:3–15)

As always, Isaiah sees arrogance and pride as the sins of Egypt. Their expression, however, is uniquely Egyptian. They are monotheists who worship Ra, the sun god, and they are idolaters who exalt Pharaoh to divine prominence. While not symbolizing the essence of evil as Isaiah portrayed Babylon, Egypt is a difficult case because the Egyptians are believers and worshipers who might well ask, "We have our god, why do we need another?"

God strikes in judgment right at the heart of Egyptian pride. To start, God divided Egypt into warring factions at every level of society—Egyptian against Egyptian, brother against brother, neighbor against neighbor, city against city, and kingdom against kingdom (v. 2). Egypt boasted not only of its high religion but also of its high culture. A visit to the monuments and museums of Egypt dazzle the modern visitor with exquisite artwork, inventive engineering, and sophisticated knowledge. These cultural advancements were accompanied by a national pride that perceived Egypt as the center of the universe and superior to all other cultures. God's judgment will confound all of these products of human ingenuity and out of confusion they will turn to their idols, charmers, mediums, and sorcerers for the answer. A nation that had all of the answers will now have none and will fall under the boot of a cruel master and fierce king (v. 4).

Along with its high religion, culture, and technology, Egypt prided itself in its rich environment created by the rise and fall of the Nile River. In fact, the cycle of their seasons and their annual festivals coincided with the flood times of the Nile because their agriculture and economy depended upon the fertile deltas created by the rising and falling waters. The sin of trusting the river rather than God brought sharp punishment upon them. Isaiah tells us that the waters will run dry and stagnant so that *"everything sown by the River, will wither, be driven away, and be no more"* (v. 7). The industries of fishing and textiles, upon which the Egyptian economy depends, will also be affected by God's judgment. Commercial fishing hooks and nets will come up empty and the quality of the woven cloth will become so inferior that the spinners and the weavers will be ashamed to take their wages.

Still another punishment is prophesied for proud, proud Egypt. Isaiah says that the superior wisdom of which the Egyptians bragged will be exposed as foolishness (v. 11). Especially those princes, wise men, and counselors upon whom the Pharaoh counted for wise decisions will be unable to explain God's purpose for Egypt. Instead of wise counsel, they will either be dumbfounded, deceived, or deluded (vv. 12–13). Worse yet, when they do offer counsel, it will send Egypt in the wrong direction staggering like a *"drunken man . . . in his vomit"* (v. 14). A once unified nation with a clear sense of direction is now spinning out of control without any answer to civil strife, economic depression, and national unemployment (v. 15).

THE WAVE OF GOD'S HAND (19:16–25)

Isaiah again uses his favorite word device to project a long-term prophecy for Egypt. *"In that day"* introduces five predictions for the future of the nation. First, he says Egypt will be as terrified of Judah as Judah is now terrified of Egypt. The turning of the tables is likened to helpless women under threat from a marauding army (v. 16). The fear will be so great that even the waving of the Lord's hand will strike terror into the heart and no one will dare speak of Judah without quaking inside (v. 17). Egypt will be so terrified of Judah that the very mention of the name will bring on a panic attack. Proud Egypt will be paralyzed by fear.

"In that day," Isaiah says for a second time, *"five cities in the land of Egypt will speak the language of Canaan and swear by the LORD of hosts; one will be called the City of Destruction"* (v. 18). Some scholars conjecture that the prophecy refers to the children of Israel who remained in Egypt after the Exodus. Isaiah is not one to look back without good reason. Although the outcome of the prophecy is uncertain, Isaiah may be using the five cities as symbols of the Egyptians turning toward the Lord.

"In that day," Isaiah goes on, *"there will be an altar to the LORD in the midst of the land of Egypt, and a pillar to the LORD at its border"* (v. 19). The prophet's message is now clear. He is referring to the coming of the Savior for the Egyptian people and their response of worship to Him. Although Egypt is still a Muslim nation today, Christianity has established a strong foothold among the people and has not faced the same total resistance that is found in other Muslim nations. Perhaps the residual influence of the Jews from the time of the Exodus makes the difference. Otherwise, the accord of Camp David in which ancient enemies of Egypt and Israel came together to bring peace to their borders could never have been accomplished. Compared to the hostility between the Jews and Arabs along the north and east banks of the Jordan River, Egypt points forward to the fulfillment of Isaiah's prophecy.

204

"In that day," Isaiah says for a fourth time, *"there will be a highway from Egypt to Assyria, and the Assyrian will come into Egypt and the Egyptian into Assyria, and the Egyptians will serve with the Assyrians"* (v. 23). Is this the first freeway in human history? In sharp contrast to the roads along which invading armies marched back and forth from Assyria to Egypt, Isaiah predicts a time of peace when there is free intercourse without tolls or checkpoints between the ancient enemies of Egypt and Assyria. Best of all, Egyptians and Assyrians will mutually serve each other rather than subjugating each other. Without doubt, Isaiah is foreseeing at the same time the reign of the Messiah in righteousness, justice, and peace.

"In that day," Isaiah speaks one more time. Miracle of miracles! In his vision, he sees Israel, Egypt, and Assyria as members of one body and serving as a blessing in the tumultuous land of the Middle East. Needless to say, Isaiah's vision is yet to be fulfilled. While Egypt and Israel are at peace, modern Assyria or Iran remains a mortal enemy of the Jews. But those who have followed the prophecies of Isaiah in the annals of history must believe that the time will come when we will witness a wonder of wonders. God will honor the spiritual union of Egypt, Assyria, and Israel with the prophet's words, *"Blessed is Egypt My people, and Assyria the work of My hands, and Israel My inheritance"* (v. 25). Never doubt. The time will come when God claims Egypt and Assyria as well as Israel with the strongest word of love that our language permits—*my* people, *my* work, and *my* inheritance. God's future should bring us to our tiptoes in eager anticipation.

CHAPTER TEN

The Role of the Watchman

Isaiah 20:1–21:17

When Isaiah speaks of the distant future, he uses the phrase, "In that day," but when he comes back to current history, he sets the time "In that year." He is now reporting an event that takes place in his lifetime and in which he plays a significant role. Rare as it is, the role of the watchman gives us new insight into the personality of Isaiah and his role as a communicator of the prophetic message.

THE DRAMA OF THE WATCHMAN (20:1–6)

1 In the year that Tartan came to Ashdod, when Sargon the king of Assyria sent him, and he fought against Ashdod and took it,

2 at the same time the LORD spoke by Isaiah the son of Amoz, saying, "Go, and remove the sackcloth from your body, and take your sandals off your feet." And he did so, walking naked and barefoot.

3 Then the Lord said, "Just as My servant Isaiah has walked naked and barefoot three years for a sign and a wonder against Egypt and Ethiopia,

4 "so shall the king of Assyria lead away the Egyptians as prisoners and the Ethiopians as captives, young and old, naked and barefoot, with their buttocks uncovered, to the shame of Egypt.

5 "Then they shall be afraid and ashamed of Ethiopia their expectation and Egypt their glory.

6 "And the inhabitant of this territory will say in that day, 'Surely such is our expectation, wherever we

flee for help to be delivered from the king of Assyria;
and how shall we escape?'"

Isaiah 20:1–6

Few would dispute the fact that Isaiah is reporting an actual event with accuracy when he cites the conquest of Ashdod by Tartan, the commander in chief of Sargon's Assyrian army (v. 1). Sometime around 713 B.C., the Philistines mounted a revolt against their Assyrian captors. In swift response, Sargon ordered Tartan to lay siege to Ashdod, the royal city of Philistia along the Mediterranean Coast. When the city surrendered in 711 B.C. Yamani, the king of Philistia, fled to Egypt for refuge. The Egyptians, however, wanted to avoid an Assyrian invasion of their own land. So, instead of offering asylum to Yamani, they turned him over to the Assyrians as a form of tribute.

WALKING NAKED THROUGH THE STREETS (20:1–2)

As we recall from Isaiah's oracle against Ethiopia (chapter 18), ambassadors had come from Egypt to persuade Hezekiah to join in a mutual defense pact against Assyria. Isaiah, of course, opposed such an alliance as evidence of a failure to trust in God. To communicate his opposition, he resorted to the dramatic sign of walking naked and barefoot through the streets of Jerusalem. Whether he was stark naked or not, Isaiah humiliated himself by this action. To bare the buttocks was a sign of shame reserved for captives on a forced march into exile (v. 4).

Isaiah had to be an unwelcome sight along the streets of Jerusalem for three years. Passersby must have scoffed at his nakedness, and even the faithful must have wondered about his persistence for so long. Some prophecies need drama to get the attention of the people. In modern telecommunications, there is the problem of viewers seeing so many starving children in Africa that they become immune to its impact, especially if the famine is distant. Even less response follows predictions of disaster in the future.

Late in the 1960's, the Club of Rome predicted that trends in population growth would lead to economic and ecological disaster sometime in the early twenty-first century. At first, the public reacted with concern at the startling statistics. Then, other social scientists questioned the predictive techniques and the hypothetical assumptions.

Consequently, the Club of Rome fell into disrepute and the public became inoculated against similar predictions from other statistical reports. Today, world population growth is low on the list of public concerns even though famine and poverty in the Two-Thirds World are directly related to overpopulation. At home, another connection has been drawn between population density and crime statistics in our major cities. No one likes to listen to prophets of gloom, particularly if you meet them on the street every time you go out for a walk!

ANNOUNCING THAT DOOM IS NEAR (20:3–6)

To add to the drama of Isaiah's nakedness, he must have shouted God's message as he walked, *"So shall the king of Assyria lead away the Egyptians as prisoners and the Ethiopians as captives, young and old, naked and barefoot, with their buttocks uncovered, to the shame of Egypt. Then they shall be afraid and ashamed of Ethiopia their expectation and Egypt their glory"* (vv. 4–5). Behind his warning is a moral. Isaiah foresees the decline of Egypt from its glory and the failure of Ethiopia to reach its expectation as a world empire. While he is saying that the children of Israel should put their trust in God alone, he is also seeing the evidence of decline of the Egyptian and Ethiopian civilizations.

All human institutions, whether world civilizations or local organizations, carry within themselves the seeds for their own demise. Max DePree, in his best-selling book *Leadership Is An Art*, cautions executive leaders against the signs of entropy in their organizations.[1] One chapter is entitled, "What Do We Weep About?" Depree suggests that you can tell whether an organization is rising or declining by the reason for its weeping. He notes that the loss of vision and compassion are reasons for weeping, and I am sure that Isaiah would add the loss of personal righteousness and social justice to the list.

An astute observer of Egypt and Ethiopia in Isaiah's day would have seen other signs of entropy. A desperate search for allies out of sheer fear might well have been the sign that Isaiah saw. To abandon Philistia as a member of a mutual defense pact and turn its king, Yamani, over to the Assyrians is also evidence of a civilization that has lost its integrity and its spirit. At least that is the way in which the people of Philistia would view their last hope as naked and barefooted

Egyptians and Ethiopians marched past them on the way to Assyrian exile. Isaiah hears them say, *"Surely such is our expectation, wherever we flee for help to be delivered from the king of Assyria, and how shall we escape?"* (v. 6). Futility echoes through their question. Reinforcing his theme, Isaiah lets the question answer itself—there is no escape outside of trust in God.

THE VISION OF THE WATCHMAN (21:1–10)

1 The burden against the Wilderness of the Sea.
As whirlwinds in the South pass through,
So it comes from the desert,
    from a terrible land.
2 A distressing vision is declared to me;
The treacherous dealer deals treacherously,
And the plunderer plunders.
Go up, O Elam!
Besiege, O Media!
All its sighing I have made to cease.
3 Therefore my loins are filled with pain;
Pangs have taken hold of me,
    like the pangs of a woman in labor.
I was distressed when I heard it;
I was dismayed when I saw it.
4 My heart wavered,
    fearfulness frightened me;
The night for which I longed
    He turned into fear for me.
5 Prepare the table,
Set a watchman in the tower,
Eat and drink.
Arise, you princes,
Anoint the shield!
6 For thus has the Lord said to me:
"Go, set a watchman,
Let him declare what he sees."
7 And he saw a chariot
    with a pair of horsemen,
A chariot of donkeys,
    and a chariot of camels,
And he listened diligently with great care.

8 Then he cried, "A lion, my Lord!
   I stand continually on the watchtower in the daytime;
   I have sat at my post every night.
9 And look, here comes a chariot of men
     with a pair of horsemen!"
   And he answered and said,
   "Babylon is fallen, is fallen!
   And all the carved images of her gods
   He has broken to the ground."
10 Oh, my threshing
     and the grain of my floor!
   That which I have heard
     from the LORD of hosts,
   The God of Israel,
   I have declared to you.

Isaiah 21:1–10

Isaiah is a master of multiple meanings in his oracles. He can hide the future in current events, send spiritual meaning through common symbols, and project a global view in a local situation. The oracle against the Wilderness of the Sea adds another dimension of different meanings in the same proclamation. Most obvious is the repeated prediction that Babylon will fall. Scholars are divided over the interpretation of the *"Wilderness of the Sea."* Except for its symbolic nature, the ascription does not fit Babylon, a city on the Euphrates but far distant from either the Mediterranean Sea or the Persian Gulf. Perhaps its location in the land between the rivers Tigris and Euphrates, which flow into the Persian Gulf, gave it the euphemistic name of the Wilderness of the Sea. Prophetic history, however, is clear in its meanings. The oracle confirms that the conquerors of Babylon are Elam and Media (v. 2), that the attack will come during Nebuchadnezzar's orgy of eating and drinking (v. 5), that the city and its idols will be crushed (v. 9), and that Judah will be consoled by the news that God's promise has been fulfilled (v. 10).

Beneath the facts of history are tonal words that reveal the deep feelings of Isaiah in his prophetic role. Because the prophet has already spoken in detail about the fall of Babylon (chs. 13 and 14), the personalized meaning of this oracle may be the major message that he wants to convey. Using the tonal words of Isaiah's feelings as a guide, the glamour of the prophetic role gives way to grinding dilemmas that a truth-teller faces.

DISTRESSING TRUTH (21:1–2)

A prophet of God is witness to *distressing* truth. To see a vision from the Lord is a high and privileged calling. Isaiah's experience in the temple (ch. 6) is the model for that calling. Despite his humility before the Holy God and his confession of sin, the focus tends to shift to the high moments of cleansing and consecration when the prophetic mantle fell upon Isaiah's shoulders. But we also learned that God did not commission Isaiah for an easy task. His message would fall upon deaf ears and his signs would be hidden to blinded eyes. Furthermore, his faith would be stretched to foresee events that would take place long after his death and even into the endtime when God's redemptive promise would be fulfilled.

But what about the lonely days of prophetic ministry when the sensitive spirit of Isaiah is stung by criticism as he remains faithful to the truth? Not by coincidence, this oracle follows immediately after his account of walking naked and barefoot for three years through the streets of Jerusalem. Put yourself in the prophet's place. Accusations of insanity would be mixed with guffaws of ridicule. In such moments, it is hard to be faithful.

With this picture in mind, Isaiah's feelings are understood when he says, *"A distressing vision is declared to me; the treacherous dealer deals treacherously, the plunderer plunders. Go up, O Elam! Besiege, O Media! All its sighing I have made to cease"* (v. 2). Suddenly, we see that he is with us in the dilemma of God's choice of the pagan nations of Elam and Media as the instruments of His judgment upon Babylon. To declare God's word, "Go up, O Elam! Besiege, O Media!" must have been the most difficult message of his ministry. Without asking *why* he had to be faithful to the word of God that distressed him. The Bishop of Cambry echoed Isaiah's feelings when he wrote,

> Smite or heal
> Depress or build me up;
> I adore thy purposes without
>   knowing them.

FRIGHTENING TRUTH (21:3–5)

A prophet of God also wrestles with *frightening* truth. The depth of Isaiah's distress is revealed in his confession that he became physically sick as he contemplated what he heard and saw in the vision. *"Therefore, my loins are filled with pain; pangs have taken hold of me, like the pangs of a woman in labor"* (v. 3). To follow the analogy of the woman in labor, Isaiah's distress is caused by more than the question *why* God would chose Elam and Media to bring down Babylon. Even deeper distress comes from the question *how* do I deliver the message of doom when it seems so contradictory to the current glory of Babylon. It is like setting a death watch over a person who is a specimen of health. Yet Isaiah must speak the frightening truth that the princes of Babylon will be caught by surprise as they eat and drink at a banquet table (Daniel 5). It is not easy to speak the truth of severe judgment in the midst of a joyous celebration.

JUSTIFYING TRUTH (21:6–7)

Further, Isaiah teaches us that a prophet of God watches for *justifying* truth. The role of a prophet as a watchman high in a tower, who is constantly on alert for the approach of the enemy and is the first to call the warning, takes us even deeper into Isaiah's sensitive soul. He foresees no delight in being the one to announce, *"Babylon is fallen, is fallen! And all the carved images of her gods He has broken to the ground"* (v. 9). To most hearers, the announcement will sound like the self-justifying taunt, "I told you so." Although Isaiah accepts his role as a watchman, who will be faithful to his post day and night with responsibility to announce the prophetic fulfillment of Babylon's downfall, he does not relish the moment. Only a sadist would take glee in watching for the proof of punitive truth and announcing the consequences of divine judgment.

PUNISHING TRUTH (21:8–10)

Still further and deeper into the heart of Isaiah the oracles go when we learn that a prophet of God weeps over *punitive* truth. "O, my threshing floor and the grain of my heart!" is a cry that rises from the bottom of the prophet's heart. At one and the same time, it is a hymn of joy for Judah and a dirge of death for Babylon. As much as Isaiah loved his people and his nation, his tears of joy were mixed with tears of sorrow.

Jesus had the same heart for Jerusalem when He wept, "O, Jerusalem, Jerusalem, the one who kills the prophets and stones those who are sent to her! How often I wanted to gather your children together, as a hen gathers her chicks under her wings, but you were not willing!" (Matthew 23:37). Contrary to all his wishes, then, Jesus announced, "See, your house is left to you desolate" (Matthew 23:38). Neither His love nor His judgment stopped with Jerusalem. Echoing Isaiah's call, He said, "Come to Me, all you who labor and are heavy laden, and I will give you rest" (Matthew 11:28 and Isaiah 55:l). At the same time, He announced that in the final day of judgment, "all nations" will be gathered before Him (Matthew 25:32). Isaiah's tears flowed from a heart like Christ's.

All of this runs contrary to our human expectations for the prophetic ministry. We want to limit our message to the "Good News of the Gospel" and draw people to Christ with the announcement of His love. Certainly, this is the primary message of the prophet, but the witness to distressing truth, the pain of frightening truth, the watch for justifying truth, and the weeping over punishing truth cannot be avoided. No issue illustrates the depth of our dilemma better than the AIDS epidemic. To witness the truth of God's Word, wrestle with the responsibility for warning the people, watch for the evidence of judgment, and weep over the victims is a prophetic task that drives us into distress and makes us sick to think about it. How do we witness to the truth without being bigots? How do we wrestle with the warning without being doomsayers? How do we announce the judgment that we see from our watchtower? How do we weep in love for its victims? AIDS may well be the Babylonian issue for modern-day prophets.

Isaiah weeps, *"Oh, my threshing and the grain of my floor!"* (v. 10). Both God and he use the word *my* to express their love and loyalty to Judah and Jerusalem. As they see the devastation of war, symbolized by the violence of threshing and the wasted grain on the floor, they weep—not just for Judah and Jerusalem, but for all nations and people who are victims of war's violence and waste. When my twelve-year-old son and I visited Pearl Harbor and the memorial for those who died on December 7, 1941, we stood among the crowd in a hush broken only by the sobs of weeping people. For those who die in battle there are those who live with scars. We weep for the survivors of Hiroshima who carry in their genes the death of a nuclear bomb. We see the pictures of naked children fleeing the fire of napalm bombs in Vietnam and we weep again. War is not only inhuman, it is unproductive. There are no signs, "USED TANKS FOR SALE," after the war is over. Saddest of all is the fact that the economy of modern Israel is artificially sustained by a national budget that is 80 percent military expenditures. "Oh, my threshing and the grain of my floor!" Isaiah has reason to weep again.

THE WORD OF THE WATCHMAN (21:11–17)

11 The burden against Dumah.
　　He calls to me out of Sier,
　　"Watchman, what of the night?
　　Watchman, what of the night?"
12 The watchman said,
　　"The morning comes, and also the night.
　　If you will inquire, inquire;
　　Return! Come back!"
13 The burden against Arabia.
　　In the forest in Arabia you will lodge,
　　O you traveling companies of Dedanites.
14 O inhabitants of the land of Tema,
　　Bring water to him who is thirsty;
　　With their bread they met him who fled.
15 For they fled from the swords,
　　　　from the drawn sword,
　　From the bent bow,
　　　　and from the distress of war.
16 For thus the LORD has said to me: "Within a
year, according to the year of a hired man, all the
glory of Kedar will fail:
17 and the remainder of the number of archers,
the mighty men of the people of Kedar, will be
diminished; for the LORD God of Israel has spoken it."

Isaiah 21:11–17

Three obscure oracles continue Isaiah's geographical sweep of judgment upon the nations surrounding Judah (vv.11–12; 13–15; and 16–17). In this case, the connector among the three cities of Dumah, Dedan, and Tema is their common location in Arabia, the vast desert land three hundred miles southwest of Judah. The third oracle (vv. 16–17) identifies the people of this region as the families of Kedar, a clan of Ishmael.

Repent of Sin (21:11–12)

All of Arabia eventually fell under Assyria and Babylon to suffer the devastation predicted by Isaiah. While Arabians did not become a partner in military oppression of Judah, they prided themselves in their reputation as wealthy merchants with caravans plying the trade routes, east and west through Dumah and north and south through Tema. Dumah served Babylon to the east and Tema served Egypt to the West. As commercial cohorts in self-glory with these antagonists of Judah and Jerusalem, Isaiah has a word of warning.

In addition to the geographical connector among the three cities, there is a link between this oracle against Arabia and the one immediately preceding—the oracle against the Wilderness of the Sea. Isaiah likens his prophetic role to that of a "watchman" at his post on the tower day and night (v. 8). From this lofty position, the watchman has a panoramic view of the landscape and by being diligent and faithful to his duty he is the first to sight the approach of the enemy and sound the warning.

In the oracle against Dumah, Isaiah is the watchman of whom the inquiry is made, *"Watchman, what of the night?"* (v. 11). Because the question comes from Seir, the highest peak in the land of Dumah, the inference is that Isaiah the prophet has a perspective on forthcoming danger that is above and beyond a human viewpoint. A mixed response is given. The watchman looks out to see both the hope of morning and the fear of night. He does this to put forward the more important answer, *"Return! Come back!"* (v. 12). The call to repentance is heard in the word "Return!"; and God's invitation for the wayward children of Ishmael to come home is sounded in the call, "Come back!"

TRUST IN GOD (21:13–15)

A working principle for prophetic inquiry is found in the watchman's response. We humans have a natural desire to know the future. Especially in moments of crisis, we ask the prophets to tell us what is ahead. During the 1991 war of Desert Storm in the Persian Gulf, for instance, books on prophecy became best-sellers overnight. However, Isaiah, the watchman, would say that we are asking the wrong question. Rather than wanting to know the details of the future out of a sense of fear, we need to repent of our sins and trust in the Father. Our song will then be, "I know not what the future holds, but I know Who holds the future."

The oracle against Dedan and Tema (vv. 13–15) speaks of the judgment that will come upon them for their pride in a reputation as wealthy traders of the world and suppliers of goods for the glory of Babylon and Egypt. A picture is drawn of the time when the trade routes are controlled by marauding armies who force the caravans to take cover in the sparse forests of the Arabian mountains. Their plight will be aggravated by the lack of food and water, which the Temanites are urged to sneak to them (v. 14).

HEAD THE WARNING (21:16–17)

An oracle against Kedar summarizes the warning of the watchman, "*Within a year, according to the year of the hired man, all the glory of Kedar will fail; and the remainder of the number of archers, the mighty men of the people of Kedar, will be diminished*" (vv. 16–17). The army of marchers in which Kedar found its glory has now become their burden and downfall. If the original question, "Watchman, what of the night?" came from them, they got an answer they did not want to hear. But, as Isaiah says, "*the LORD God of Israel has spoken it*" (v. 17).

NOTES

1. M. DePree, *Leadership is an Art* (New York: Doubleday, 1989).

CHAPTER ELEVEN

The Valley of the Vision

Isaiah 22:1–23:18

Another look into the heart of Isaiah as God's watchman comes from a well-documented event in history that will occur during the prophet's lifetime. The title Oracle or Burden of Isaiah is symbolic. Just as we sought the meaning of the oracle against the Wilderness of the Sea and suggested that the name may have been a colloquial expression for the land of Arabia, so "The Valley of the Vision" may have local meaning for Isaiah's time that is now lost to us. Most scholars agree that the reference is to the Valley of Hinnom just west of Jerusalem, which had the reputation for being the place where prophets had visions. This explanation is logical because the oracle revolves around the city of Jerusalem and its immediate environs where an army of siege would be encamped.

THE VALLEY: PLACE OF PRESUMPTUOUS SINS (22:1–14)

1 The burden against the Valley of
   Vision.
   What ails you now that you have
      all gone up to the housetops,
2 You who are full of noise,
   A tumultuous city, a joyous city?
   Your slain men are not slain with the sword,
   Nor dead in battle.
3 All your rulers have fled together;
   They are captured by the archers.
   All who are found in you are bound together,
   Who have fled from afar.

4 Therefore I said, "Look away from me,
   I will weep bitterly;
   Do not labor to comfort me
   Because of the plundering of the daughter of my
      people."
5 For it is a day of trouble
      and treading down and perplexity
   By the Lord GOD of hosts
   In the Valley of Vision—
   Breaking down the walls
   And of crying to the mountain.
6 Elam bore the quiver
   With chariots of men and horsemen,
   And Kir uncovered the shield.
7 It shall come to pass that your choicest valleys
   Shall be full of chariots,
   And the horsemen shall set themselves in array at
      the gate.
8 He removed the protection of Judah.
   You looked in that day to the armor of the House of
      the Forest;
9 You also saw the damage to the city of David,
   That it was great;
   And you gathered together the waters of the
      lower pool.
10 You numbered the houses of Jerusalem,
   And the houses you broke down
   To fortify the wall.
11 You also made a reservoir
      between the two walls
   For the water of the old pool.
   But you did not look to its Maker,
   Nor did you have respect for Him who fashioned it
      long ago.
12 And in that day the Lord GOD of hosts
   Called for weeping and for mourning,
   For baldness and for girding with sackcloth.
13 But instead, joy and gladness,
   Slaying oxen and killing sheep,
   Eating meat and drinking wine:
   "Let us eat and drink,
      for tomorrow we die!"

14 Then it was revealed in my hearing by the
        LORD of hosts,
    "Surely for this iniquity there will be no atonement
        for you,
    Even to your death," says the Lord GOD of hosts.
                                                Isaiah 22:1–14

Well-chronicled history backs up Isaiah's burden against the Valley of the Vision. Isaiah 36 and Second Kings 18 concur in the report that in the fourteenth year of Hezekiah (701 B.C.) Sennacherib, king of Assyria, captured forty-six cities of Judah and threatened to put Jerusalem under siege. King Hezekiah, to save his capital city, paid tribute to King Sennacherib by sacking both the house of the Lord and the house of the king in order to garner three hundred talents of silver and thirty talents of gold. Although the actual story of Isaiah's protest against the king's failure to trust in God is yet ahead, we need this background to understand the oracle against the Valley of Vision.

Rather than reading the oracle as just another judgment against Judah and Jerusalem, we can profit by studying the prophecy from the perspective of Isaiah himself. Earlier, we felt our way into the feelings of Isaiah as he wept over the violence and waste of war, which affected not just the children of Israel but all nations and peoples. Now, as Isaiah foresees Sennacherib's threat of siege against Jerusalem and Hezekiah's tribute to the pagan king, he says, "I will weep bitterly" (v. 4). His tears of sympathy have now turned sour.

Sin comes in many forms and perhaps many degrees. Isaiah had already charged the children of Israel with rebellion against the Father's love in the opening words of his prophecy (1:2). Although the people of Judah and Jerusalem refused to repent of this sin and continued to rebel against God, they had not yet extended their arrogance to the presumptuous sins of spurning God's grace or disdaining His judgment in the face of the evidence. For Isaiah, the sins of presumption would be particularly painful. At the time of his calling, God had warned him that the people would hear, but not understand; and see, but not perceive (6:9). Now, as he confronts an arrogance that flaunts the evidence of prophecy fulfilled, he knows what God meant when He also warned him about dull hearts, heavy ears, and closed eyes that keep the children of Israel from returning to trust in God and being healed (6:10).

PRESUMING ON THE GRACE OF GOD (22:1–4)

Isaiah has good reason to weep bitterly for the people of Jerusalem and to reject their attempts to console him. With Hezekiah's payment of tribute to Sennacherib came a brief respite from the threat of attack on the city. As the Assyrians withdrew, Jerusalem went into noisy, tumultuous, and joyous celebration over what appeared to be a diplomatic victory (v. 2). Isaiah could not stand the sight of what he saw and heard because he knew that Hezekiah's tribute violated God's command and put trust in human instrumentality. Isaiah wept because by deliberately flaunting God's warning, the people of Jerusalem presumed upon the grace of God. While treating the temporary truce like a decisive victory, they overlooked the fact that their rulers and warriors had exposed them to slaughter by fleeing in fear and falling into the hands of the enemy. Rather than shouting from the housetops and dancing in the streets, the people of Jerusalem should have been humbly thanking God for the respite. Instead, their wild celebration flew in the face of His grace and turned the prophet's tears to bitterness because he knew that they were setting up the plundering of Jerusalem (v. 4).

PRESUMING ON THE WORD OF GOD (22:5–7)

As further aggravation of their presumptuous sin, the people of Jerusalem quashed the Word of God. Like Nero, who fiddled while Rome burned, the people of Jerusalem partied when doom was near. Isaiah had been faithful in speaking the vision of God, pleading with the people to trust in Him alone, and warning them of the consequences if they disobeyed. Symbolically, if not literally, The Valley of the Vision served as the site from which he spoke the Word of God. So, when the people of Jerusalem reveled in Hezekiah's tribute, which even required stripping the gold from the doors of the Temple, they not only repudiated the vision of God, but tromped on it (v. 5). Isaiah's bitterness becomes obvious as he foretells the return of the Assyrian army with the reinforcements of crack troops, chariots, and cavalry from Elam and Kir tromping over the choicest valleys around Jerusalem and even up to the city's gate (vv. 6–7).

PRESUMING ON THE TRUST OF GOD (22:8–11)

One presumptuous sin builds upon another. Along with the sins of presuming on the grace of God and quashing His Word, the people of Jerusalem spurned the trust of God. Misreading the cue of their temporary relief from an Assyrian siege, they presumed that Jerusalem was an impregnable fortress that could not be conquered by Sennacherib. In a series of scathing denunciations, Isaiah tells of their elaborate preparation of the city for siege. Six times he thrusts out an accusing finger to say,

> You . . . looked to the armor of the House of the Forest,
> You . . . saw the damage to the city of David
> You . . . gathered together the waters of the lower pool
> You . . . numbered the houses of Jerusalem
> You . . . broke [them] down to fortify the wall
> You . . . made a reservoir between the two walls.
>
> *Isaiah 22:8–11*

Historical references confirm these preparations for siege. King Saul developed the forest of Lebanon as an arsenal for military weapons. Earlier we met King Ahaz at the upper pool checking the water supply in anticipation of an Assyrian siege. Hezekiah added a second wall to the city (2 Chronicles 32:5) and a tunnel for a new water supply (2 Kings 20:20). Jerusalem, presumably the impregnable city, took the place of God as the source of their trust. *"But,"* Isaiah says, *"you did not look to its Maker, nor did you have respect for Him who fashioned it long ago"* (v. 11). To trust our creation rather than the Creator is a presumptuous sin that brings bitter tears to the eyes of the prophet.

PRESUMING ON THE PROMISE OF GOD (22:12–14)

Presumptuous sins are subject to the domino effect. Once one presumptuous sin is committed, others fall one after the other and each becomes more arrogant than the last one. When Isaiah invokes the words, *"And in that day,"* we know that he is ringing down the curtain of divine wrath upon the people of Jerusalem who disclaimed the promise of God (v. 12). A forced march into the shame of exile is ahead of them because they have refused to trust in God. But, instead of weeping in repentance and mourning for sin, the people of Jerusalem will give the world the motto for hedonists, *"Let us eat and drink, for tomorrow we die!"* (v. 13).

Presumptuous sins have led to apostasy. God promised the people of Jerusalem the leading role in bringing righteousness and justice to the earth. At first they rebelled against His love; then they refused to listen to His prophet and put their trust in Him alone. Now, by presumptuous sins, they set the tone for generation after generation of hedonists who laugh in the face of God and live as if there is no tomorrow. Isaiah is most severe when he reports God's response to these revelers, *"Surely for this iniquity there will be no atonement for you"* (v. 14). Is this the sin against the Holy Spirit for which Jesus said there is no forgiveness? If so, we understand why Isaiah wept bitterly and no one could comfort him.

SHEBNA: THE PRESUMPTUOUS STEWARD (22:15–25)

15 Thus says the Lord GOD of hosts:
   "Go, proceed to this steward,
   To Shebna, who is over the house, and say:
16 'What have you here,
     and whom have you here,
   That you have hewn a sepulcher here,
   As he who hews himself a sepulcher on high,
   Who carves a tomb for himself in a rock?
17 Indeed, the LORD will throw you away violently,
   O mighty man,
   And will surely seize you.
18 He will surely turn violently
     and toss you like a ball
   Into a large country;
   There you shall die,
     and there your glorious chariots
   Shall be the shame of your master's house.
19 So I will drive you out of your office,
   And from your position he will pull you down.
20 'Then it shall be in that day,
   That I will call My servant Eliakim the son of Hilkiah;
21 I will clothe him with your robe
   And strengthen him with your belt;

> I will commit your responsibility into his hand.
> He shall be a father to the inhabitants of Jerusalem
> And to the house of Judah.
> 22 The key of the house of David
> I will lay on his shoulder;
> So he shall open,
>   and no one shall shut;
> And he shall shut,
>   and no one shall open.
> 23 I will fasten him as a peg in a secure place,
> And he will become a glorious throne
>   to his father's house.
> 24 'They will hang on him all the glory of his
> father's house, the offspring and the issue, all vessels
> of small quantity, from the cups to all the pitchers.
> 25 'In that day,' says the LORD of hosts, 'the peg
> that is fastened in the secure place will be removed
> and be cut down and fall, and the burden that was on
> it will be cut off; for the LORD has spoken.'"

Isaiah 22:15–25

MAYOR OF THE PALACE (22:15)

Individuals, as well as nations, who are accomplices in sin against God must stand in judgment. After Isaiah's sweep of the nations surrounding Judah with oracles of judgment, he returns home to foresee the local scene where King Hezekiah will seek the counsel of his chief advisers, Eliakim and Shebna (ch. 36). Eliakim is identified as second in command to the king and entitled "Mayor of the Palace" (2 Kings 18:18). Shebna's role as a scribe would most likely be similar to a Secretary of State. But, according to Isaiah's prophecy, Eliakim and Shebna were once in opposite roles. Shebna is addressed as the *"steward,"* a term used nowhere else in the Old Testament but synonymous with the title "Mayor of the Palace."

The term also anticipates Jesus' choice of the word *steward* in His teaching about servanthood. A steward is a person who owns nothing, manages all the household, and is directly accountable to the master of the house. Closely related to this term is the word *economics* or the "law of the household" that Jesus used to describe the guiding principles for the steward's responsibility. In combination, these two terms have both temporal and eternal meaning. As a steward owns nothing, so a servant of the Lord holds in trust any power, position, or money as a gift from God. Furthermore, as a steward is given the responsibility as chief executive officer for managing all of the policies, people, and programs of the organization, so God trusts His servant with all of the physical, human, and spiritual resources with which the organization is endowed. Finally, as a steward is accountable to the master of the household for prudent and ethical action that fulfills the mission of the organization, so God holds His servant to an accounting of the temporal and eternal outcomes of his leadership.

VIOLATOR OF TRUST (22:16)

Shebna violated the trust of his stewardship as the Master of the Palace. According to Isaiah's charge, he used the role to advance his own agenda and make his mark on history. His arrogance is sealed in stone as Shebna sculpts on a monument on a high place and carves out a tomb in the rock as his final resting place (v. 16). Obsessed with his own self-glory, Shebna tried to preserve his place in history and in so doing, betrayed the trust of his high office.

Yet he is not alone. Kings and presidents, chiefs of staff, and secretaries of state have been obsessed with the judgment of history. Leadership theory confirms the fact that the quality of servanthood is best determined by the "tombstone test" after the leader is no longer in office. If the assessment of history becomes an obsession, however, it has demonic control over the decisions of the leader. Richard Nixon, for instance, is reputed to have tape recorded the conversations in the Oval Office with the idea of preserving his role in American and world history. But his tape became his tomb with the revelations of the Watergate scandal.

SUBJECT OF DEMOTION (22:17–19)

Because of Shebna's sin of pride, God will treat him like a ball that he turns over, tosses up, and throws away (vv. 17–18). The analogy vividly describes Shebna's demotion to Secretary of State and Eliakim's elevation to Mayor of the Palace. Leaders who are intoxicated by high office cannot withstand humiliation of demotion. George Bush, former President of the United States, was said to go into post-election depression when he lost his position to Bill Clinton. To the very end, Bush was convinced that he would pull off another upset victory. Only persons who have held chief executive roles can understand the emotional reaction when power and position are lost. For persons who are obsessed with their place in history, or whose personal identity is inseparable from the position, demotion or replacement is a test of emotional stability. According to later passages in Isaiah, Shebna survived demotion. The monument and tomb that he carved out for himself, however, became hollow reminders of his ill-fated arrogance. Shebna would die in shame in a distant land, perhaps as one of the first exiles to Babylon, like the words on the pedestal of the trunkless statue of Ozymandias in the desert as pictured in Shelby's poem:

> "My name is Ozymandias, king of kings:
> Look on my works, ye Mighty, and despair!"
> Nothing beside remains. Round the decay
> Of that colossal wreck, boundless and bare
> The lone and level sands stretch far away.[1]

Driven out of office and pulled down from his position, Shebna paid both a temporal and eternal price for his sin of pride.

LOSER OF HONOR (22:20–24)

Eliakim, formerly the Secretary of State, is announced as the successor to Shebna, the deposed Mayor of the Palace (v. 20). Isaiah is most precise in describing the symbols of the office Shebna lost. The Master's robe, representing the honor of the lofty position, will be put upon Eliakim's shoulders. Similar robes are worn by clergy, judges, and professors in our day when they perform their official functions in administering church sacraments, presiding over court trials, or conferring degrees on graduates at academic commencements. The robes symbolize both the credentials of their profession and the trust of their office. In keeping with the meaning of steward and servant, the robe also means that the wearer has responded to the divine call and consecration to the vocation of the church, the court, or the school. While the inroads of secularism and egalitarianism have undermined the historical and spiritual meaning of the robe in our day, profound meaning filled the symbol in Isaiah's day.

Eliakim will also receive the belt Shebna wore around his waist as the sign and seal of his authority over the whole household of his master, the king (v. 21). And with the authority of the steward comes accountability. To Shebna, Isaiah writes, *"I will commit your responsibility into his hand"* as a reminder that Eliakim will be held accountable just as Shebna had to answer to the king for the results of his work.

The transition goes on to include a revered title that Shebna sought for himself when he built his own stone monument and carved out his own tomb from the rock. Eliakim, not Shebna, will be remembered as one of the patriarchs to the people of Jerusalem and Judah (v. 21). "Patriarch" is a title that must be earned by a lifetime of faithful service, wise decisions, and a caring spirit. Shebna learned that the honor of being a patriarch cannot be artificially created by one's own scheme; it must be spontaneously given by the people who are served.

Best of all, Eliakim will be invested with the *"key of the house of David,"* which puts him in the line of royalty to inherit the spirit of the King "after God's own heart" and leads toward the Messiah who will come from the "Root of Jesse." Whereas Shebna would become a "bouncing ball" in the hands of God because of his sin, Eliakim was characterized as a "peg in a secure place" upon whom would be hung all of the garlands of glory that Shebna sought for himself—a ruler and a patriarch remembered through the generations as a model of a steward who remained true to his trust and brought glory to his master (vv. 23–24). Jesus' commendation to the man who multiplied his talents through wise investments fits Eliakim, "Well done, good and faithful servant" (Matthew 25:21).

SYMBOL OF HUMAN LEADERSHIP (22:25)

Yet, in what appears to be quick and complete reversal, the LORD of hosts speaks one last word through Isaiah. *"In that day . . . the peg that is fastened in the secure place will be removed and be cut down and fall, and the burden that was on it will be cut off; for the LORD has spoken"* (v. 25). Are we to assume that Eliakim will go the way of Shebna? No. The last we hear about Eliakim, he is leading the delegation that includes Shebna and Joah to inform the Assyrian Ambassador that King Hezekiah rejects the offer of a protective alliance with the king of Assyria and he will trust in God alone (37:20).

God's word, then, is consistent with Hezekiah's decision. As a "steward" of the Lord, Eliakim is a human being in whom the children of Israel cannot put their ultimate trust. As trustworthy as Eliakim might be, he is a mortal being responsible to God and due to die in his time. Through the brief biographies of Shebna and Eliakim, Isaiah has reinforced his dominant theme: Our trust must be in God and God alone.

TYRE: THE PRESUMPTUOUS CITY (23:1–18)

1 The burden against Tyre.
 Wail, you ships of Tarshish!
 For it is laid waste,
 So that there is no house, no harbor;
 From the land of Cyprus it is revealed to them.
2 Be still, you inhabitants of the coastland,
 You merchants of Sidon,
 Whom those who cross the sea have filled.
3 And on great waters the grain of Shihor,
 The harvest of the River,
   is her revenue;
 And she is a marketplace
   for the nations.
4 Be ashamed, O Sidon;
 For the sea has spoken,
 The strength of the sea, saying,
 "I do not labor, nor bring forth
 children;
 Neither do I rear young men,
 Nor bring up virgins."
5 When the report comes to Egypt,
 They also will be in agony at the report of Tyre.
6 Cross over to Tarshish;
 Wail, you inhabitants of the coastland!
7 Is this your joyous city,
 Whose antiquity is from ancient days,
 Whose feet carried her far off to sojourn?
8 Who has taken this counsel against
 Tyre, the crowning city,
 Whose merchants are princes,
 Whose traders are the honorable of the earth?

9 The LORD of hosts has purposed it,
   To bring to dishonor the pride of all glory,
   And to bring into contempt all the
   honorable of the earth.

10 Overflow through your land like the River,
   O daughter of Tarshish;
   There is no more strength.

11 He stretched out His hand over the sea,
   He shook the kingdoms;
   The LORD has given a commandment against Canaan
   To destroy its strongholds.

12 And He said,
   "You will rejoice no more,
   O you oppressed virgin daughter of Sidon.
   Arise, cross over to Cyprus;
   There also you will have no rest."

13 Behold, the land of the Chaldeans,
   This people which was not;
   Assyria founded it for wild beasts of the desert.
   They set up its towers,
   They raised up its palaces,
   And brought it to ruin.

14 Wail, you ships of Tarshish!
   For your strength is laid waste.

15 Now it shall come to pass in that day that Tyre
will be forgotten seventy years, according to the days
of one king. At the end of seventy years it will happen
to Tyre as in the song of the harlot:

16 "Take a harp, go about the city,
   You forgotten harlot;
   Make sweet melody, sing many songs,
   That you may be remembered."

17 And it shall be, at the end of seventy years, that
the LORD will visit Tyre. She will return to her pay,
and commit fornication with all the kingdoms of the
world on the face of the earth.

18 Her gain and her pay will be set apart for the
LORD; it will not be treasured nor laid up, for her gain
will be for those who dwell before the LORD, to eat
sufficiently, and for fine clothing.

Isaiah 23:1–18

228

Isaiah's oracles against the nations of the world come to a poetic conclusion with wide-ranging implications in the oracle against Tyre. By exact location, Tyre is the southernmost city of Phoenicia on the Mediterranean coast. Usually the city is linked with Sidon, its northern twin, which Isaiah also mentions three times in the oracle (vv. 2, 4, and 12). The inclusion of other names of cities, such as Tarshish (vv. 1, 6, 10, and 14) and surrounding regions, such as the isle of Cyprus (vv. 1 and 12), Shihor in Egypt (v. 3), Canaan (v. 11), Egypt (v. 5), and the River Nile (vv. 3, 10) signify the worldwide sweep of the oracle. Still, Tyre is the focus of the prophecy because the city symbolizes a cosmopolitan spirit of commercialism through world trade that has become another point of pride and self-glory subject to the judgment of God.

MARKETPLACE FOR THE NATIONS (23:1–3)

Isaiah, a prophet from the small, rural land of Judah, waxes eloquent in his vision of Tyre. Anticipating the high-sounding, contemporary terms of *world-class cities* and a *global economy*, he calls Tyre a *"marketplace for the nations"* (v. 3). Even though his prophecy opens with the lament, *"Wail, you ships of Tarshish!"* for the judgment to come, Isaiah sees Tyre as the seaport for world trade. Shipping lanes from Egypt, Cyprus, Sidon, and Shihor are plied by the ships of Tarshish to bring grain and goods to Phoenician shores where caravans take them far and wide across the Eastern world. Rich revenues fill the coffers of the merchants of Tyre who take pride in their reputation as a sophisticated seaport of world import.

Isaiah pays Tyre a backhanded compliment when he describes the reputation of the city. If a chamber of commerce brochure were written according to Isaiah's description, it would highlight Tyre as a crowning city of joy, antiquity, world influence, merchant princes, and honorable traders (vv. 7–8). With these qualities, Tyre had good reason to bask in its reputation as a world-class city—Jewel of the Coastland.

THE POINT OF PRIDE (23:4–5)

Tyre's pride in its reputation suffered a spiritual flaw that proved to be fatal. In its dependence upon the *"strength of the sea"* to sustain its economy and its reputation, the inhabitants of the city failed to thank God for His special blessing upon them and to trust Him for the future. The "strength of the sea," in effect, became their god. Isaiah appeals to the sea itself to call Tyre into judgment. The sea says, *"I do not labor, nor bring forth children; neither do I rear young men, nor bring up virgins"* (v. 4).

Once again, God has called upon His physical creation as a witness against human pride. The testimony of the sea recalls the opening words of Isaiah when God calls the cosmic court into session, "Hear, O heavens, and give ear, O earth" (1:2). No greater indictment could be put upon the people of Tyre than to hear the source of their pride take the witness stand against them. Even the sea knows that its strength and glory come from God.

THE MERCENARY SPIRIT (23:6–9)

Tyre's pride also has a moral flaw. God-substitutes come in many forms. Whenever human pride is elevated to self-glory in either deliberate or tacit defiance of God, it is targeted for divine judgment. Isaiah's commendation of Tyre as the "marketplace for the nations" and the "Jewel of the Coastland" illustrates the insidious danger of legitimate enterprises that can become gods in themselves. Undoubtedly, Tyre stood as the envy of the ancient world. And when compared with the aggressive military spirit of Assyria, its aggressive mercantile spirit would seem to be rather innocent. But God shows Isaiah that whenever the driving force of human motivation becomes an end in itself, it is sin.

Contrary to some opinions, there is nothing wrong with an enterprising spirit in business ventures that produce wealth. If, however, the enterprising spirit, the business venture, or the production of wealth becomes a habit and then a drive that captivates the soul, the sin of idolatry has been committed. In the momentum of its economic success and worldwide reputation, Tyre committed the sin of a mercenary spirit and provoked God's wrath *"to bring to dishonor the pride of all glory"* (v. 9).

THE WAILING SHIPS (23:10–15)

God's judgment strikes right at the heart of Tyre's pride. Isaiah foresees the time when the huge, loaded merchant *"ships of Tarshish"* will arrive at Tyre and find no port, no harbor, no loading docks, and no warehouses for their goods. Tyre's reputation as a "marketplace for the nations" will be lost. At the sources of its riches in Cyprus and Egypt, word will go out that Tyre has been *"laid waste"* (v. 1). The sea, defined as its strength, will become its weakness (v. 10), and the citizens of Tyre will wander over the earth finding no refuge even in the cities and lands, such as Cyprus, that they helped to prosper (vv. 11–13). In a reprise of his opening lament, Isaiah cries again, *"Wail, you ships of Tarshish! For your strength is laid waste"* (v. 14).

THE HARLOT'S SONG (23:16–18)

After Tyre's period of judgment, which will continue through the cycle of seventy years, or the time of one king's reign, the contrasting spirit of the city befits the song of a harlot whose physical beauty has faded. In what might have been a popular song of the day, her plaintive lament will be:

> Take a harp, go about the city,
> You forgotten harlot;
> Make sweet melody, sing many songs,
> That you may be remembered.
>
> *Isaiah 23:16*

Memories of better days are all that the harlot and Tyre have left to sing about. The mercenary's glory is compared to a prostitute's beauty: fleeting and soon forgotten. When that happens, both the mercenary and the prostitute will forsake the money and give themselves away in fornication just for the sake of being remembered (v. 17). Like the desperate king who cried, "My kingdom for a horse," Tyre will give anything to recapture the gleam of its former glory.

Although Tyre will be laid waste, all is not completely lost. Isaiah foresees the day when the strategic position of Tyre on the Mediterranean coast will be the entry point for wealth, goods, and services coming to Judah and Jerusalem (v. 18). More than that, as a point of entry to the land of Israel, Tyre will have a role in the fulfillment of Isaiah's vision of the day when the nations of the world will stream like a river to the Holy City and its temple to learn the ways of the Lord and to walk in His paths (2:3).

PART FIVE

The Vision Projected

Isaiah 24:1–35:10

CHAPTER TWELVE

The Apocalypse

Isaiah 24:1–27:13

Isaiah's vision of judgment upon the nations of the world explodes like a string of firecrackers on the prophetic landscape. The loud sounds and the brilliant light of these explosions, however, are nothing compared to his oracles of the endtime in chapters 24–27. Like a skyrocket bursting against the nighttime sky, Isaiah's vision of the final day of judgment is deafening in sound and blinding in light. In a preview of the book of the Revelation, God lifts the final curtain on the future (the Apocalypse) and shows His prophet a picture of last things (eschatology).

Not all is gloom and doom in the endtime vision of either Isaiah or John the Revelator. Like an antiphonal choir singing to each other across the sanctuary of a church, both revelators alternate the messages of judgment upon sinners and praise by the redeemed in those last days. Isaiah, of course, has a genius for communicating by contrast. He gives full vent to that gift in this outline of chapters 24–27:

    I.   Isaiah 24:1–13—Judgment

   II. Isaiah 24:14–16—Praise

  III. Isaiah 24:17–23—Judgment

  IV. Isaiah 25:1–9—Praise

   V. Isaiah 25:10–12—Judgment

  VI. Isaiah 26:1–19—Praise

 VII. Isaiah 26:20–27:1—Judgment

VIII. Isaiah 27:2–11—Praise

  IX. Isaiah 27:12–13—Summary of Judgment and Praise

Although the message of these chapters is highly catalytic, symbolic, and futuristic, we can approach them as we would listen to a great symphony. While the complex composition may escape us, we catch the rhythm of the movements, absorb the emotions of the music, and feel the impact of the message.

GOD'S GREAT REVERSAL (24:1–23)

1 Behold, the LORD makes the earth empty and makes it
   waste,
   Distorts its surface
   And scatters abroad its inhabitants.
2 And it shall be:
   As with the people,
      so with the priest;
   As with the servant,
      so with his master;
   As with the maid,
      so with her mistress;
   As with the buyer,
      so with the seller;
   As with the lender,
      so with the borrower;
   As with the creditor,
      so with the debtor.
3 The land shall be entirely emptied and utterly plun-
   dered,
   For the LORD has spoken this word.
4 The earth mourns and fades away,
   The world languishes and fades away;
   The haughty people of the earth languish.
5 The earth is also defiled under its inhabitants,
   Because they have transgressed the laws,
   Changed the ordinance.
   Broken the everlasting covenant.
6 Therefore the curse has devoured the earth,
   And those who dwell in it are desolate.
   Therefore the inhabitants of the earth are burned,
   And few men are left.
7 The new wine fails, the vine languishes,
   All the merry-hearted sigh.

8 The mirth of the tambourine ceases,
The noise of the jubilant ends,
The joy of the harp ceases.
9 They shall not drink wine with a song;
Strong drink is bitter to those who drink it.
10 The city of confusion is broken down;
Every house is shut up,
    so that none may go in.
11 There is a crying for wine in the streets,
    All joy is darkened,
The mirth of the land is gone.
12 In the city desolation is left,
And the gate is stricken with destruction.
13 When it shall be thus in the midst
of the land among the people,
It shall be like the shaking of an olive tree,
Like the gleaning of grapes when the vintage is done.
14 They shall lift up their voice,
    they shall sing;
For the majesty of the LORD
They shall cry aloud from the sea.
15 Therefore glorify the LORD in the dawning light,
The name of the Lord GOD of Israel in the coastlands of
    the sea.
16 From the ends of the earth we have heard songs:
"Glory to the righteous!"
But I said, "I am ruined, ruined!
Woe to me!
The treacherous dealers have dealt treacherously,
Indeed, the treacherous dealers have
dealt very treacherously."
17 Fear and the pit and the snare
Are upon you,
    O inhabitant of the earth.
18 And it shall be
That he who flees from the noise of the fear
Shall fall into the pit,
And he who comes up from the midst of the pit
Shall be caught in the snare;
For the windows from on high are open,
And the foundations of the earth are shaken.
19 The earth is violently broken,

> The earth is split open,
> The earth is shaken exceedingly.
> 20 The earth shall reel to and fro like a drunkard,
>   And shall totter like a hut;
>   Its transgression shall be heavy upon it,
>   And it will fall, and not rise again.
> 21 It shall come to pass in that day
>   That the LORD will punish on high the host of
>   exalted ones,
>   And on the earth
>   the kings of the earth.
> 22 They will be gathered together,
>   As prisoners are gathered in the pit,
>   And will be shut up in the prison;
>   After many days they will be punished.
> 23 Then the moon will be disgraced
>   And the sun ashamed;
>   For the LORD of hosts will reign
>   On Mount Zion and in Jerusalem
>   And before His elders, gloriously.

Isaiah 24:1–23

The final judgment of the earth will be a reversal of all the benefits of creation that God pronounced as "very good" (Genesis 1:31). When the veiled curtain of endtime revelation is lifted before the eyes of Isaiah, he sees these frightening facts.

THE EMPTY EARTH (24:1a)

To say the least, these haunting words of the endtime take us back to the beginning of the time before the Spirit of God moved over the face of the waters. The earth was "without form and void " (Genesis 1:1). In that final day, however, the destructive waste of the curse will add to the formlessness and the emptiness of the physical creation before the Spirit of God brooded over the dark waters and spoke the words of creation. More frightening still is the thought that the Spirit of God will be withdrawn so that destructive and chaotic forces are permitted to take over and wreak havoc that has never been known before.

THE SCATTERED PEOPLE (24:1b–2)

When God created Adam and Eve as the first family on earth and with complementary roles as persons, He also initiated the beginnings of human community and culture. Community is held together by the bond of personal relationships, and culture is maintained by the moral values of social roles and relationships that support the common good. Isaiah saw the essential nature of these relationships when he spoke about the family of God as the "children of Israel," "the house of Jacob," and the coming governance of the Messiah over the world community. All of this is lost in the final day of judgment. Cultures will be shattered, communities will crumble, families will be broken, and every inhabitant of the earth will be scattered without regard for position, prestige, or power (vv. 2–3). William Butler Yeats foresaw this day when he wrote in his poem, "The Second Coming":

> Things fall apart; the center cannot hold;
> Mere anarchy is loosed upon the world;
> The blood-dimmed tide is loosed, and everywhere
> The ceremony of innocence is drowned;
> The best lack all conviction, while the worst
> Are full of passionate intensity.

THE DEVOURING CURSE (24:3–6)

In Genesis, the curse of sin made physical nature an enemy of human creation. The ground was cursed, thorns and thistles grew up in the Garden of Eden, the soil resisted human efforts to bring forth fruit, and the dirt of the earth covered the bodies of those who died (Genesis 3:17–19). Yet, the curse was not complete. With hard work and sweat equity, the earth produced the fresh water and edible fruits required for human survival. But in the great reversal of the final day of judgment, the earth and its people will suffer the consequences of total contamination by sin. According to Isaiah, the original curse of sin is aggravated by the inhabitants who defile God's earth, transgress His Laws, change His commands, and break His everlasting covenant (v. 5). *"Therefore,"* Isaiah writes, *"the curse has devoured the earth, and those who dwell in it are desolate"* (v. 6).

Only the most vivid imagination can picture a time when the earth is the archenemy of humanity with every element aimed at destruction. Anyone who has lived through a tornado, an earthquake, or a hurricane knows the violence of nature when it is unleashed. To live constantly under the dread of these destructive forces is the revelation of the endtime that Isaiah sees. If the curse of sin can literally devour the earth, it means that we have never yet felt the full power of evil unleashed upon our lives. Only Jesus Christ has had that experience. But what if His Spirit is withdrawn from the earth in that final day? Utter desolation and unquenched fire will be the fate of the inhabitants (v. 6). Or because humanity has broken the everlasting covenant God made with Noah, He would no longer be under the vow to keep the earth from another flood of worldwide proportions. A deluge may be the curse that devours the earth.

THE BROKEN SPIRIT (24:7–13)

Isaiah employs the analogy of wine to convey the vibrancy of the human spirit—merry-hearted, mirthful, jubilant, joyous, and singing (vv. 7–9). But alas, in the final day of judgment, confusion and fear will break down the human spirit, darken the joy, and drive out the mirth (vv. 10–12). The *"city of confusion"* (v. 10) may well have reference to the chaos of tongues in the city of Babel, and *"the city desolation"* (v. 12) calls up the burning of Sodom and Gomorrah. In any case, Isaiah envisions a violent convulsion of the human spirit similar to the force required to shake down an olive or two from the top of an olive tree after the yield has already been taken (v. 13).

THE SHATTERED NATIONS (24:14–16)

Isaiah foresees the day when God's desire will be fulfilled and all ends of the earth will sing His praise, *"Glory to the righteous!"* (v. 16). But in the final day of judgment, those who sing will hear a countering voice crying, *"I am ruined, ruined! Woe to me!"* (v. 16). Like the "Amen" that stuck in MacBeth's throat when he tried to pray, the treachery of sin has stifled the song. All of the instances cited by Isaiah, in which the people were misled by leaders who refused to put their trust in God, will come forward to spoil the unified voice of the masses praising the Lord for His righteous character and His glorious works. Because no other person or power can unify all nations, all hope for world peace will lie in rubble.

THE OPEN PIT (24:17–18)

Reminiscent of an earlier prophecy (5:14), in the final day of judgment the pit of hell will enlarge its appetite, expand its jaws, and set its traps for those who flee in fear of the wrath to come (vv. 17–18). Here we learn that the hint of deluge due to the broken covenant has become a fact. Floods will come when the *"windows from on high are open,"* and earthquakes will follow as the *"foundations of the earth are shaken"* (v. 18b). Those who assume that death must give them respite from these natural disasters are in for a surprise. Fear on earth may be unbearable, but the pit of hell is eternal.

THE DRUNKEN GLOBE (24:19–20)

Earthquakes, as dreadful as they may be, are still natural phenomena within the balance of nature. As pressure builds between the plates and along a fault under the earth, the tension must be released so that balance can be restored. Isaiah foresees more than a natural earthquake shaking the earth in the final day of judgment. To see the earth *"reel to and fro like a drunkard, and . . . totter like a hut"* is a cataclysm of nature the universe has never known. In the image of a drunkard reeling to and fro is an earth *"violently broken," "split open,"* and *"shaken exceedingly"* (vv. 19–20). This is a picture of a globe spinning out of orbit because it has fallen off its axis and lost its equilibrium. Obviously, no human beings can survive the catastrophe and the earth itself, once it falls, cannot rise again (v. 20b). Later in his prophecy, Isaiah will see the rise of a new heaven and new earth (65:17). His description of a globe spinning off its orbit leaves no alternative. Once its equilibrium is lost, the imbalance reverberates irretrievably throughout the whole universe. A new heaven and a new earth must be created by God.

THE HUMBLED MIGHTY (24:21–22)

In the final day of judgment, God will convene a high court in heaven and on earth to punish angels and kings who have risen against Him (v. 21). Isaiah's earlier oracle comes back to mind, "How are you fallen from heaven, O Lucifer, son of the morning!" (Isaiah 14:12). Consistent with that vision, Lucifer and his host of fallen angels will be brought together with the kings of the earth who pretended to be God before the highest of tribunals for sentencing. With the verdict of "guilty," they will be put in solitary confinement in the pit of hell to await their fate. Evil, at its satanic source and in its personal manifestation, will be bound forever.

THE DARKENED LIGHT (24:23a)

God's first act of creation was to pronounce, "'Let there be light'; and there was light" (Genesis 1:3). His second act was to divide the night from the day (Genesis 1:4–5). On the fourth day, then, God created the sun as the greater light to rule the day and the moon as the lesser light to rule over the night (Genesis 1:14–19). As primal as these creative acts may be, they are now reversed so that the moon is *"disgraced"* and the sun is *"ashamed,"* by the events on earth. As Jesus predicted for the time of tribulation, "The sun will be darkened, and the moon will not give its light . . ." (Matthew 24:29). Creation is reversed and once again, darkness shall cover the earth.

THE REIGNING LORD (24:23b)

Winston Churchill gained his fame when he strode through the rubble of London after a Nazi bombing and encouraged the survivors, "We have just begun to fight." A similar picture with eternal dimensions comes to mind when Isaiah concludes this prophecy with the triumphant promise, *"For the LORD of hosts will reign on Mount Zion and in Jerusalem, and before His elders, gloriously"* (v. 23). No contrast that Isaiah uses is more pronounced. Against the total devastation of the earth and its people, due to the curse of sin, God reigns to fulfill His purpose—not just effectively, but gloriously. Over His new creation He will again speak the words, "It is very good."

GOD'S LONG-RANGE PLAN (25:1–12)

1 O LORD, You are my God.
  I will exalt You,
  I will praise Your name,

For You have done wonderful things;
Your counsels of old are faithfulness and truth.
2 For You have made a city a ruin,
A fortified city a ruin,
A palace of foreigners to be a city no more;
It will never be rebuilt.
3 Therefore the strong people
will glorify You;
The city of the terrible nations
will fear You.
4 For You have been a strength to the poor,
A strength to the needy in his distress,
A refuge from the storm,
A shade from the heat;
For the blast of the terrible ones is as a storm against
the wall,
5 You will reduce the noise of aliens,
As heat in a dry place;
As heat in the shadow of a cloud,
The song of the terrible ones
will be diminished.
6 And in this mountain
The LORD of hosts will make for all people
A feast of choice pieces,
A feast of wines on the lees,
Of fat things full of marrow,
Of well-refined wines on the lees.
7 And He will destroy on this mountain
The surface of the covering cast over all people,
And the veil that is spread over all nations.
8 He will swallow up death forever,
And the Lord GOD will wipe away tears from all
faces;
The rebuke of His people
He will take away from all the earth;
For the LORD has spoken.
9 And it will be said in that day:
"Behold, this is our God;
We have waited for Him,
and He will save us.
This is the LORD;
We have waited for Him;

We will be glad and rejoice
   in His salvation."
10 For on this mountain the hand
   of the LORD will rest,
And Moab shall be trampled down under Him,
As straw is trampled down for the refuse heap.
11 And He will spread out His hands in their midst
As he who swims spreads out his hands to swim,
And He will bring down their pride
Together with the trickery of their hands.
12 The fortress of the high fort of your walls
He will bring down, lay low,
And bring to the ground,
   down to the dust.

Isaiah 25:1–12

Judgment has reached its peak and the LORD of hosts reigns "on Mount Zion and in Jerusalem and before His elders, gloriously" (24:23). It is time to sing. Isaiah joins with the children of Israel to praise and exalt the name of their God who has done wonderful things and whose word is faithful and true (25:1). As distant as it may seem, the time will come when the people of Judah and Jerusalem will see what God has been trying to do throughout their history. They will return to Him in the relationship of love that prompts them to sing, "O LORD, You are my God;" they will praise Him for the miracles of "wonderful things" including the return from exile and the restoration of the Holy City and its temple; and they will exalt His name because He has been faithful to every promise and true to every word. With good reason, Isaiah and Israel sing praises to God for the fulfillment of His plan for them and the world.

Long-range planning can answer either the question *"What* do we want to be?" or *"How* do we get there?" The answer to the first question, comes from looking into the future and envisioning goals to be reached. Persons who are involved in long-range planning for their churches, businesses, or schools, for instance, are asked to imagine themselves riding in a helicopter at some specific point of time in the future, looking down and describing the church, business, or school as they believe it should be. After answering "What do we want to be?" attention can then be turned to the question "How do we get there?" Usually this means specifying the steps required to get from the present position to the future goals. What? is a question of ends; How? is a question of means. Long-range planning in churches, businesses, and schools often fails because the people are preoccupied with *how* and forget that *what* is the most important question.

We tend to approach God's long-range plan in the same way. Rather than seeing *what* God wants us to be, we are preoccupied with *how* He is working to get us there. Israel succumbed to the same error. Preoccupied with the short-term view of God's will, they failed to see the long-range view of His redemptive purpose. But "In that day" when the LORD of hosts reigns in Mount Zion and Jerusalem, the children of Israel will sing His praises as they see, for the first time, His redemptive will for them and realize that He has been wonderful, faithful, and true in all of His ways with them. Isaiah takes us intimately into the mind and heart of God as he answers the question *what* for the children of Israel by specifying His long-range goals for them.

ALL NATIONS WILL WORSHIP HIM (25:1–3)

In the oracles against the nations of the world, the *how* of God's judgment fell with devastating force. Possibly referring back to the oracle against Babylon (ch. 13), Isaiah cites the utter *"ruin"* of *"a city,"* *"a fortified city,"* and *"a palace of foreigners"* (v. 2). The reference may sum up God's judgment in history against the pride of the nations of the world or it may mean God's ultimate triumph over Babylon as the symbol of evil in its essence. In either case, the *how* of judgment quickly gives way to the *what* of God's redemptive purpose. His goal is to bring all *strong* or foreign people to glorify Him and the *"city of the terrible [hostile] nations"* to *fear* Him (v. 3). Such a goal is consistent with Isaiah's oft-stated theme that the purpose of God's judgment upon sin is to redeem the sinner.

ALL THE POOR WILL HAVE REFUGE (25:4–5)

Try as we might, we cannot get away from the fact that poor, needy, and helpless people are closest to the heart of God. Biblical scholars agree that the *"poor"* and *"needy"* identified in this passage are especially, but not exclusively, the children of Israel. Exile had cast God's chosen people into the ranks of the poor and needy who suffered from helplessness, persecution, and ridicule. But, no more. Anticipating the prophecies of comfort in the second half of the book of Isaiah (chs. 40–66), Isaiah sees God as the strength for their weakness, support during their distress, refuge from the storm of war, and shade from the heat of persecution (v. 4). Comparing their plight to driving rain or icy hail hitting a wall, God understands the oppression of the *"terrible ones"* against His children.

Today, the poor and needy are expanded to include the boat people of Haiti and Somalia, the refugees of Croatia and Iraq, the victims of apartheid in South Africa, the outcasts of India, and the homeless of America to name just a few of those who are God's afflicted people. He will be their comfort, but we must be their help.

In this same vein of thought, Isaiah includes God's role in reducing the noise of ridicule from *"aliens"* and *"terrible ones"* who oppress the children of Israel with their taunts (v. 5). The child's rhyme, "sticks and stones may break my bones, but names can never hurt me," is only half true. Sticks and stones can break bones, but names may hurt more. Moments ago, a telephone call came from a distraught mother who asked advice about a situation involving her ten-year-old son. On a overnight outing, he became the butt of the jokes of the boys with whom he stayed. Crushed by the ridicule, he would have preferred broken bones to a broken heart.

Jewish people around the world and across the generations have been victims of taunting songs and cruel jokes. Hitler, we are told, was a master at telling Jewish jokes. He illustrates a sobering fact. Ridicule of poor, needy, and helpless people can be the prelude to persecution. When the LORD of hosts reigns, however, the ridicule will be silenced.

ALL PEOPLE WILL BE INVITED TO HIS TABLE (25:6)

Newly crowned kings always host coronation banquets, and, likewise, the LORD of hosts. He has the goal of inviting all of the people of the world to Mount Zion for a feast of *"choice pieces,"* *"fat things full of marrow"* and *"well-refined wines"* of highest quality (v. 6). John the Revelator saw the same vision in the Marriage Supper of the Lamb when all the redeemed of the ages will gather to sing, "Hallelujah!

For the Lord God Omnipotent reigns! Let us be glad and rejoice and give Him glory . . ." (Revelation 19:6–7). God's ultimate triumph over sin is cause for celebration, but we cannot forget His desire to bring all people to the banquet table. Even though Isaiah and the children of Israel are the singers of the song, they are not the only guests at the feast. "*All people*" includes the Gentiles who are identified as "strangers," "aliens," and even the "terrible ones" earlier in the song. With a prophetic sweep into the distant future, Isaiah foresees faith in God as the way in which a person, Jew or Gentile, receives an invitation to the feast. Whether the prophet knew it or not, he forecast a spiritual revolution that would shake the Jewish community to the core. As they closed their ranks on Old Testament beliefs and rejected Jesus Christ as the Messiah, they limited the kind of persons and the number of places at God's banquet table.

Yet the Jews are not alone. At the end of the twentieth century in America, the Christian church still tends to be white, middle-aged, Protestant, Anglo-Saxon, English-speaking, educated, and affluent. Statistics of a changing population, however, reveal new majorities rising from the ranks of people of color, youth, and ethnic origin who struggle for education, employment, economic survival, self-esteem, and social justice. They are hungry, not just for food and jobs, but for personal salvation and spiritual community. We must make room at the Lord's table for them.

In our home, we eat our family meals at a round table. When our four children were home, we comfortably seated six around the table. Then when the older ones got married and brought home spouses we simply scooted our chairs closer together to make room for the newcomers to our family. Admittedly, we ran out of space when ten grandchildren arrived, but leaves in the dining room table made it possible for all the family to eat holiday meals together. God expects the same of His people and His Church at His table where the choicest, richest, and most delectable foods are served. We must scoot over and make room for the newcomers whom we invite to the table of His grace.

ALL SUFFERING WILL END (25:7–8)

We, as humans, live with the reality of suffering, the fear of death, and the burden of tears for both our suffering and our death. We know the comfort of God for these harsh and, often unexplainable facts of human existence, but they are still inevitable because we are human. God, however, anticipates the day when He will destroy the "cover" of suffering *"cast over all people,"* lift the *"veil"* of death *"spread over all nations,"* *"swallow up death forever,"* and *"wipe away tears from all faces"* (vv. 7, 8). Is it any wonder that the poet, Robert Burns, with his sensitive, soul, wept whenever he read these words? We have entered into the deepest and innermost desires of the heart of God. He yearns for the day when He will end our suffering, release us from death, and turn our sorrows into joy. With Robert Burns, as we read these words of God's compassion and join in the song to praise Him, the tears will flow.

ALL WILL SING THE SONG OF TRUST (25:9)

At long last, Isaiah's plea for the children of Israel to put their total trust in God will be realized when the LORD of hosts reigns on Mount Zion and in Jerusalem. To their hymn of praise the verse is added, *"Behold, this is our God. We have waited for Him, and He will save us"* (v. 9). What a turnaround for the children of Israel! Their history in Isaiah's time is written as rebellion against God, impatience with His ways, and refusal to trust His saving power. *"In that day,"* however, the children of Israel will return to the family, claim God as their father, wait with patient trust as His good will unfolds, and hope only in Him for their salvation. God Himself has set the goal and awaits the moment of accomplishment.

ALL GOD'S ADVERSARIES WILL BE FRUSTRATED (25:10–12)

Moab is the proverbial thorn-in-the-flesh for the children of Israel. Born as the son of Lot out of his incestuous relationship with his daughter, Moab and his descendants never stopped causing trouble for Israel. Isaiah's earlier oracle against Moab (15:1–16:14) occupied more space and pinpointed more judgment than the oracles against Philistia and Edom, greater and more powerful nations. Biblical history bears out the reason why Moab represents the major adversary of Judah and Jerusalem. Just as the children of Israel were about to enter the Promised Land, King Balak of Moab hired Balaam to seduce Israel into sexual immorality with the Moabite women and invite them to make sacrifices to their idol, Baal of Peor (Numbers 25:1–3). Even though Moses was buried in an unknown grave in the land of Moab (Deuteronomy 34:6) and Ruth was a Moabite woman (Ruth 1:4), the hostility between the nations never ended. Isaiah's oracle against Moab, for instance, may have been provoked by Moabite raiders who made forays into Israel every spring (2 Kings 13:20).

All will change, however, when the LORD of hosts reigns from Mount Zion. Instead of the Moabites frustrating Israel, God will frustrate Moab. Isaiah reserves his choicest metaphor for God's judgment upon Moab. *"And Moab shall be trampled down under Him, as straw is trampled down for the refuse heap. And he will spread out his hands in their midst as he who swims spreads out his hands to swim"* (vv. 10–11). Moab will be like a man trying to swim in a dung heap! No frustration could be greater. The more the hands flay, the deeper the man sinks. All of Moab's pride, trickery, and defensiveness will be brought down, laid low, and ground into the dust (v. 12). As the adversary of Israel and God, it is not enough for Moab just to be brought down. The nation will be conquered, humiliated, and made the lowest of the low. Sinking through these three deepening levels of judgment, the destruction of Israel's ancient adversary, whether Moab or the evil it represents, will be complete.

SONGS OF THE FUTURE (26:1–21)

1 In that day this song will be sung
  in the land of Judah:
  "We have a strong city;
  God will appoint salvation for walls and bulwarks.
2 Open the gates,
  That the righteous nation which keeps the truth may
    enter in.
3 You will keep him in perfect peace,
  Whose mind is stayed on You,
  Because he trusts in You.
4 Trust in the LORD forever,
  For in YAH, the LORD,
    is everlasting strength.
5 For He brings down those
    who dwell on high,
  The lofty city;
  He lays it low,

He lays it low to the ground,
He brings it down to the dust.
6 The foot shall tread it down—
The feet of the poor
And the steps of the needy."
7 The way of the just is uprightness;
O Most Upright,
You weigh the path of the just.
8 Yes, in the way of Your judgments,
O LORD, we have waited for You;
The desire of our soul is for Your name
And for the remembrance of You.
9 With my soul I have desired You in
      the night,
Yes, by my spirit within me
   I will seek You early;
For when Your judgments
   are in the earth,
The inhabitants of the world
   will earn righteousness.
10 Let grace be shown to the wicked,
Yet he will not learn righteousness;
In the land of uprightness
   he will deal unjustly,
And will not behold the majesty of the LORD.
11 LORD, when Your hand is lifted up, they will
      not see.
But they will see and be ashamed
For their envy of people;
Yes, the fire of Your enemies
   shall devour them.
12 LORD, You will establish peace for us,
For You have also done all our works in us.
13 O LORD our God,
      other masters besides You
Have had dominion over us;
But by You only we make mention of Your name.
14 They are dead, they will not live;
They are deceased, they will not rise.
Therefore You have punished
   and destroyed them,
And made all their memory to perish.

15 You have increased the nation,
    O LORD,
You have increased the nation;
You are glorified;
You have expanded all the borders of the land.
16 LORD, in trouble they have visited You,
They poured out a prayer when Your chastening was
    upon them.
17 As a woman with child
Is in pain and cries out in her pangs,
When she draws near the time
    of her delivery,
So have we been in Your sight,
    O LORD.
18 We have been with child,
    we have been in pain;
We have, as it were,
    brought forth wind;
We have not accomplished any
    deliverance in the earth,
Nor have the inhabitants
    of the world fallen.
19 Your dead shall live;
Together with my dead body
    they shall arise.
Awake and sing,
    you who dwell in dust;
For your dew is like the dew of herbs,
And the earth shall cast out the dead.
20 Come, my people,
    enter your chambers,
And shut your doors behind you;
Hide yourself, as it were,
    for a little moment,
Until the indignation is past.
21 For behold, the LORD comes
    out of His place
To punish the inhabitants of the earth
    for their iniquity;
The earth will also disclose her blood,
And will no more cover her slain.

Isaiah 26:1–21

To bring together the Oracles of the Endtime, God gives Judah a song to sing. It is a Song of Salvation intended to keep fresh in the minds of the people through the generations the lessons that the children of Israel learned from the judgments and the promises of God. Words and verses connect with other oracles of Isaiah and, in keeping with his style of communication, unmistakable contrasts are drawn between good and evil, righteousness and wickedness, sin and salvation.

OUR STRENGTH IS IN YOUR TRUST (26:1–6)

Taking his cue from the downfall of the high and fortressed city of the Moabites, a symbol of defiance against God, Isaiah gives the people of Judah a verse of song about the restoration of Jerusalem, the Holy City. Borrowing from Charles Dickens, some have called this contrast "The Tale of Two Cities." Whereas the city of Moab found its strength in a walled fortress on high ground, Jerusalem has unequalled strength because *"God will appoint salvation for walls and bulwarks"* (v. 1b). Moreover, while the city of Moab showed its fear by closing its gates behind high walls between bulwarks of protective space, Jerusalem will open its gates for all peoples and nations who keep the truth to enter in. Such a daring venture can be taken because the peace of Jerusalem does not depend on closed gates, but upon a mind of disposition and direction fixed in trust upon *YAH*, the immovable and everlasting rock of salvation (vv. 3–4).

Stephen Covey, in his book *Seven Habits of Highly Effective People*, tells the story of a battleship sailing through the fog during the dark of night. A lookout spots the weak ray of flashing light ahead and warns the captain on the bridge. Sending out a radio message the captain orders the other vessel to change course because (he signals), "I am a battleship." However, the message comes back with the counter-command to the captain of the battleship, "I am a lighthouse."[1] We know who changed course.

Isaiah might have issued the same command. God, the everlasting rock, envisioned Jerusalem as the city that would be the light of the world. All other cities and nations that trust in the strength of high places, solid walls, and wide bulwarks are on a collision course with God's chosen city. They, not Jerusalem, must change their course to enter into its gates. Otherwise, like the fortress city of Moab, they will be laid low, low to the ground, and trampled in the dust (25:12 and 26:5). Ironically, the poor and the needy whom the Moabites oppressed will be the participants in a peasant's revolt, and they will do the trampling.

Our Righteousness Is in Your Trust (26:7–11)

Isaiah has already announced the opening of the gates of Jerusalem to the "righteous nation which keeps the truth" and promised perfect peace to the inhabitant of the city whose mind is fixed in constant trust upon the Lord (26:2, 3). To these never-ending spiritual lessons, he goes on to make it clear that righteousness is not an exercise in self-discipline and justice is not a creation of human law. Rather, when Isaiah offers the verse, *"The way of the just is uprightness, O Most Upright"* (v. 7), he leaves no doubt that our righteousness comes from the righteousness of God and our justice comes from the justice of God. Otherwise, as Isaiah will say later, "And all our righteousnesses are like filthy rags" (64:6).

God makes the way of the righteous level and straight by building upon His judgments and our desires. Divine sovereignty and human freedom work hand in hand to make us holy. In His judgments, Israel has learned that God's only purpose in the purging of its soul through the suffering of exile is preparation for redemption. If, then, Israel has the spiritual hunger to wait for the return of the Lord, to yearn for the privilege of bearing His name, and to remember His glorious deeds, then the promise is given, *"The inhabitants of the world will learn righteousness"* (v. 9b).

A startling truth is before us when Isaiah goes on to note that the wicked do not learn righteousness when the grace of God is shown to them (v. 10a). Whereas the judgments of God revive spiritual hunger for the children of Israel, the grace of God teaches the wicked no lessons. *"In the land of uprightness he will still deal unjustly, and will not behold the majesty of the Lord"* (v. 10b). Neither will the wicked respond when God's hand of judgment hangs over their heads like a sword of Damocles (26:11a). Why? The answer is in the direction of the mind and the disposition of the soul. Even though the children of Israel had rebelled against the love of God and had denied their thirst for His name, they could not escape their spiritual heritage and their miraculous history. Like the prodigal son who came to his senses in a pigpen, they remember the Father's house and want to come home.

Today, Christian parents of prodigal children can live with that promise. A letter just came from a Christian couple who have given their life and dedicated their children to the service of the Lord. Their only daughter left home, denied her faith, and practiced a lifestyle that contradicted everything she had been taught and once professed. After years of strained relationships, news came that her body was filled with aggresive, terminal cancer. When her parents rushed to her bedside, they were held away by the wishes of their daughter and her friends. The call for fervent prayer went out to the community of faith. Within hours, the daughter mellowed, received her parents, heard their prayers, and reached out to hold their hands as she rested peacefully just before death. The direction of her life and the disposition of her soul in the love and care of a Christian family could not be denied. While her friends remained skeptical in the presence of God, she responded to the love of her Christian family.

Our Peace Is in Your Lordship (26:12–15)

In a prayer of confession, the people of Judah acknowledge that all of their efforts to win peace by trusting in kings and rulers, armies, and alliances have failed. All those who held dominion over them are destroyed, dead, and forgotten (v. 14). Only trust in God has brought them permanent peace through His glorious deeds. More than that, God has added the bonus of doing what other rulers promised to do and failed. Keeping His promise to Abraham, He has increased the numbers of the nation and expanded all of its borders. Prosperity is the bonus of God's peace for Judah (v. 15).

Charles Colson has often said that many contemporary Christians claim Jesus Christ as the Savior of their soul, but do not permit Him to be the Lord of their life. Israel learned that they could not be spiritual schizophrenics. Isaiah condemned them for continuing the habit of worshiping God in the temple but accommodating the idols of the marketplace. The tension between the two worlds brings no peace to the soul. All other masters will be destroyed, die, and disappear. Only the lordship of Jesus Christ will bring us the peace we desire and fulfill the promises of enlarging our witness and expanding our world. With Judah, then, we will sing, "*You are glorified*" (v. 15).

OUR DELIVERANCE IS IN YOUR POWER (26:16–18)

Judah's prayer of confession continues. As the people of Judah confessed that they found no peace under the dominion of other masters in whom they put their trust, they now confess that their turning to God during times of trouble was not genuine repentance, but efforts at self-deliverance (v. 16). Likening themselves to a pregnant woman nearing the time of delivery, their cries of pain gave them some relief but had no bearing on the delivery. Pressing the analogy to its limit, they confess that all of their efforts gave birth only to "*wind*" or gas (v. 18).

Isaiah had already spoken scathing words against Judah for religious pretense. In his opening prophecy, he spoke for God, "When you spread out your hands, I will hide My eyes from you; even though you make many prayers, I will not hear. Your hands are full of blood. Wash yourselves, make yourselves clean" (1:15–16). Now, Judah confesses the sin against which Isaiah prophesied. They had used their religion as a means of saving themselves in times of crisis. We make our God too small when we use Him like a spare tire in the trunk of the car. Until we have an emergency, we live as if we did not need him. In the past, at least spare tires were full size and capable of long use once they were installed on the car. Today, the spare is a temporary tire with the warning, "Do not drive over 100 miles." The analogy may still hold. The God to whom we turn only in emergencies may be small, but the God who is just a "quick fix" is even smaller.

Brutal honesty is heard in Judah's confession of using God as a "quick fix" in time of trouble. They admit that they had not "*accomplished any deliverance in the earth, nor have the inhabitants of the world fallen*" (v. 18b). What a tragic conclusion. Judah is like a person nearing the end of life who confesses that he or she missed the very purpose for which they were born. With Judah, all of their own attempts to be the deliverer and ruler of nations had brought forth nothing but a gust of wind that is instantly gone. Now they know that only their total trust in the Lord, the Lord alone, can deliver them and nurture them in their birthright as the hope of the world for salvation when the LORD of hosts reigns.

Our Hope Is in Your Life (26:19)

A contrast of eternal proportions is drawn between the Moabites, who will be brought down to the very dust of the earth (25:12 and 26:5) to die and live no more (26:14), and the people of Judah, who find their hope in the life of the Lord for the resurrection of the dead. When Isaiah wrote these word of prophecy, the children of Israel's concept of life after death was still limited to the shadowy realm of spirits known as Sheol. But with prophetic insight reaching far ahead of his time, Isaiah puts the sound of a trumpet to the lips of Judah, *"Awake and sing, you who dwell in the dust"* (v. 19b). This note of victory is the natural follow-up to Isaiah's grand vision of the Lord who will "swallow up death forever" (25:8). Now, he takes the vision a step farther to identify the source of the resurrection. *"Your dew is like the dew of herbs, and the earth shall cast out the dead"* (v. 19).

As dust symbolizes death throughout the Scriptures, so dew symbolizes life. Before God created the rain to fall upon the earth from the clouds above, He provided the dew of the ground to water the earth and bring forth its fruit. Dew, then, is the life from heaven and the source of resurrection power. Scholars argue over the general resurrection of the dead as implied in the verse, *"the earth shall cast out the dead,"* and the prior resurrection of believers as inferred in the words, *"Your dead will live; together with my dead body they shall arise"* (v. 19). Isaiah, however, has a message that cannot be argued or denied: God is the source of our hope for resurrection into eternal life.

Our Future Is in Your Time (26:20–21)

Fulfillment of all of these Oracles of the Endtime is yet ahead. Isaiah returns from the glorious future to the dreadful present when he advises Judah to *"enter your chambers, and shut your doors behind you; hide yourself, as it were, for a little moment"* (v. 20). God's exact timing for the endtime is not known. All those who attempt to predict the time of His glorious coming claim a spiritual insight that neither Isaiah nor Jesus claimed. Both left us one message: Be prepared for His coming by trusting in His care and living righteously in His presence. No other protection is needed from the wrath of God, which will come sharply upon the wicked of the earth and then pass by. As the children of Israel remembered the protection of the blood on the doorpost when the

Angel of Death swept through Egypt during their exile there, so Isaiah brings back the memory of history to communicate the truth that those who trust in the Lord will be at peace in the time of tempest as they await His coming.

EPIC OF THE ENDTIME (27:1–13)

1 In that day the LORD with His
 severe sword, great and strong,
 Will punish Leviathan the fleeing serpent,
 Leviathan that twisted serpent;
 And He will slay the reptile
  that is in the sea.
2 In that day sing to her,
 "A vineyard of red wine!
3 I, the LORD, keep it,
 I water it every moment;
 Lest any hurt it,
 I keep it night and day.
4 Fury is not in Me.
 Who would set briers and thorns
 Against Me in battle?
 I would go through them,
 I would burn them together.
5 Or let him take hold of My strength,
 That he may make peace with Me;
 And he shall make peace with Me."
6 Those who come He shall cause
  to take root in Jacob;
 Israel shall blossom and bud,
 And fill the face of the world with fruit.
7 Has He struck Israel as He struck those who struck
  him?
8 In measure, by sending it away,
 You contended with it.
 He removes it by His rough wind
 In the day of the east wind.
9 Therefore by this the iniquity of Jacob will be covered;
 And this is all the fruit of taking away his sin:
 When he makes all the stones of the altar
 Like chalkstones that are beaten to dust,

When wooden images and incense altars do not
   stand up.
10 Yet the fortified city will be desolate,
The habitation forsaken
   and left like a wilderness;
There the calf will feed,
   and there it will lie down
And consume its branches.
11 When its boughs are withered,
   they will be broken off;
The women come and set them on fire.
For it is a people of no understanding;
Therefore He who made them will not have mercy
   on them,
And He who formed them will show them no favor.
12 And it shall come to pass in that day
That the LORD will thresh,
From the channel of the River
   to the Brook of Egypt;
And you will be gathered one by one,
O you children of Israel.
13 So it shall be in that day.
That the great trumpet will be blown;
They will come, who are about to perish in the land
   of Assyria,
And they who are outcasts in the land of Egypt,
And shall worship the LORD in the holy mount at
   Jerusalem.

Isaiah 27:1–13

One last prophecy of epic proportions closes down Isaiah's Oracles of the Endtime. "In that day," he warns, the "great and strong" sword of the Lord will strike a final and fatal blow to the forces of evil in the world. Although no date for the confrontation is given, Isaiah's prophecy has both temporal and eternal interpretations.

GOD WILL SLAY EVIL (27:1)

Temporal and local history are inferred in Isaiah's image of Leviathan, the legendary, multiheaded monster of the sea whom ancients feared as the cause of chaos on the earth. Consistent with that image,

Isaiah gives personality to the three archenemies of Judah according to the distinctive characteristics of the waterways that coursed through their land. (1) The *"fleeing serpent,"* or the Elusive One, represents Assyria, a nation located on the swift flowing Tigris River; (2) The *"twisted serpent,"* or the Torturous One, calls up the setting of Babylon, the city on the winding Euphrates River; and (3) The *"reptile that is in the sea,"* or the Rushing One, identifies Egypt with its dependence upon the mighty flow of the Nile. Each of these empires, in its turn and in keeping with its personality, had struck Judah and Jerusalem. By their attacks they continued to frustrate the purpose of God for His people. Therefore, their ultimate defeat was absolutely necessary for the peace of Israel if it were to fulfill its God-appointed mission as the home of the Savior and the instrument through whom salvation was to come. Not by coincidence, Jesus Christ was born after the defeat of these three empires and in the small gap of time in Roman history when the doors of the Temple Zeus were closed to signal *Pax Romana* (peace in Rome) when no legion was at war anywhere in its world empire. As preparation for the coming of Christ, the monster of chaos had to be slain.

Isaiah's choice of the word *"Leviathan"* links his prophecy with wisdom literature as well as with epic poetry. In Job's humbling encounter with God, the wise and righteous man is asked if he could put a hook in Leviathan and control him, a crocodile-like creature who personifies evil in all of its vicious attacks and incorrigible nature (Job 41). After an exacting description of this snorting, sneezing, and fiery monster that no human can control, God reminds Job, "On earth there is nothing like him, which is made without fear. He beholds every high thing; he is king over all the children of pride" (Job 41:33–34). Job is quick to confess his pride and acknowledge his inability either to explain evil in the world or to defeat it by his own righteousness.

Following the meaning of Leviathan in wisdom literature, Isaiah's vision takes on cosmic proportions. In seeing the swift and sure stroke of the Lord's sword severing the multiple heads of the monster of chaos, his small snapshot of local history is projected onto the wide screen of endtime history. We see the utter defeat of the chaos caused by sin. The three-headed monster adds to this meaning. Using the perfect tense of the verb "to punish," and applying it three times,

Isaiah employs a favorite literary device of the Hebrews when they wanted to speak of an act of perfect completion. For the monster of three heads but the same heart, the great and strong sword of the Lord will sever the heads and penetrate the heart. Once again, Isaiah has struck a resounding note for God's ultimate triumph over the forces of evil.

GOD WILL RESTORE ISRAEL (27:2–5)

New hope springs into Isaiah's vision with the announcement of Satan's final downfall. Utilizing the phrase "In that day" as an introduction to last things or eschatology, the prophet adds emphasis to his view of Israel's future by describing the new things God will do for Israel following the purging of the Babylonian Exile. To help understand the oracle, note that several threads of the thought are pulled through earlier oracles and tied more specifically into the promise of the restoration of Israel. The Parable of God's Vineyard, for instance, which Isaiah introduced earlier to communicate the disappointment of God with His children, now comes back in the context of promise after punishment (ch. 5).

Whenever Isaiah pulls through these connecting threads, he creates a contrast between punishment and promise that makes both sides of the prophecy stand out in our minds. In the first Parable of God's Vineyard, the garden is overgrown with "briers and thorns," a symbol of the ravaging effects of punishment for sin (5:6), but in the new parable, there are no briers and thorns because of God's promise of personal care for His garden (v. 4). Some scholars find punishment and promise mixed in the sections of this oracle. Certainly, Isaiah holds to his theme that punishment is the purging of sin that will lead to the fulfillment of God's promise. The overall tone of the oracle, however, is positive, not negative, and deserves to be read as a series of affirmations of God's promise for the restoration of Israel.

As the first Parable of God's Vineyard began as a song of rejected love in a minor key (5:1), so the new Parable is a song of faithful love sung in a major key (v. 2). Contrasting chords strike the promises of the new Parable. *"A vineyard of red wine,"* rather than a harvest of bitter grapes, is now the product of the vineyard. During the time that the children of Israel have gone through the punishment of exile for their rebellion against the love of God, He has remained faithful to them, waiting for the time when they will again put their full trust in Him. With that trust, then, comes the nurturing love of the Father for His children as typified by the tender care of the Keeper for His beloved vineyard. *"I, the LORD, keep it, I water it every moment; lest any hurt it, I keep it night and day"* (v. 3).

In contrast, we remember God lifting the protective hedge around the vineyard and breaking down the walls because of the bitter grapes that set His teeth on edge (5:5). All the fury will be gone when Israel is restored. The "briers and thorns," which He permitted to grow and ruin the vineyard, are now envisioned as enemies against whom God will do battle. Rather than forbidding the clouds to rain upon the vineyard, He will personally see to a constant flow of life-giving water. And, best of all, anyone who tries to trample on the vineyard will have to deal directly with the strength of God Himself and make peace with the Keeper (v. 5).

No human need is greater than to know that God protects us from harm and nurtures us to grow with the care of a loving Father. Our hearts break at the thought of our sin, which has flaunted His love and frustrated His purpose in our lives. Many young people who have sown their wild oats feel as if they will forever be second-class citizens in the community of faith. Women who have had abortions, for instance, may suffer from the nagging guilt of post-abortion trauma. Or men may live in mortal fear of testing HIV positive after early years of promiscuity. While it is true that each of us has a past for which we must pay the consequences, the Parable of the Vineyard is the promise that God has not given up on us. Punishment for our sins is a purging to bring us to trust in Him so that the past is forgiven and the future is under His care. The beauty of the gospel is found in the promise that He will keep us in His faithful love and nurture us in His good will toward the purpose for which we were born. Every day we need to claim the promise of the Parable of God's Vineyard.

GOD WILL PROSPER ISRAEL (27:6)

Extending the analogy of the vineyard from its protection and nurture to its product, Isaiah draws upon another analogy of an earlier oracle, namely the root of Jesse (11:1). What began as a "Holy Seed" in a stump (6:13) had grown into a "Branch" out of the root of Jesse. Isaiah now sees the "Branch" blossoming, budding, and producing fruit that will *fill the face of the world* (v. 6). What a promise for a smidgen of space on the face of the earth called Israel! What a promise for a rural, agricultural people in the midst of an urban world of cultural sophistication, commercial wealth, and military strength! What a promise for a fearful people headed toward years of exile! Only God could see such a vision and make such a promise.

Prosperity is ahead for Israel, but not the prosperity of the world. To think of Israel and Jewish people as representatives of commercial genius is not God's intention for their fame. His vision is to see Israel grow to world stature as the source of the Savior and the hope of His salvation. Other forms of prosperity may follow, but they must always be a distant second in the reputation and influence of the nation. If they begin to compete with God's primary purpose for their prosperity, Israel has defaulted on its destiny.

Isaiah continues to demonstrate the contemporary application of his ancient prophecy. Prosperity is grossly misinterpreted for Christians in Western culture, especially in North America. Economic wealth, political power, cultural sophistication, and military strength tend to usurp the only reputation and influence worthy of God's purpose. Unless the Church and Christians are known first for the message and spirit of Christ the Savior, we too default on our destiny.

GOD WILL SAVE ISRAEL (27:7–9)

Isaiah is responding to a hard question that the children of Israel would certainly ask, *"Has he struck Israel as He struck those who struck him?"* (vs. 7). God's answer, while neither simple nor easy, seems to be that divorce is better than death. In the language of divorce proceedings, He says that He sent Israel away into exile on a rough, east wind as a lesser punishment than the fiery burning with which He consumed Assyria, Babylon, and Egypt. But that explanation is almost incidental to the purpose of His punishment. God purges Israel of its sins and atones for its iniquity through the ameliorated judgment of exile (v. 9). He has no other purpose than to bring His people back to Himself as their one and only God. The proof will come when the stone altars erected to idols are ground into chalk dust and the wooden poles of Asherim topple over (vs. 9). So the punishment of exile is less severe than the dust of death that awaits the enemies of Israel and proof of the people's trust in God will be the destruction of idols. But both punishment and proof turn upon Isaiah's most important point. God will cover the iniquity of the House of Jacob and take away, or atone for, the sins of His people. Exile, however, is not a substitute for the atonement of Christ. While serving as a symbol for the purging of sins leading to repentance, only God can forgive those sins through the death of His son.

GOD WILL PROTECT ISRAEL (27:10–11)

Biblical scholars disagree on the interpretation of the words, *"Yet, the fortified city will be desolate"* (v. 10). The preference tends toward Jerusalem and its future punishment. Isaiah's pattern in this oracle, however, is to affirm God's promises to Israel. Furthermore, the image of the "fortified city" is more fitting to the same name that is given to the stronghold of the enemy, over whom God has triumphed, in 25:2. From that perspective, we see another of God's promises fulfilled, namely that He will guarantee the peace of Israel by putting down and burning up every attempt of the enemy to rise against His people. According to the text, the "fortified city" has already been destroyed so thoroughly that its habitation is a "wilderness" where only cattle feed (v. 9). But if there is the slightest evidence of food or kindling left over from the evil, calves will eat the branches and women will burn the boughs (vv. 10b–11a).

Isaiah has introduced a new thought of great comfort for the children of Israel. Having lived under the boot of evil empires for centuries, the residual fear of revolt and reprisal must have haunted them. God's promise is to "nip in the bud" the slightest sign of the return of evil. Saints of the ages have lived holy with the same promise. Thomas a'Kempis, in his classical book of devotion, *The Imitation of Christ*, prays for the sensitivity of spirit to catch the first hint of word, thought, or deed that would lead him into sin.[2] God is equally sensitive to these impulses and, by His Spirit, will guard us from their potential for destruction if we share the prayer of Thomas a'Kempis.

GOD WILL PRESERVE ISRAEL (27:12)

The gathering of a remnant of Israel is not a new prophecy. In fact, Isaiah has already spoken similar words time and time again. The phrase, "the Lord will thresh," for instance, takes us back to the "shaking of the olive tree" in the oracle of Final Judgment (24:13) and to "gleaning . . . two or three olives at the top of the uppermost bough, four or five in its most fruitful branches . . ." in Isaiah's oracle against Israel (17:6). "Threshing" is Isaiah's word for judgment and implies the violence that will go along with Babylonian exile and the dispersion of the Jews to every corner of the earth. Through the pain, however, His promise will be fulfilled. From the *"channel of the River to the Brook of Egypt,"* or every corner of the earth, the children of Israel will be gathered to return home.

The extent of the scattering is evident in the phrase *"one by one."* Wherever the Jews have gone, individually or en masse, they are proud to retain their ethnic and spiritual origin. But a greater truth is on the other side of their relationship with God. As a loving father keeps track of a prodigal child who leaves home for distant places, God follows the steps of each of His children and gives His personal attention to bring them home "one by one." Jesus showed us this expression of God's love when He spoke the parables of the Lost Sheep, the Lost Coin, and the Lost Son (Luke 15). The common point of these parables is the persistence of God in searching and waiting for one person who is lost. "One by one" He finds us and brings us home.

GOD WILL FULFILL ISRAEL (27:13)

With the grand finale of a great trumpet, Isaiah closes his Oracles of the Endtime on the note of salvation for those who are *"about to perish in the land of Assyria"* and *"they who are outcasts in the land of Egypt"* (v. 13). To this heart-stopping promise, Isaiah implies a caution. God will not lead the return of His people and promise the restoration of Jerusalem for ethnic, political, economic, or social purposes. Singularly, He says that the goal of all His glorious works is to bring His people home to *"worship the LORD in the holy mount at Jerusalem."* Such worship will then lead to God's ultimate purpose when all nations and all people will stream to Mount Zion saying, "Come, and let us go up to the mountain of the LORD, to the house of the God of

Jacob; He will teach us His ways, and we shall walk in His paths" (2:3). Isaiah has written his own commentary.

NOTES

1. S. Covey, *The Seven Habits of Highly Effective People* (New York: Simon & Schuster, 1989), 33.

2. T. a'Kempis, *The Imitation of Christ* (Chicago; New York: Belford, Clarke, 1887).

CHAPTER THIRTEEN

Oracles of Wisdom—Book I

Isaiah 28:1–29:24

Another book of prophecies is opened as Isaiah narrows his focus in time from the distant to the near future and in space from the corners of the earth to the land of Zion. Even though the book opens with the ominous sound of "woe" and repeats the word at the opening of chapters 29, 30, 31, and 33, the overriding tone of the book is not punishment upon Zion. Rather, filtering through the text and setting the tone is the promise of a glorious future for the people of Zion as they return to the Lord and learn of His ways.

Wisdom is the primary subject of Isaiah's message in chapters 28–33. Underneath the lessons of history is the same insight that guided the writers of the Wisdom Literature, "The fear of the Lord, that is wisdom" (Job 28:28). Other Wisdom writers tend to use proverbs, parables, and poetry to communicate the meaning of this nugget of truth. Isaiah adds a new dimension to the literature by seeing the wisdom learned in the perspective of history. Along with other writers of the Wisdom Literature, his goal is to see the fear of the Lord as the basis for personal righteousness and social justice. Isaiah's model might well have been Job who was "blameless and upright, and one who feared God, and shunned evil" (Job 1:1). But the prophet would also confess that even Job, the wise man, had a lot to learn when wisdom met reality.

Current history comes back into view as Isaiah foresees events in the reign of King Hezekiah (725–697 B.C.). Historians place the events of the prophecy within the time frame of Samaria's fall (722 B.C.) and Hezekiah's continuing temptation to enter into a protective alliance with Egypt against Assyria. Isaiah's warning against such an alliance covered a span of time following Samaria's fall to 701 B.C. when

Sennacherib, King of Assyria, mysteriously pulled his troops from the siege of Jerusalem and returned home in fulfillment of Isaiah's prophecy that an alliance with Egypt was foolish because Assyria would never attack Jerusalem.

Historical records support Isaiah's prophecy, but history is not the primary message. The prophet still has a special message for Zion that he has seen in his vision from the Lord. His tone of speaking and style of writing become more intense as he communicates with his own people. God's word of judgment is more stern and His word of promise is more glorious than ever before. Isaiah's style rises to this challenge as he unleashes his full repertoire of literary devices, especially in rich metaphors, sharp contrasts, witty epigrams, and pointed parables. George Adam Smith, in his commentary on Isaiah in *The Expositor's Bible*, was so impressed by these sections of the book that he called it "one of Isaiah's greatest prophecies . . . distinguished by regal versatility of style."[1] A moving and stretching experience awaits us.

THE STANDARD OF WISDOM (28:1–22)

1 Woe to the crown of pride,
    to the drunkards of Ephraim,
  Whose glorious beauty is a fading flower
  Which is at the head of the verdant valleys,
  To those who are overcome with wine!
2 Behold, the Lord has a mighty and strong one,
  Like a tempest of hail
    and a destroying storm,
  Like a flood of mighty waters
    overflowing,
  Who will bring them down
    to the earth with His hand.
3 The crown of pride, the drunkards of Ephraim,
  Will be trampled under foot;
4 And the glorious beauty is a fading flower
  Which is at the head of the verdant valley,
  Like the first fruit before the summer,
  Which an observer sees;
  He eats it up while it is still in his hand.
5 In that day the LORD of hosts will be

For a crown of glory
  and a diadem of beauty
To the remnant of His people,
6 For a spirit of justice to him
    who sits in judgment,
And for strength to those who turn back the battle at
  the gate.
7 But they also have erred through wine,
And through intoxicating drink are out of the way;
The priest and the prophet have erred through intoxi-
  cating drink,
They are swallowed up by wine,
They are out of the way through intoxicating drink;
They err in vision,
  they stumble in judgment.
8 For all tables are full of vomit
  and filthiness,
So that no place is clean.
9 "Whom will he teach knowledge?
And whom will he make to understand the message?
Those just weaned from milk?
Those just drawn from the breasts?
10 For precept must be upon precept,
  precept upon precept,
Line upon line, line upon line,
Here a little, there a little."
11 For with stammering lips
  and another tongue
He will speak to this people,
12 To whom He said,
  "This is the rest with which
You may cause the weary to rest,"
And, "This is the refreshing";
Yet they would not hear.
13 But the word of the LORD was to them,
  "Precept upon precept,
  precept upon precept,
Line upon line, line upon line,
Here a little, there a little,"
That they might go and fall backward,
  and be broken
And snared and caught.

14 Therefore hear the word of the L<small>ORD</small>,
    you scornful men,
Who rule this people who are in Jerusalem,
15 Because you have said,
    "We have made a covenant with death,
And with Sheol we are in agreement.
When the overflowing scourge passes through,
It will not come to us,
For we have made lies our refuge,
And under falsehood we have hidden ourselves."
16 Therefore thus says the Lord G<small>OD</small>:
"Behold, I lay in Zion a stone for a foundation,
A tried stone, a precious cornerstone, a sure
    foundation;
Whoever believes will not act hastily.
17 Also I will make justice the measuring line,
And righteousness the plummet;
The hail will sweep away
    the refuge of lies,
and the waters will overflow
    the hiding place.
18 Your covenant with death
    will be annulled,
And your agreement with Sheol
    will not stand;
When the overflowing scourge passes through,
Then you will be trampled down by it.
19 As often as it goes out it will take you;
For morning by morning it will pass over,
And by day and by night;
It will be a terror just to understand the report."
20 For the bed is too short for a man to stretch out on,
And the covering so narrow that he cannot wrap
    himself in it.
21 For the L<small>ORD</small> will rise up as at Mount Perazim,
He will be angry as in the Valley of Gibeon—
That He may do His work,
    His awesome work,
And bring to pass His act,
    His unusual act.
22 Now therefore, do not be mockers,
Lest your bonds be made strong;

> For I have heard from the Lord GOD of hosts,
> A destruction determined even upon the whole earth.
>
> *Isaiah 28:1–22*

While Isaiah's lofty style always matched the grandeur of his prophetic theme, he never let his style overrun the meaning of his message. As a preview of chapter 28, we discover that Isaiah is dealing with the eternal questions that have intrigued and confounded religious and secular thinkers in every generation. Those eternal questions are: What is beauty?, What is good?, and What is true? The answers to these questions make up the meaning of wisdom. In their turn, Isaiah infers each question, gives an answer, and sums up his prophecy with a parable of wisdom.

WHAT IS BEAUTY? (28:1–6)

Addressing the Jews in the Northern Kingdom of Israel who are the descendants of Ephraim, Isaiah commands their attention with the words of *"woe"* against the city of Samaria, which wore its reputation for beauty as a *"crown of pride,"* and against the leaders of the nation, who wallowed as drunkards either in the literal wine of alcohol or in the figurative wine of privilege and power (v. 1). Wasting no words, the prophet likens the glorious beauty of their city *"at the head of the verdant valleys"* to a *"fading flower"* and infers that the garland of flowers worn at orgies by reveling leaders was dying on their heads.

Drunkenness, whether from alcohol or pride, is a sin that comes under severe judgment from God. To his pronouncement of *"woe"* Isaiah sounds another note of alarm when he calls out *"behold"* and announces the judgment of God upon the city of Samaria. Likening the punishment to a *"tempest of hail"* followed by a *"destroying storm"* and capped by a *"flood of mighty waters,"* Isaiah employs the triple threat of destruction from three forces of nature to prophesy the complete downfall of Samaria.

History tells us that the prophesy came true in 724 B.C. when Shalmaneser laid siege to Samaria for three years until the city fell in 721 B.C. Resorting to every tactic of siege, Shalmaneser subjected the city and its citizens to all of the terrors implied in Isaiah's prophecy of hail, storm, and flood. The city was *"trampled under foot"* because the moral breakdown of its drunken leadership had produced a vacuum of vision and direction. Likened to a choice olive that ripens early in the season, Samaria was a city ready for the picking by the Assyrian army.

Neither cities nor civilizations die from external conquest without moral breakdown within the culture and among its leadership. Rome, for example, fell when the drunken orgies of mad emperors undermined the moral code and the legal system that had served as foundations for the empire. Alcohol and anarchy go hand in hand when the leaders lose their moral bearings, sense of direction, and perspective for wise decisions. In reading the moral quality of a culture, the questions are asked, "At what do we laugh?" "At what do we weep?" and "What do we reward?" The answers to these questions are all distorted by drunkenness. Under the influence of alcohol, a person laughs at things that are not funny, weeps over things that are not important, and rewards things that are usually punished. If this moral distortion is elevated to leadership decisions involving the destiny of a nation or a civilization, the garland of past glory will quickly become a fading flower.

True beauty is found in the LORD of hosts who will be recognized *"in that day"* as a *"crown of glory and a diadem of beauty to the remnant of His people"* (v. 5). Quite in contrast to the garland of fading flowers, the crown of glory and diadem of beauty worn by the Lord is imperishable and serves to empower human leaders to make decisions in the spirit of justice and find strength to turn back enemy forces before they can mount their attack. Isaiah's oft-spoken message is heard once again with the nuance of new truth—to trust in the Lord is the basis for beauty.

WHAT IS GOOD? (28:7–15)

Isaiah has already scored the leaders of Ephraim for their malfeasance in office due to drink-induced errors in decision-making and direction-setting. His harshest words, however, are reserved for the priests and prophets who have become equally stupefied by alcohol so that their faulty wisdom and counsel contributes equally to the leaders' sins. Every culture counts upon its priests and prophets for *"vision"* and *"judgment"* as the lodestar for steering a true course. Even more fundamental than the decision-making and the direction-setting role of leaders who are responsible for governance, the priests who set the moral tone and prophets who see the meaningful future must be true to their sacred calling. But if they too are *"swallowed up by wine"* and *"out of the way through intoxicating drink"*—whether it is alcohol or power—they will *"err in vision"* and *"stumble in judgment"* (v. 7b).

The picture gets worse when Isaiah tells us that *"all tables are full of vomit and filthiness, so that no place is clean."* He must mean the sacred tables in the sanctuary where sacrifices are offered and communion is taken. Like the priests and prophets who were expected to be pure even if all other leaders around them were polluted, the tables of the sanctuary were expected to be clean in honor of the Holy One of Israel. To imagine drunken priests vomiting on those tables during the ritual of worship means that the culture is polluted to the core.

Another severe indictment falls from Isaiah's lips when he asks those who are supposed to be holy and wise, *"Whom will he teach knowledge? And whom will he make to understand the message?"* (v. 9a). Deliberately using hyperbole to make a point, Isaiah answers his own questions by other questions, *"Those just weaned from milk? Those just drawn from the breasts?"* (v. 9b). What more scathing condemnation could be leveled against those who are responsible for holy living and wise counsel? Isaiah's message is so simple and clear that even the smallest of infants can understand its meaning. Perhaps as a taunt, he twists the blade that he has driven into the hearts of the priests and prophets by reciting a nursery rhyme. You can almost hear little children chanting as they skip along,

> *Precept must be upon precept*
> *Precept upon precept,*
> *Line upon line,*
> *Line upon line,*
> *Here a little,*
> *There a little.*
>
> *Isaiah 28:10*

Still the spiritual leaders of Ephraim will not hear. God's only alternative is to speak with *"stammering lips and another tongue,"* namely, the military language of Assyrian hordes. Both words and deeds have a language of their own. Through His words God offered Ephraim rest and refreshment from external assault, but because *"they would not hear"* the clear and simple truth, He will now speak through the atrocious deeds of a foreign army. Ephraim prefers the whip to words as its instrument of learning.

As impossible as it seems, the worst gets worse. The political and spiritual leaders of Ephraim responded to the Word of the Lord through His prophet with bitter scorn. With a perversity that smacks of a Faustian drama in which they sell their soul to the devil, the leaders boast, *"We have made a covenant with death, and with Sheol we are in agreement"* (v. 15). In league with the devil! Scoffing at God's covenant of life with His children, they brag about a "covenant with death." Cynically defying God's promise to them for rest and refreshment in His will, they flaunt their agreement with hell.

The path from drunkenness to damnation has bottomed out. Mimicking the words of Isaiah, the leaders of Ephraim foolishly claim to be safe from the *"overflowing scourge"* of the Assyrian whip in the refuge of their lies and in the hiding place of their falsehood. One would expect God's wrath to strike like a bolt of lightning upon such mockery. But no, God has made His point. In clear and simple language that even children can understand, God has shown that His will and His way are good. The truth needs no defense. Scornful leaders, even priests and prophets, have made fools of themselves.

Deeper sadness comes through Isaiah's denunciation of leaders when he includes the rulers of Jerusalem among the scornful rulers who have made a covenant with death and an agreement with hell (v. 15). Sharing the deceit, lies, and falsehood with their drunken compatriots in Ephraim, they stand equally condemned.

WHAT IS TRUE? (28:16–22)

Against the background of blasphemy by drunken and cynical leaders in Ephraim and Jerusalem, Isaiah raises one of God's monumental promises for the glory of Zion. Beginning with the clarion call of *"Behold"* to His children, He announces the laying of a stone as the foundation upon which Zion will be built. The qualities of the stone will stand in sharpest contrast to the lies and falsehood the leaders of Ephraim and Jerusalem hid behind for refuge. First, it will be *"a tried stone"* or a stone of testing hewn so true that other stones can be measured against it. Second, it will be a *"precious cornerstone"* against which all other stones can be laid to assure a completed structure that is true in height, breadth, and depth. Third, it is a *"sure foundation"* or a solid rock that will not crumble under internal weight or external pressure.

As late as the 1960s, the height of buildings in Seattle, Washington was restricted because of fear of earthquakes. Engineers then invented a system of vertical poles and cross beams that would withstand the shock of high magnitude earthquakes. Almost overnight, the skyline of Seattle changed. Smith Tower, long a landmark of thirty-six stories, soon became dwarfed by scores of new buildings that scraped the sky at fifty, sixty, and seventy stories or more. The foundation made the difference. Like the cornerstone that the Lord God laid in Zion, the strength of the building and the trueness of its structure depends upon the starting point.

An architectural analogy continues as God says that He will make *"justice"* the measuring line and *"righteousness"* the plummet (v. 17). When applied to the *"refuge of lies"* and *"hiding place"* concocted by the leaders of Ephraim and Jerusalem, the hail and the flood will sweep away and overflow their false security. By the same measuring line of justice and plummet of righteousness, their covenant with death will be *"annulled,"* and their agreement with hell will not stand under the lashing of the *"overflowing scourge"* or Assyrian whip (v. 18). Nor will their cynicism be any protection for them. Shivers of terror will chill their souls just at the report of the wrath to come (v. 19).

Shortsightedness is a special sin of the drunken leaders of Ephraim and Jerusalem. A short bed and narrow sheet convey the inadequacy of their policies and decisions for the long-term protection of the people. Referring back to King David's defeat of the Philistines at Mount Perazim and to Joshua's victory in the Valley of Gibeon, the prophet reminds them that when God takes the field in battle against falsehood, He is the victor. Only the longsighted view of the truth will save them.

The federal deficit in the United States is a classic example of the same shortsightedness. Politicians continue to add billions of dollars of debt to the deficit each year and citizens take a live-now-pay-later attitude toward their share of the responsibility. Anyone who sounds the warning that we are mortgaging the future of our children is subjected to the kind of scorn that Isaiah received from the rulers of

Ephraim and Jerusalem. Economically, at least, we have "made lies our refuge and under falsehood we have hidden ourselves" (v. 15).

Isaiah's warning against mockery is sobering. Those who mock, he says, will only make their bonds stronger. Mockery is a form of ridicule that irretrievably alienates people. Furthermore, once a person resorts to mockery, the scorn must be escalated with each encounter in order to be effective. So, those who mock God alienate themselves from Him and find themselves making more and more radical statements from which they cannot retreat. Mockery, then, joins lies and falsehood as a futile defense against the measuring line of justice and the plummet of righteousness. Worse yet, those who mock, lie, and deceive themselves are building a structure "out of true" and therefore are destined to crumble from the inside if not from external attack. Against the foundation stone that God had laid in Zion, they failed the test of truth.

THE PARABLE OF WISDOM (28:23–29:24)

23 Give ear and hear my voice,
   Listen and hear my speech.
24 Does the plowman keep plowing all day to sow?
   Does he keep turning his soil
      and breaking the clods?
25 When he has leveled its surface,
   Does he not sow the black cumin
   And scatter the cumin,
   Plant the wheat in rows,
   The barley in the appointed place,
   And the spelt in its place?
26 For He instructs him in right judgment,
   His God teaches him.
27 For the black cumin is not threshed with a threshing
      sledge,
   Nor is a cartwheel rolled over the cumin;
   But the black cumin is beaten out with a stick,
   And the cumin with a rod.
28 Bread flour must be ground;
   Therefore he does not thresh it forever,
   Break it with his cartwheel,
   Or crush it with his horsemen.

29 This also comes from the LORD of hosts,
Who is wonderful in counsel
and excellent in guidance.

1 "Woe to Ariel, to Ariel,
    the city where David dwelt!
Add year to year;
Let feasts come around.

2 Yet I will distress Ariel;
There shall be heaviness and sorrow,
And it shall be to Me as Ariel.

3 I will encamp against you all around,
I will lay siege against you with a mound,
And I will raise siegeworks against you.

4 You shall be brought down,
You shall speak out of the ground;
Your speech shall be low,
    out of the dust;
Your voice shall be like a medium's,
    out of the ground;
And your speech shall whisper
    out of the dust.

5 "Moreover the multitude of your foes
Shall be like fine dust,
and the multitude of the terrible ones
Shall be as chaff that passes away;
Yes, it shall be in an instant, suddenly.

6 You will be punished by the LORD of hosts
With thunder and earthquake
    and great noise,
With storm and tempest
And the flame of devouring fire.

7 The multitude of all the nations
    who fight against Ariel,
Even all who fight against her
    and her fortress,
And distress her,
Shall be as a dream of a night vision.

8 It shall even be as when a hungry man
    dreams,
And look—he eats;
But he awakes,
    and his soul is still empty;

276

Or as when a thirsty man dreams,
And look—he drinks;
But he awakes, and indeed he is faint,
And his soul still craves:
So the multitude of all the nations shall be,
Who fight against Mount Zion."
9 Pause and wonder!
Blind yourselves and be blind!
They are drunk, but not with wine;
They stagger, but not with intoxicating drink.
10 For the LORD has poured out on you
The spirit of deep sleep,
And has closed your eyes,
namely, the prophets;
And He has covered your heads,
namely, the seers.

11 The whole vision has become to you like the words of a book that is sealed, which men deliver to one who is literate, saying, "Read this, please"; and he says, "I cannot, for it is sealed."
12 Then the book is delivered to one who is illiterate, saying, "Read this, please"; and he says, "I am not literate."
13 Therefore the LORD said:

"Inasmuch as these people draw near to Me with their
mouths
And honor Me with their lips,
But have removed their hearts far from Me,
And their fear toward me is taught by
the commandment of men,
14 Therefore, behold, I will again do a marvelous work
Among this people,
A marvelous work and a wonder;
For the wisdom of their wise men shall perish,
And the understanding of their prudent men shall be
hidden."
15 Woe to those who seek deep to hide
their counsel far from the LORD,
And their works are in the dark;
They say, "Who sees us?"
and, "Who knows us?"

16 Surely you have things turned around!
    Shall the potter be esteemed as the clay;
    For shall the thing made say of him who made it,
    "He did not make me"?
    Or shall the thing formed say of him who formed it,
    "He has no understanding"?
17 Is it not yet a very little while
    Till Lebanon shall be turned into a fruitful field,
    And the fruitful field be esteemed as a forest?
18 In that day the deaf shall hear the words of the book,
    and the eyes of the blind shall see out
    of obscurity and out of darkness.
19 The humble also shall increase their joy in the LORD,
    And the poor among men shall rejoice
    In the Holy One of Israel.
20 For the terrible one is brought to nothing,
    The scornful one is consumed,
    And all who watch for iniquity are cut off—
21 Who make a man an offender by a word,
    And lay a snare for him who reproves in the gate,
    and turn aside the just for a thing of naught.

22 Therefore thus says the LORD, who redeemed
Abraham, concerning the house of Jacob:

    "Jacob shall not now be ashamed,
    Nor shall his face now grow pale;
23 But when he sees his children,
    The work of My hands, in his midst,
    They will hallow My name,
    And hallow the Holy One of Jacob,
    And fear the God of Israel.
24 These also who erred in spirit
        will come to understanding,
    And those who murmured
        will learn doctrine."

                                Isaiah 28:23–29:24

THE WAY OF WISDOM (28:23–29)

To summarize his comparison between the leadership of God and
the rulers of Ephraim and Jerusalem, Isaiah tells the Parable of the

Wise Plowman. A series of rhetorical questions provide the setting for the lesson God wants to teach. *"Does the plowman keep plowing all day to sow?"* (v. 24). Obviously not. Common sense says that the farmer who always plows and never sows is unwise. *"Does he keep turning his soil and breaking the clods?"* Obviously not. Common sense says that a smooth but unseeded field will never produce a crop. "Does he not sow, scatter, or plant according to the nature of the crop?" Obviously, yes. Common sense says that black cumin is sown, cumin is scattered, wheat is planted in rows, barley in plots, and spelt around the edges. Every peasant farmer knows and obeys these principles of *"right judgment"* that God has given as His instruction and teaching. To know *when* to plow, harrow, and sow, *what* to sow, and *how* to sow are fundamentals not just for peasant farmers, but for God Himself.

Speakers of parables usually do not take the time to explain the meaning of their story. Jesus, for instance, let those who had "ears to hear and eyes to see" understand the meaning of His parables. At the same time, He took His disciples aside and explained to them in detail the meaning of His teaching. God shows similar patience with the leaders of Ephraim and Jerusalem. Despite their scorn for His Word, they are still His children. "Precept upon precept, line upon line, and here a little, there a little," the parable is explained.

God is the plowman who not only knows when, what, and how to plow, harrow, and sow, He also knows how to thresh according to the nature of the crop. The instrument of threshing varies from beating with a stick, grinding in a mill, and dividing with a blade, to rolling under a cartwheel. Even then, there is timing for the threshing so that the value of the seed or grain is not lost. Of course, God is referring to the differential nature and limits of time for His punishment of sin in Israel and among the nations of the world. For those in Israel who have questioned whether or not God has punished them with the same severity as pagan nations, He has already assured them that His moderated punishment is still "double for all her sins" (40:2).

But the parable makes another point. The children of Israel are assured that God knows what He is doing. In contrast with the drunken leaders of Ephraim and Jerusalem who have erred in judgment and misguided the people (28:7), the LORD of hosts is *"wonderful in counsel and excellent in guidance"* (v. 29). Not only does He have a clear and bright vision of the future, but He is the sure and safe guide into that future. On the cornerstone of the beautiful, good, and true foundation that He will lay in Zion, God lets His children know that He can be trusted.

THE WOE OF WISDOM (29:1–8)

Having addressed the issue of the drunken leaders of Samaria, capital of the Northern Kingdom, Isaiah turns his attention to Jerusalem, capital of the Southern Kingdom, where its leaders also erred in their judgment and led the people astray with lies and falsehood (28:15). More than one story can be traced through the prophecy. The historical story line revolves around the Assyrian threat to Jerusalem in 701 B.C.; the moral story line involves the failure to trust in God for deliverance; and the spiritual story line condemns the prophets and seers who are deaf to the Word and blind to the vision of God for His people.

Wisdom, then, is still the primary subject of Isaiah. The intoxicated leaders of Jerusalem share the guilt with the drunken leaders of Samaria. They do not fear the Lord and they do not want to understand His Word or learn of His ways so that they might be wise in judgment and excellent in counsel. Their situation in Jerusalem may be different, but their sin is the same. They hide behind lies and resort to falsehood as a defense against the truth. God's punishment is inevitable, but His promise is still good. In that day, wisdom will be recovered and will rule the house of Jacob.

As a loyal citizen of Jerusalem, Isaiah shared the notion that the Holy City was an impregnable fortress and an inviolable sanctuary under the protection of God. Something of a cultic character had developed around this notion. As the city where King David dwelt, the inhabitants were convinced that God would never allow a pagan enemy to be its conqueror. Moreover, as the city where the holy temple was located and the Lord God was honored in the cycle of feasts throughout the year, the inhabitants believed that the hedge of their spiritual heritage would never be breached. So, secure within the cult of David's personality, Jerusalem's festive air of confidence kept the city from facing the reality of intoxicating pride among its leaders who scoffed at God's warning of impending judgment.

"Woe to Ariel" is a warning appropriate for the seriousness of the situation. Whenever Isaiah begins an oracle with the lament of "woe," he is sending out a distress signal not unlike the S.O.S. that is sent from sinking ships. "Ariel" adds a special symbol to the call of distress. As a code name for Jerusalem, it means either "altar hearth" or "lion of God." If "altar hearth" is the meaning, Isaiah is foreseeing the city becoming the altar of sacrifice to the Assyrian hordes; if the meaning is "lion of God," he is refuting the cultic notion that Jerusalem is so strong it can sin without punishment.

As the oracle advances, the meaning of Ariel as altar hearth comes to the forefront. God Himself will use the Assyrians to put the Holy City under siege and raise the most sophisticated towers of siege against the city (v. 3). Jerusalem's heady confidence will fall as the voice of the city is heard *"out of the dust"* from *"out of the ground"* (v. 4). A military siege of ancient times has that effect upon the survivors of the besieged city. A voice "out of the dust" symbolizes the mournful sound of death within the city and "out of the ground" signifies the muffled sound of those who are cowering in trenches and catacombs waiting for the next salvo of siege.

God is full of surprises. *"In an instant, suddenly,"* He turns from punishing Jerusalem to blowing away her enemies like *"fine dust"* and windblown *"chaff"* (v. 5). What has happened? In the mystery of His sovereign will, God has reversed all systems to punish the enemies of Jerusalem whom He had called to its gates. Is the city inviolable or has His lesson been taught? Not even history gives us a clear answer. We do know that Sennacherib encamped around the city in 704 B.C. and laid siege to it for three years while testing the most advanced siegeworks as Isaiah had predicted. We also see that strange circumstances, as unfathomable as a plague of mice eating the bowstrings of Sennacherib's archers, caused him to withdraw his forces and return home never to mount a serious threat against Jerusalem again. Not that the Holy City was inviolable, for in 586 B.C. Jerusalem fell under the onslaught of the Babylonian army. The answer must be that for the sake of God's timing and teaching, the fall of Jerusalem in 701 B.C. was not within His long-term plan for the redemption of His children.

Natural phenomena of thunder, earthquake, great noise, storm, tempest, and devouring fire (v. 6) explain what happened to the Assyrian army that laid siege to Jerusalem. Whether these threats of nature are real or representative expressions of God's judgment, the result is the same. The Assyrians felt the frustration of a person awakening from a dream in which he or she has eaten heavily and drunk fully. But upon awakening, the stomach is empty and the thirst is maddening (v. 8). An earlier analogy also fits Isaiah's description of Assyria's frustration. Jerusalem is likened to the first and sweetest fruits of an olive tree, ripe for picking. But as the hand reaches for the succulent morsel, it is gripped by paralysis and withdraws in empty-handed frustration. *"So the multitude of all the nations shall be, who fight against Mount Zion"* (v. 8).

The Word of Wisdom (29:9–16)

Despite God's miraculous intervention on behalf of Jerusalem, the city must still be punished for the practiced resistance of its leaders against the Word of God. Calling them to *"pause and wonder"* or stop and think, Isaiah cites reason after reason why the leaders are deaf and blind to the truth.

Self-Induced Blindness (29:9a)

"Blind yourselves and be blind" states the fact that we can become blind to the truth by choice of habit. Continuous rejection of the Word of God can cause a blindness that is more than a periodic defense. Spiritual blindness can become a way of life and the nature of being. Jesus may have had this fact in mind when He said, "But if your eye is bad, your whole body will be full of darkness. If therefore the light within you is darkness, how great is that darkness!" (Matthew 6:23). John added to this warning in his epistle when he wrote, "If we say that we have fellowship with Him, and walk in darkness, we lie and do not practice the truth" (1 John 1:6).

Psychology also confirms these warnings. If a person persists in a habit over a long period of time, the habit can become a drive in itself. Addictions are explained this way. Alcoholism begins as a habit in which the person persists until the need for a drink becomes a driving force that dominates the person. An addiction has a 3-D description—dependence, denial, and disability. An alcoholic, for instance, is dependent upon alcohol, denies the problem, and suffers disability in functioning with regard to job, relationships, and family.

As the drunken leaders of Ephraim and Jerusalem were described, they too were victims of self-induced spiritual blindness (28:7–15). Having rejected the truth time and time again, they became dependent upon rejection as evidenced by their scoffing at the Word of God. Otherwise, just one ray of acknowledged truth would have toppled all of the defenses against truth that they had built. Naturally, they would deny that they were wrong by hiding behind the self-deceit of lies and falsehood. The end result was disability as leaders of the people, erring in judgment and misleading the people. Sir Walter Scott described them well when he wrote, "O what a tangled web we weave, when first we practice to deceive."[2]

God-Induced Stupor (29:9b)

Prophets and seers are persons called of God who are endowed with the special gift of seeing His vision and entrusted with the responsibility to speak His truth. If these same prophets and seers become part of the company of drunken leaders in Ephraim and Jerusalem who resort to scoffing, lies, and falsehoods, God does not wait for the consequences of self-induced blindness. According to Isaiah, He pours upon their spirits a deep sleep so that their eyes are closed to the truth and their heads are covered against the truth (v. 10).

Every person who is called of God to see and speak His truth should pay heed. The same Spirit of God that awakens us to His Word can blind us to His Word if we betray our trust. Nothing is more tragic than a prophet or seer who continues to speak out of blindness. The personal penalty is minimal in comparison to the consequences suffered by the people who count upon the prophet and seer to lead them. Isaiah says, "The whole vision has become to you like the words of a book that is sealed" (v. 11). When the people plead, "Read this, please" and the prophet or seer answers, "I cannot, for it is sealed," they turn in desperation to their own ranks with the same plea and get the pitiful answer, "I am not literate" (vv. 11–12). If the prophet or seer who is expected to be literate in the Word of God cannot read it, who can? Tragedy stalks the society where divine truth is sealed against its prophets and seers and where the masses are illiterate to that truth.

As incredible as it may seem, Western culture is perilously close to spiritual illiteracy among the masses of the people. Andrew Greeley, in the book *Religion In America*, reports on a survey of religious attitudes among young adults coming into their forties in the last decade of the twentieth century. To paraphrase his findings, Greeley reports that this is the first generation in American history to come into adulthood and the child-rearing years without a word of Scripture in their minds, a verse of a hymn in their hearts, and a memory of prayer in their homes.[3] If Greeley is right, it means that the spiritual destiny of our society depends almost exclusively upon our prophets and seers for seeing God's vision, hearing God's Word, and speaking God's truth. Awesome responsibility rests upon our biblical scholars, religion professors, preaching pastors, and teaching ministers for interpreting, communicating, and modelling God's Word in the years ahead.

Religiously-Induced Blindness (29:10a)

When blind prophets and seers go through the ritualistic motions of mouthing God's word and giving lip service to His Name, God will bypass them for the sake of His people. Severe indictments are directed against the prophets and seers who teach the people to speak the language of worship and control the people by commandments of fear. Pretending to be wise, their wisdom will perish and, posing as prudent, their understanding will be hidden (v. 14b). But for the people whom they have deluded, God has a note of exuberant promise. He announces, *"Behold, I will again do a marvelous work among this people, a marvelous work and a wonder"* (v. 14a). Just when it appears as if the gloom of spiritual darkness will overcome the nation because of the hypocrisy of its spiritual leaders, God has a surprise in store. Through the coming of the Messiah, He will show them wisdom and give them understanding.

The prophets and seers who forfeited their gifts and betrayed their trust in Isaiah's time are the forefathers of the Pharisees in Jesus' time who mouthed their spirituality, offered lip service to the Lord in ritualistic worship, and dominated the people by regulations based upon fear. We must not forget that these prophets and seers became the archenemies of Jesus, plotted His death, and gloated at His crucifixion. Religiously-induced blindness is the darkest of all. Atrocities blight the history of the Church when blinded leaders provoke illiterate people into horrendous acts in the name of God.

Ego-Induced Blindness (29:10b–16)

Perpetrators of lies and masters of trickery must develop defenses for their sins to avoid detection. No device is more often used than the classic "cover-up." Behind closed doors in the dark of night, they plot their strategy for manipulation and their tactics for concealment while gloating, *"Who sees us?"* and *"Who knows us?"*

The Watergate scandal that brought down President Richard Nixon immediately comes to mind. Behind closed doors, and probably under the cover of darkness, a politically-motivated scheme of dirty tricks was concocted to gather damaging evidence against the Democratic Party. The arrogance of political power assured the perpetrators that they would never be discovered. But when the Watergate break-in was botched, all of the tactics for damage control went into operation. As the scandal spread and the denials mounted, the President himself became involved when he protested to the American people, "Your President is no crook." The same subterfuge, however, brought him down when one knowledgeable member code-named "Deep Throat" leaked the truth to the reporter Robert Woodward who then published his story in the Washington Post. Richard Nixon, who assumed that he was untouchable in the office of the President, resigned in shame.

Prophets and seers who snicker, "Who sees us?" and "Who knows us?" as they try to conceal their lying and cheating behind closed doors and under the cover of darkness are guilty of more than the dirty tricks of politics. According to Isaiah, they are denying the role of God as their creator and defying His understanding of what is best for them. *"Surely you have turned things around"* is Isaiah's gentle way of condemning the ego-induced twist that caused their blindness. Whether they knew it or not, spiritual leaders who assumed that they could hide their sins from God also had to play God and tell Him what to do in order to justify their false counsel and evil deeds. When Jesus encountered such deception, He spoke candidly, "This is the condemnation, that the light has come into the world, and men loved darkness rather than light because their deeds were evil" (John 3:19). Isaiah goes a step farther. Those who love darkness do more than cover their sins. They become practical atheists by twisting the roles of the potter and the clay. Only spiritual blindness caused by an exaggerated ego dares to fling out the challenge against God, *"He did not make me"* and *"He has no understanding"* (v. 16).

THE RESTORATION OF WISDOM (29:17–21)

God's redemptive purpose for Israel includes more than the return of the remnant from exile and the restoration of Jerusalem as the seat of Mount Zion. *"In that day"* He will also restore the sight of those who have been deaf to His Word and blind to His vision for Israel and the world. A logical progression leads to the restoration of wisdom among His people. First, *"the deaf shall hear the words of the book, and the eyes of the blind shall see out of obscurity and out of darkness"* (v. 18). More than the recovery of physical hearing and eyesight is implied in this promise. Prophets and seers, those who are expected to be literate in His word and insightful of His vision, will have their gifts restored and their calling renewed.

Second, as a consequence of their restoration, *"the humble also shall increase their joy in the LORD, and the poor among men shall rejoice in the Holy One of Israel"* (v. 19). As noted earlier, when leaders sin, the people suffer. Conversely, when leaders are restored to their trust, the people are renewed in spirit. The equation is fundamental to our homes, our churches, our communities, and our civilization. As the leaders go, the people go. And the cycle keeps turning. When the people are blind because of blind leaders, they get the leaders they deserve and *"both fall into the ditch"* (Luke 6:39).

Third, when the *"terrible one"* or Satan is brought down in that day, leaders who scorn God's Word and *"watch for [the opportunities of] iniquity"* will be *"consumed"* and *"cut off"* (v. 20). Alexander makes the observation that whenever truth is proclaimed, these three classes of opposition arise: (a) those who do violent wrong; (b) those who show contempt for the truth; and (c) those who are constantly looking for the opportunity to do evil.[4] Special cases are cited as evidence of the intentionality of those who use the legal system as a tool of their iniquity. In one case, they bring false testimony against an innocent person, in another case the snares of legalism are set to entrap an unsuspecting person, and in still another case a filibuster of empty words is used to cancel the cause of justice. All those who exploit these devices to oppress the humble and the poor will be consumed by the seeds of their own destruction or cut off from the source of their power. The restoration of wisdom will assure the cause of social justice *"in that day."*

The Recovery of Righteousness (29:22–24)

Wisdom leads to the recovery of personal righteousness as well as social justice. Isaiah foresees the house of Jacob being transformed by the hearing of His Word and the seeing of His vision. The redemptive revolution is complete. In the place of shame and weakness, the house of Jacob will show the light and the strength of the glory of God. His children, rather than denying their Creator and defying His love, will worship His name, follow after His holiness, and respect His sovereign will. But the transformation depends upon the redemption of those leaders, most likely the prophets and seers, who *"erred in spirit"* and *"murmured"* against the truth. Their redemption will mean that they personally embrace an *"understanding"* of God's Spirit and open themselves to the continuous learning of God's truth. They will then qualify as the models and the mentors of righteousness and justice for the house of Jacob. In their transformed role, the recovery of wisdom will be complete.

NOTES

1. Smith, *Expositor's Bible*, 151.

2. Sit Walter Scott, *Marmion*, Ib. xvii.

3. A. M. Greeley, *Religious Change in America* (Cambridge: Harvard University Press, 1989), 32ff.

4. J. A. Alexander, quoted in E. J. Young, *The New International Commentary on the Old Testament; The Book of Isaiah, Vol. II* (Grand Rapids, Eerdmans, 1969), 328.

CHAPTER FOURTEEN

Oracles of Wisdom—Book II

Isaiah 30:1–32:20

Blind leaders cannot function without blind people. Having analyzed the reasons for blind leaders in chapter 29, pronounced their punishment, and predicted their restoration to righteousness and justice, Isaiah turns the coin to address the children of Israel whose rebellious attitude has encouraged unrighteousness and injustice. The prophet again weaves together the record of history with the message of God. In this instance, history turns around the alliance with Egypt into which Hezekiah considered entering as a protection against Assyria. Isaiah opposed this alliance as trusting in a "paper tiger" that had neither the military power nor the national intent to protect Judah. The prophet also argued that Assyria, nemesis of both Judah and Egypt, be left in the hands of God.

Isaiah's spiritual message, however, supersedes the events of history. "Whom will you trust, God or Egypt?" is the uppermost question in the prophet's mind. Having spoken forcefully to the political and spiritual leaders of the nation, he now addresses the same question to the people.

THE SIGNS OF REBELLION (30:1–11)

1 "Woe to the rebellious children,"
  says the LORD,
   "Who take counsel, but not of Me,
   And who devise plans,
     but not of My Spirit,
   That they may add sin to sin;
2 Who walk to go down to Egypt,

And have not asked My advice,
To strengthen themselves in the strength of Pharaoh,
And to trust in the shadow of Egypt!

3 Therefore the strength of Pharaoh
Shall be your shame,
And trust in the shadow of Egypt
Shall be your humiliation.

4 For his princes were at Zoan,
And his ambassadors came to Hanes.

5 They were all ashamed of a people who could not
    benefit them,
Or be help or benefit,
But a shame and also a reproach."

6 The burden against the beasts of the South.
Through a land of trouble and anguish,
From which came the lioness and lion,
The viper and fiery flying serpent,
They will carry their riches on the
    backs of young donkeys,
and their treasures on the humps of camels,
To a people who shall not benefit them;

7 For the Egyptians shall help in vain
    and to no purpose.
Therefore I have called her
Rahab-Hem-Shebeth.

8 Now go, write it before them on a tablet,
And note it on a scroll,
That it may be for time to come,
Forever and ever:

9 That this is a rebellious people,
Lying children,
Children who will not hear the law of the Lord;

10 Who say to the seers, "Do not see,"
And to the prophets,
"Do not prophesy to us right things;
Speak to us smooth things,
    prophesy deceits.

11 Get out of the way,
Turn aside from the path,
Cause the Holy One of Israel
To cease from before us."

Isaiah 30:1–11

Reaching back to the opening verse of his prophecy, Isaiah pronounces "woe" upon the rebellious children of Judah and Jerusalem. While acknowledging the responsibility of political and spiritual leaders for the direction of the nation, Isaiah does not spare the masses of the people from their share of culpability. To label them as *"rebellious children"* is sufficient to invoke the law of Moses against a rebellious son who will not accept discipline. The penalty is death. Isaiah did not equivocate. His indictment would either strike fear in the hearts of the children of Israel or provoke the anger that would mean his death. His specific charges were even more provocative.

You Scheme in Sin (30:1–5)

Judah had entered into a secret alliance, graphically described by the prophet as weaving a web and toasting a libation of diplomatic relationships that openly defies the counsel and the Spirit of God (v. 1). Consequently, Judah's pride in this alliance only adds sin to the sin of their rebellion. By trusting in the strength of Egypt for their protection and hovering under the shadow of Egypt for their identity, the people of Judah exposed themselves to the coming shame and humiliation of an empire in decline.

Isaiah's word must have come just at the time when Hezekiah's delegation from Judah had reached the Egyptian cities of Zoan and Hanes (v. 4). Bowing before these minor powers and paying tribute to their puppet kings, rather than Pharaoh himself, served as an example of the level to which God's people had stooped.

Sin has a way of compounding itself. Once a person embarks on the path of rebellion against God, one sin adds to another. Cheaters, for instance, must lie to cover their tracks and liars must cheat to avoid detection. King David is an example. After adultery with Bathsheba, he compounded his sin by scheming for the murder of Uzziah, her husband. The rebellious children of Israel did the same thing by adding *"sin to sin"* (v. 1b). Having denied their heritage and rejected the love of God, they wove unholy alliances with a pagan power and toasted the fatal covenant with drunken libation. God disclaimed any part of the process because He knew that Egypt had neither the strength to resist Assyria nor the will to save Israel. Shame rather than salvation would be the outcome (v. 5).

An elaborate description of the negotiating team that Hezekiah sent to Egypt shows how desperate the king had become. To woo Egypt into the protective alliance, he sent his choice princes and senior ambassadors as leaders of the delegation. On the backs of donkeys and camels in the caravan Hezekiah loaded *"riches"* and *"treasures"* from Judah and Jerusalem, a pittance compared to the wealth of Egypt. Worst of all, he gambled the lives of the delegates and the value of the tribute against the hazards of the desert and wilderness of Sinai. In addition to the violent forces of nature that gave the Sinai its reputation as a *"land of trouble and anguish,"* wild animals such as *"the lioness and lion, the viper and fiery flying serpent,"* threatened the safety of the caravan. Edward Young suggests "Here is one of the saddest pictures in all of Scripture" because Hezekiah's party represented a reversal of the Exodus from Egypt.[1] Isaiah is quoting one of the celebrated texts of Israel's history that every child would know as he or she praised the God "who led you through that great and terrible wilderness, in which were fiery serpents and scorpions and thirsty land where there was no water; who brought water for you out of the rock of flint" (Deuteronomy 8:15). So, forgetting God, risking lives, wasting treasures, and flaunting history, Hezekiah chose to put his trust in an empire that Isaiah mocks as *"Rahab-Hem-Shebeth"* (v. 7).

Many meanings are attached to Rahab, the sea monster of ancient lore who is variously identified with chaos, confusion, noise, powerlessness, and immobility. Literally, the name means "Rahab who sits still." Leupold ventures a modern interpretation that sums up several meanings in the phrase, "A Big-Mouth that is a Do-Nothing."[2] The point is that Rahab represents the folly and futility of trusting in Egypt. At the most elemental level of faith, Israel knows that God does what He says He will do.

When the children of Israel refuse to hear Isaiah's word of warning, God instructs him to put his message in writing. The double record on a tablet and scroll will stand as a permanent witness against the people and as a future reference for teaching oncoming generations. Perhaps this is the origin of the Book of Isaiah. His written message has withstood centuries in which writings have been lost, destroyed, revised, and canceled. Yet, when the Dead Sea Scrolls were unearthed at Qumran, Isaiah's writings received confirming evidence of their permanence through the centuries.

God has good reason for instructing Isaiah to write his message on a tablet and in a book. In addition to their rebellion against God's Word, the people have tried to turn the prophet's message into a lie (v. 9). Four demands are made. First, they insist that the seers *"do not see."* In a tacit confession of the truth, they do not want to see God's vision for their life and destiny. Second, the people tell the prophets, *"Do not prophesy to us right things; speak to us smooth things."* Luther translated this verse, "Preach soft." In other words, the people wanted the half truth of God's promise, but not the whole truth that included His judgment. Third, they asked that the prophets deviate from the plumb line of truth with a message that is conditioned by their bias. "Political correctness" is not new to the mind that wants to rewrite the Word of God. Fourth, in order to sustain their lie, the children of Israel demanded that the prophet of God quit walking the streets and appearing in the palace because his presence served as a constant reminder of the Holy One of Israel. What started as a refusal to hear the Word of God has now become a need to eliminate from their sight the convicting presence of the prophet who represents the Holy One of Israel.

Isn't this the final lie that sinners tell themselves? Robert Bellah, in *Habits of the Heart,* says that persons in Western culture whose character is shaped by radical self-interest need therapists to help them feel good about themselves after they have insisted on being what they want to be and doing what they want to do.[3] With all of the emphasis upon therapy in our culture and the church, Isaiah might wonder whether we are trying to escape the conviction and absolve the guilt of deceiving ourselves. Is the therapeutic movement another way of saying, *"Cause the Holy One of Israel to cease from before us"* (v. 11)?

THE PRICE OF REBELLION (30:12–18)

12 Therefore thus says the Holy One of Israel:
      "Because you despise this word,
      And trust in oppression and perversity,

And rely on them,

13 Therefore this iniquity shall be to you
Like a breach ready to fall,
A bulge in a high wall,
Whose breaking comes suddenly,
   in an instant.

14 And He shall break it like the breaking of the potter's
   vessel,
Which is broken in pieces;
He shall not spare.
So there shall not be found among its fragments
A shard to take fire from the hearth,
Or to take water from the cistern."

15 For thus says the Lord GOD, the Holy
One of Israel:
"In returning and rest
   you shall be saved;
In quietness and confidence
   shall be your strength."
But you would not,

16 And you said,
   "No, for we will flee on horses"—
Therefore you shall flee!
And, "We will ride on swift horses"—
Therefore those who pursue you shall be swift!

17 One thousand shall flee at the threat of one,
At the threat of five you shall flee,
Till you are left as a pole on top of a mountain
And as a banner on a hill.

18 Therefore the LORD will wait,
   that He may be gracious to you;
And therefore He will be exalted,
   that He may have mercy on you.
For the LORD is a God of justice;
Blessed are all those who wait for him.

Isaiah 30:12–18

THE PUNISHMENT OF GOD (30:12–17)

A high price must be paid by those who *"despise"* the Word of God and *"trust in oppression and perversity"* (v. 12). Three sins against the

Word of God are listed. One is to *despise* the Word of God, or refuse to hear it. Two is to *oppress* the Word of God when seers do not see the truth. Three is to *pervert* the Word of God by speaking half-truths, pointing in the wrong direction, and stifling the presence of the prophet who symbolizes the Holy One of Israel (v. 12).

For these sins Israel will pay dearly. Isaiah likens the nation to a wall with a flaw running through its structure. Pressure from the weight of the wall will cause the flaw to open into a fissure that runs from top to bottom and results in a bulging of the wall as the weight pushes down on the widening flaw. Soon the wall will collapse under its own weight and be broken into thousands of pieces that are scattered across the floor as when an earthen jar is dropped. What was once a formidable wall is so shattered that no sizable piece can be found for any useful purpose (v. 14b).

Sad words continue as God calls out to the caravan heading for Egypt, *"In returning and rest you shall be saved"* (30:15). Following the analogy of the Exodus, the company must turn around as an act of repentance and follow in the way of the Lord that will lead them back to the *rest* of the promised land. Isaiah is appealing to one of the most significant promises in Israel's history. When the children of Israel started from Egypt for the trek across the treacherous wilderness of Sinai, God promised, "My Presence will go with you, and I will give you rest" (Exodus 33:14). His *rest* stands in contrast with Rahab, the sea monster who "sits still" and is at rest. God's *rest* is the Sabbath peace that follows His creative action; Rahab's *rest* is the paralysis of power that can create nothing good, only chaos. "Return and rest" is the call of God upon every soul and society that is running from His Word.

Israel chose flight on swift horses over *"quietness and confidence"* in the presence of God. Isaiah has already said that they were adding sin to sin. Now, sin multiplies as they rely upon the swift horses of Egypt for their safety. Alas, their flight will be filled with fear as the threat of one or five will put thousands on the run, and only a small remnant will remain like a lonely pole on a mountain or a solitary banner on a hill (v. 17b).

THE PATIENCE OF GOD (30:18)

While Israel is fleeing toward futility, God is waiting to show His grace. How typical of our humanity and His divinity! In the pivotal verse for this chapter, we see the mood swing from sin and judgment to grace and mercy. God's attributes jump out at us from the text. He is patient, gracious, merciful, and just. *"And therefore, He will be exalted."* For those who trust in Him and are willing to wait, God has blessings that cannot be counted. Our problem, of course, is our unwillingness to wait. Like Type A personalities who are driven by the "tyranny of the urgent," we join with the children of Israel in devising our own schemes, controlling our own destiny, and running from reality rather than waiting upon the Lord.

THE PROMISES OF GRACE (30:19–33)

19 For the people shall dwell in Zion at Jerusalem;
    You shall weep no more.
    He will be very gracious to you at the sound of your
       cry;
    When He hears it, He will answer you.
20 And though the Lord gives you
    The bread of adversity
       and the water of affliction,
    Yet your teachers will not be moved
       into a corner anymore,
    But your eyes shall see your teachers.
21 Your ears shall hear a word behind you, saying,
    "This is the way, walk in it,"
    Whenever you turn to the right hand
    Or whenever you turn to the left.
22 You will also defile the covering of your graven images
       of silver,
    And the ornament of your molded images of gold.
    You will throw them away as an unclean thing;
    You will say to them, "Get away!"
23 Then He will give the rain for your seed
    With which you sow the ground,
    And bread of the increase of the earth;
    It will be fat and plenteous.
    In that day your cattle will feed
    In large pastures.
24 Likewise the oxen and the young donkeys that work
       the ground
    Will eat cured fodder,

Which has been winnowed with the shovel and fan.

25 There will be on every high mountain
And on every high hill
Rivers and streams of waters,
In the day of the great slaughter,
When the towers fall.

26 Moreover the light of the moon
  will be as the light of the sun,
And the light of the sun will be sevenfold,
As the light of seven days,
In the day that the LORD binds up the bruise of His
  people
And heals the stroke of their wound.

27 Behold, the name of the LORD comes from afar,
Burning with his anger,
And His burden is heavy;
His lips are full of indignation,
And His tongue like a devouring fire;

28 His breath is like an overflowing stream,
Which reaches up to the neck,
To sift the nations with the sieve of futility;
And there shall be a bridle in the jaws of the
  people,
Causing them to err.

29 You shall have a song
As in the night when a holy festival is kept,
And gladness of heart as when one goes with a
  flute,
To come into the mountain of the LORD,
To the Mighty One of Israel.

30 The LORD will cause His glorious voice to be heard,
and show the descent of His arm,
With the indignation of His anger
And the flame of a devouring fire,
With scattering, tempest,
  and hailstones.

31 For through the voice of the LORD
Assyria will be beaten down,
Who struck with a rod.

32 And in every place where the staff of punishment
  passes,
Which the LORD lays on him,

It will be with tambourines and harps;
And in battles of brandishing He will fight with it.
33 For Tophet was established of old,
Yes, for the king it is prepared.
He has made it deep and large;
Its pyre is fire with much wood;
The breath of the LORD,
    like a stream of brimstone,
Kindles it.

Isaiah 30:19–33

One by one, God's blessings are revealed to the children of Israel. Countering all of the rebellious attitudes of the past, Isaiah envisions the day when the people who "dwell in Zion at Jerusalem" will be transformed by his grace.

YOU WILL WEEP NO MORE (30:19)

Sorrow and mourning are ahead for the house of Jacob as the aftermath of their conquest and exile. They will know moments when their weeping and crying will elicit no response from God. But "in that day" their tears will be wiped away and their cries will be answered by the *"very gracious"* Spirit of God.

YOU WILL LEARN HIS WORD (30:20–21)

After the Children of Israel have eaten the *"bread of adversity"* and drunk the *"water of affliction,"* their blind eyes will be opened to see who their true teachers are and whenever there is a tendency to veer to the right or the left their deaf ears will be unstopped to hear the Spirit whisper, *"This is the way, walk in it"* (v. 21). Isaiah would have rejoiced with Paul's sense of discipline and direction for walking in the way of the Lord: "All Scripture is given by inspiration of God, and is profitable for doctrine, for reproof, for correction, for instruction in righteousness, that the man of God may be complete, thoroughly equipped for every good work" (2 Timothy 3:16–17). The thought of the voice behind us as we walk is particularly encouraging. Like a compass always pointing true north, the Spirit of God is constant in His guidance for the direction we take and the way we walk.

You Will Rebuke Idols (30:22)

Because the children of Israel had been guilty of mixing their obedience to God with sacrifices to idols, their worship needed to be
purified. Isaiah links learning of the Word of God with throwing
away idols. Like two stars in the galaxy on a collision course, either
the worship of God or the worship of idols must go. God is not unfair. When He commanded, "You shall have no other gods before
Me," He set down the ground rules for His worship. Anything less
than full trust in the sovereign Lord is a form of blasphemy against
His nature. He is not jealous because of competing gods as much as
He is frustrated in the accomplishment of His redemptive purpose.
Unless divergent parties of different faiths agree on this primary
principle of the Word concerning Christ, all attempts to short-circuit
the redemptive process will encounter resistance from God Himself.
As Jesus said, "Get behind Me, Satan," we must say to our idols, "Get
away" and worship them no more.

You Will be Healed (30:23–26)

Healing comes with obedience to His instruction and the elimina-
tion of idols. The land itself will be healed. God will give rain in the
land of drought for sowing the seed and reaping the harvest. Large
green pastures will provide grazing land for herds of cattle and provide choice fodder for the oxen and young donkeys that *work the
ground*" (v. 24). Mountain streams will flow again and empty into rivers of life-giving water. And the moon and sun, whose light has been
darkened by judgment, will shine with greater splendor than ever before. Rain, food, water, and light are the fundamental elements
needed for binding up the bruises and healing the cuts that God's
people have suffered in punishment for their sins. Virtue and well-
being go hand in hand with God's promise.

You Will See God Act (30:27–28)

At the same time the children of Israel are being healed, God will
bring the full force of His anger upon Assyria, the archenemy of
Judah. Burning anger, a heavy burden, indignant lips, a tongue of devouring fire, and breath like an overflowing stream bespeak the

wrath of God that will sift the nations like a sieve and put a bridle in the jaws of people (v. 28). Isaiah leaves no doubt about God's moderation in the punishment of Judah and Jerusalem. Yes, they will be conquered and exiled as punishment for their sins, but the return of a remnant and the restoration of Jerusalem is a promise of grace that God has reserved for His children. As for Assyria, it will be shaken like flour in a *"sieve of futility"* and left desolate among the nations of the world.

You Will Sing a Song (30:29–33)

Assyria's defeat will bring a song to the lips of the children of Israel. They are not gloating over their enemy's downfall but praising God for His deliverance. With each downward stroke from the arm of the Lord, Assyria will be *"beaten down"* and Israel will celebrate with the *"gladness of heart"* that goes along with the sound of a flute exalting the Lord and leading a processional into the temple on Mount Zion (v. 29b). The final verse will be sung when Assyria's funeral pyre is lighted in Tophet, the place of burning outside the walls of Jerusalem that symbolizes the pit of hell for the wicked. The breath of God's brimstone anger will kindle the fuel of *"much wood"* that has been building with each act of arrogance on the part of Assyria and its kings. With the burning, the children of Israel will come full cycle from rebellion to redemption.

The Wisdom of God (31:1–9)

1 Woe to those who go down to Egypt for help,
   And rely on horses,
   Who trust in chariots
      because they are many,
   And in horsemen
      because they are very strong,
   But who do not look to the Holy One of Israel,
   Nor seek the LORD!
2 Yet He also is wise
      and will bring disaster,
   And will not call back His words,
   But will arise against the house of evildoers,

And against the help of those who work iniquity.
3 Now the Egyptians are men,
    and not God;
And their horses are flesh,
    and not spirit.
When the LORD stretches out His hand,
Both he who helps will fall,
And he who is helped will fall down;
They all will perish together.
4 For thus the LORD has spoken to me:
"As a lion roars,
And a young lion over his prey
(When a multitude of shepherds is summoned against
    him,
He will not be afraid of their voice
Nor be disturbed by their noise),
So the LORD of hosts will come down
To fight for Mount Zion and for its hill.
5 Like birds flying about,
So will the LORD of hosts defend Jerusalem.
Defending, He will also deliver it;
Passing over, He will preserve it."
6 Return to Him against whom the children of Israel
    have deeply revolted.
7 For in that day every man shall throw away his idols of
    silver and his idols of
gold—sin, which your own hands have made for
    yourselves.
8 "Then Assyria shall fall
    by a sword not of man,
And a sword not of mankind shall devour him.
But he shall flee from the sword,
And his young men shall become forced labor.
9 He shall cross over to his stronghold for fear,
And his princes shall be afraid of the banner,"
Says the LORD,
Whose fire is in Zion
And whose furnace is in Jerusalem.

Isaiah 31:1–9

At first reading, it appears as if Isaiah is repeating himself. With slight variation, chapter 31 addresses the same subject as chapter 32:

Judah's folly in going down to Egypt for help against the Assyrians. Scholars cannot agree on the interpretation of chapter 31 and Martin Luther concluded that Isaiah's prophetic warning against the Egyptian alliance had now become boring. It is true that the new historical insights seem limited to the introduction of Judah's reliance upon Egyptian horses and chariots, superior weapons of war that the smaller and weaker nations lacked. But if Isaiah is using this fact of history to support another lesson in the meaning of wisdom, the oracle opens up with new spiritual insights that intrigue and mystify us at the same time.

THE FOOLISHNESS OF HUMAN WISDOM (31:1)

From a human standpoint, Hezekiah's decision to send a delegation down to Egypt to get help against Assyria appears to be wise. Egypt and Assyria were the superpowers of the ancient East. As nuclear weapons created the superpowers of the United States and the Soviet Union during the Cold War in our day, so horses and chariots made Egypt and Assyria the superpowers of their day. Judah had neither the size nor wealth to equip its army with horses and chariots. Ironically, Judah's location in the hills and mountains nullified the threat of invasion by troops mounted on horses and riding in chariots. The battle between Egypt and Assyria would be fought elsewhere, but if Egypt lost, Hezekiah feared an attack against Jerusalem by the Assyrian infantry. In fear of such an attack, Hezekiah sought an alliance with Egypt.

On the surface, Hezekiah's tactic looks wise. Why not protect your pawns in the deadly chess game of the Middle East? Isaiah's answer is pointed. Hezekiah did not *"look to the Holy One of Israel, nor seek the LORD!"* (v. 1b). Instead, he put his trust in the Egyptians and their horses without consulting God. Each of us can identify with Hezekiah. When we submit to our fears and refuse to trust God, we studiously avoid His counsel.

THE SUPERIORITY OF DIVINE WISDOM (31:2–3)

Isaiah counters the alleged human wisdom of Hezekiah by saying of God, *"Yet, He also is wise."* Always before in Scripture, wisdom is identified as a human virtue given by God. So for Isaiah to speak of the wisdom of God in a comparative sense is unusual. The distinction between the wisdom of God and the wisdom of man offered by Isaiah, however, quickly dispels the notion that the two can be compared. God's wisdom is superlative because it is transcendent.

Three characteristics distinguish the wisdom of God. First, he *"will bring disaster"* (v. 2). Other translations read, "He will bring evil." Only the wisdom of God can sort out the difference between "evil" and "disaster." As the Holy One of Israel, God cannot be the source of moral evil in the universe, but He can utilize forces of nature and the events of history to exercise judgment and punish sin. His wisdom, then, is the ability to discriminate between moral evil and natural disaster as instruments of His will. Human wisdom fails this test of discrimination. Whenever we humans take judgment into our own hands, we run the risk of our own sin motivating the punishment. For this reason, God says, "Vengeance is Mine, I will repay" (Romans 12:19). Only the wisdom of God can "bring disaster" without evil intent.

Second, Isaiah characterizes the distinct wisdom of God by the assurance that He *"will not call back His words"* (v. 2). Human wisdom requires revision as learning continues and insights develop. Humility is the mark of a wise man or woman. God's wisdom, however, needs no revision. His truth stands firm and forever. After He speaks, He "will not call back His words." While we do not worship His Word, we know that what He says will stand to the end with His promise, "These words are faithful and true" (Revelation 22:6) along with the warning, "If anyone adds to these things . . . and if anyone takes away from the words . . . God shall take away his part from the Book of Life, from the holy city, and from the things which are written in this book" (Revelation 22:18–19).

Third, God's wisdom is distinguished from human wisdom by His even-handedness in rising *"against the house of evildoers, and against the help of those who work iniquity"* (v. 2b). Both Judah and Egypt will feel the wrath of God. Judah will be punished because of King Hezekiah's sin of seeking Egypt's help, and Egypt will be punished for giving the help. At the same time, the punishment will fit the sin. Discretionary judgment is a virtue of the wisdom of God that is lacking in human wisdom. Without the perspective of human history—past, present, and future—against the backdrop of eternity, human wisdom can never be fully fair in exercising judgment. The bias of a limited perspective and human motivation will invariably creep into the punishment. God and God alone can exercise wrath against His people and their enemies with the wisdom of His eternal purpose.

Isaiah goes on to tell us why human wisdom is faulty. *"Now the Egyptians are men, and not God; and their horses are flesh, and not spirit"* (v. 3). Hidden in the words are the questions, "Will you trust in the living God or in dying men?" and "Will you trust in the strength of horses or in the power of the Spirit of God?" With just a stretch of the Lord's hand in human events, both men and horses, those who help and those who are helped—*"They all will perish together"* (v. 3b).

The Mystery of God's Wisdom (31:4–9)

Isaiah takes the superlative nature of God's wisdom one more step into the mystery of His ways, which even the wisest of humans cannot understand. Two proofs are given in the context of the forthcoming judgment upon Judah and Assyria. The first proof is the mystery of God being a tenacious lion and a hovering mother bird over Judah at the same time. Although God will permit Assyria to come to the gates of Jerusalem, He will then take on the role of a roaring young lion ready to devour a lamb. Nothing the Assyrian shepherds can do will turn Him from His purpose. With the tenacity of a young lion, God will *"fight for Mount Zion and for its hill"* (v. 4b).

Instantly, the image of God changes from a devouring lion to a hovering bird. Strength gives way to compassion as God again shows His love for the children of Israel. Like a mother bird, He will defend Jerusalem against the Assyrians, deliver the city from their hands, and preserve His people by passing over them when death strikes their enemies. Memories of the Passover in Egypt are refreshed in the minds of Isaiah's hearers. As in Egypt, when the Angel of Death passed over the Israelites who had smeared the blood of the lamb on their doorposts, God reinforces His promise of their preservation in the unforgettable picture of the hovering mother bird. With the promise of the Passover fresh in mind, Isaiah pleads with the children of Israel to return to the Father against whom they have *"deeply revolted"* and *"throw away"* the silver and gold idols that they have made as the symbols of their insolence.

303

A second proof of the mystery of God's unfathomable wisdom is the promise that Assyria will fall by a sword that is not a human weapon. God calls in the supernatural to put the Assyrians to flight, enslave their crack troops, send them home in shameful retreat, and strike fear into the hearts of their princes at the mere sight of His banner (vv. 8–9a). To this day, history does not tell us why the Assyrians withdrew their siege against Jerusalem and retreated in disarray. Of all the explanations, the consistency between Isaiah's prophecy and reporting gives his account the most credibility. "Then the angel of the LORD went out and killed in the camp of the Assyrians one hundred and eighty-five thousand . . . so Sennacherib king of Assyria departed and went away, returned home, and remained at Nineveh" (37:36).

Behind the mystery of His will is the assurance of His wisdom. Jerusalem, the city where His fire burns both on the altar hearth of His worship and in the *"furnace"* of Tophet for His wrath, is special to His purpose, but not exempt from His wrath. Human wisdom cannot fathom the mystery.

THE REIGN OF WISDOM (32:1–20)

1 Behold, a king will reign in righteousness,
   And princes will rule with justice.
2 A man will be as a hiding place from
   the wind,
   And a cover from the tempest,
   As rivers of water in a dry place,
   As the shadow of a great rock in a weary land.
3 The eyes of those who see
      will not be dim,
   And the ears of those who hear
      will listen.
4 Also the heart of the rash
      will understand knowledge,
   And the tongue of the stammerers
      will be ready to speak plainly.
5 The foolish person will no longer be called generous,
   Nor the miser said to be bountiful;
6 For the foolish person will speak foolishness,
   And his heart will work iniquity:
   To practice ungodliness,

To utter error against the LORD,
To keep the hungry unsatisfied,
And he will cause the drink of the thirsty to fail.

7 Also the schemes of the schemer are evil;
He devises wicked plans
To destroy the poor with lying words,
Even when the needy speaks justice.

8 But a generous man devises generous things,
And by generosity he shall stand.

9 Rise up, you women who are at ease,
Hear my voice;
You complacent daughters,
Give ear to my speech.

10 In a year and some days
You will be troubled,
    you complacent women;
For the vintage will fail,
The gathering will not come.

11 Tremble, you women who are at ease;
Be troubled, you complacent ones;
Strip yourselves, make yourselves bare,
And gird sackcloth on your waists.

12 People shall mourn upon their breasts
For the pleasant fields,
    for the fruitful vine.

13 On the land of my people will come up thorns and
    briers,
Yes, on all the happy homes in the joyous city;

14 Because the palaces will be forsaken,
The bustling city will be deserted.
The forts and towers
    will become lairs forever,
A joy of wild donkeys,
    a pasture of flocks—

15 Until the Spirit is poured upon us
    from on high,
And the wilderness
    becomes a fruitful field,
And the fruitful field
    is counted as a forest.

16 Then justice will dwell in the wilderness,
And righteousness remain in the fruitful field.

17 The work of righteousness will be peace,
     And the effect of righteousness,
         quietness and assurance forever.
18 My people will dwell in a peaceful habitation,
     In secure dwellings,
         and in quiet resting places,
19 Though hail comes down on the forest,
     And the city is brought low in humiliation.
20 Blessed are you who sow beside all waters,
     Who send out freely the feet of the ox and the donkey.
                                        Isaiah 32:1–20

The fall of Assyria under the supernatural sword of God's intervention prepares the way for the advent of the Kingdom of Righteousness. Rising in comparison with a nation in rebellion against the love and will of God, the Kingdom of Righteousness is governed by wisdom, empowered by the Spirit, and characterized by peace.

THE GOVERNANCE OF WISDOM (32:1–8)

Joy springs into Isaiah's words whenever he shifts from punishment to promise. "Woe" gives way to "behold" as he announces the coming of the Kingdom of Righteousness. In contrast to the governance of foolish kings, cynical princes, deaf prophets, and blind seers, the prophet sees the evidence of wisdom at every level of society.

The King Reigns in Righteousness (32:1a)

Isaiah establishes a principle of truth that applies to every nation: The leader sets the tone for the quality of governance. Peters and Waterman's book *In Search of Excellence* tells the stories of business leaders whose vision for the future, valuing of human resources, and modelling of moral values created the climate for excellence in their corporations.[4] Nordstrom's clothing stores, for instance, have built a reputation for personalized service to the customer. Not by accident, the tone was set many years ago when Lloyd Walter Nordstrom opened a shoe store in Seattle, Washington, with the motive of personalized service. Since then, generation after generation of the Nordstrom family has carried on the heritage as leaders of the company. From the chairman of the board to the clerk behind the counter, customers can count upon personalized service. The character of the business is set by the quality of the leader.

As the character of a business is set by the personality of the leader, so the quality of a kingdom is set by the character of the king. Not by accident, Isaiah notes that a righteous kingdom needs a righteous king. Character, then, becomes the primary qualification for leadership. In his earlier denunciations of the leaders of Judah and Jerusalem, the prophet noted that character no longer counted. Drunkenness, lies, and trickery were standard operations for the leaders who misled the people. As a consequence, rebellion replaced righteousness and oppression replaced justice at every level of government. Added meaning is given to the Scripture, "Righteousness exalts a nation, but sin is a reproach to any people" (Proverbs 14:34).

The Princes Rule with Justice (32:1b)

Another important principle of wisdom is established when Isaiah reports that the princes rule with justice: Righteousness precedes justice in the equation of good governance. It is false to assume that a leader can do justice without being righteous. Sooner or later, there will be moral decisions that test the caliber of the leader's soul and expose the flaw. Conversely, if the leader is right with God, he or she will respect the rights of others. Another principle of wisdom is established for us: Righteousness not only precedes justice, but righteousness guarantees justice. The king who reigns in righteousness, then, has princes who rule in justice. In the clearest terms, Isaiah has laid the stone of justice upon the cornerstone of righteousness for the building of the nation and the guidance of the people.

The Masses are Protected (32:2)

Government's first responsibility is the health and safety of its people. This is the structure of good government built upon righteousness and justice. We are not surprised, then, to learn that "*a man*," or every individual person in the Kingdom of Righteousness, will find a "*hiding place*" from the wind of adversity, "*a cover*" from the tempest of catastrophe, "*rivers of water*" for the times of sickness, and *"the shadow of a great rock"* in the moments of malaise. If government limited its functions to the health and safety of the people, its agenda would be full. At the end of the twentieth century and into the twenty-first century, government must return to these basics. Whether it is the health issue of AIDS, or the safety issue of crime in the streets, people need protection. Yet, without the moral foundation of righteousness and justice, can health and safety be assured? Isaiah would answer, no.

The People are Enlightened (32:3–4)

After health and safety, good government has the responsibility for the welfare of its people. Education is considered the leading edge of welfare. At the fundamental level is literacy and at the highest level is wisdom. Isaiah may well have literacy in mind when he foresees that *"the eyes of those who see will not be dim, and the ears of those who hear will listen"* (v. 3). We know from an earlier oracle (30:11–12) that he made literate leaders, especially prophets and seers, responsible for reading the words of a sealed book. When they could not read, the illiterate people could not read. In the Kingdom of Righteousness, however, the opposite is true. The literate will have both open eyes and a listening ear for the word of truth so the illiterate can be taught to read and learn the way. Also, the rash who rush to judgment will become patient to understand knowledge and *"the tongue of the stammerers will be ready to speak plainly"* (v. 4). To see clearly, listen perceptively, understand thoroughly, and speak plainly the word of truth—these are qualities of a wise people.

The Foolish are Exposed (32:5–8)

All of the values are tipped in a kingdom that is not founded on righteousness, ruled by justice, and guided by wisdom. A fool who rejects God and His teaching is called *"generous"* and the miser is said to be *"bountiful"* (v. 5). But when righteousness, justice, and wisdom rule the kingdom, the ruse is lifted. The fool will be exposed as a person who speaks foolishly, works iniquity, practices ungodliness, and utters errors against the Lord (v. 6). Just as righteousness is a pervasive influence upon thinking, speaking, and doing, so foolishness travels like a microbe in the bloodstream to every part of the personality. And the consequences are evil. With wicked intent, the fool keeps the hungry unsatisfied and the thirsty unfulfilled (v. 6b). By the fool's evil schemes and wicked plans, the poor are destroyed and the needy oppressed. Along with the fool, the miser will be exposed. Pretending to be generous, the miser is motivated by self-interest. But, in the Kingdom of Righteousness, the generous person will be known by generous plans and generous deeds that need no defense.

A secular nation has been described as a society in which all of the values have been reversed. Imagining the nation as a large department store filled with merchandise, a secular society is like a prankster who sneaks into the store in the middle of the night and changes all of the price tags. Cheap things are now valuable and valuable things are now cheap. Topsy-turvy values are a sure indicator that righteousness no longer reigns and justice no longer rules.

THE SPIRIT OF WISDOM (32:9–15)

Why does Isaiah seem to interrupt his train of thought by inserting an appeal to the women of Judah who are charged with ease and complacency (v. 9)? Perhaps the answer comes in his inclusive sweep through the nation and its people. He has spoken to kings, princes, common people, prophets, seers, and fools. Why not women who represent a significant influence in the life of the nation? True, they are addressed last among the groups and scolded for their complacency about the happenings in Judah, but on the other hand, they are recognized for the role they play in setting attitudes for the nation.

Isaiah's challenge, *"Rise up . . . Hear my voice . . . Give ear to my speech,"* is a compliment to the power they wield. His warning is that their ease will turn to trembling and their complacency will give way to trouble when the Lord brings judgment upon Judah. Perhaps only they will remain when the men of the nation are marched into exile. With the people who remain, they will mourn the loss of *"pleasant fields,"* the *"fruitful vine,"* *"happy homes,"* festive *"palaces,"* the *"bustling city,"* and protective *"forts and towers"* along the city walls (vv. 12–14). The implication is that the women of Judah took these blessings for granted, but if they arose, they could make a difference. Rather than criticizing Isaiah for chauvinism, he deserves to be the complimented for his confidence in the latent power of the women of Judah.

One thing is certain. Isaiah saw that the Kingdom of Righteousness could not come by any human power, male or female. Rather, foreseeing Pentecost, he waits *"until the Spirit is poured on us from on high"* (v. 15). Some scholars dispute the thought that Isaiah is referring to the power of the Spirit of God. I disagree. Just as God showed Isaiah that the supernatural sword of the Lord would put the Assyrians into retreat from the walls of Jerusalem, so He gives His prophet a perspective of the only power that can bring righteousness and justice to the nation. "Until the Spirit is poured upon us from on high" leaves no doubt. Supernatural power is essential to the transformation of a nation steeped in rebellion, foolishness, and complacency.

The Peace of Wisdom (32:16–20)

Make no mistake. The outpouring of the Spirit is necessary for the peace that God promises in the Kingdom of Righteousness. The women of Judah and Jerusalem took their "ease" in the false sense of peace in their nation and their homes. But with the outpouring of the Spirit, true peace will come. Justice will be present but righteousness will lead the way. *"The **work** of righteousness will be peace and the **effect** of righteousness, quietness and assurance forever"* (v. 17). We may not fully understand the pervasive power and positive effect of righteousness. Isaiah began with the simple statement "Behold, a king will reign in righteousness" (32:1). The concept expanded with revolutionary effect into every level of society and every group in the nation—affirming some, exposing others, and challenging still others. But now we see righteousness coming to its final effect—peace in heart and peace in the nation.

God promises *"My people will dwell in a peaceful habitation"* (v. 18). How distant from that promise modern Israel still seems. Rather than peace, the nation is an armed camp beset on every side by hostile neighbors. Israelis do not have *"secure dwellings"* or *"quiet resting places"* (v. 18a). Yet, the promise is still good for Israel and for us. The outpouring of His Spirit not only transforms our lives, clears our vision, and empowers our witness, but He also gives us peace in the midst of the noxious hail or devastating storm (v. 19). For all of us, Isaiah's closing beatitude is the word of wisdom, *"Blessed are you who sow beside all waters, who send out freely the feet of the ox and the donkey"*

(v. 20). By sowing beside all waters, we tap the source of His life, and by freely sending out the feet of the ox and the donkey, we show our confidence in His promise. If the fear of the Lord is the beginning of wisdom, the water of His Spirit and the freedom of His promise are steps toward maturity.

NOTES

1. Young, *New International Commentary*, 340–341.

2. H. C. Leupold, *Exposition of Isaiah, Vol. I* (Grand Rapids: Baker, 1971), 471.

3. R. Bellah, *Habits of the Heart* (Berkeley: University of California Press, 1985), 41ff.

4. T. J. Peters and R. H. Waterman, *In Search of Excellence: Lessons from America's Best-Run Companies* (New York: Harper & Row, 1982).

CHAPTER FIFTEEN

The Reign of Righteousness

Isaiah 33:1–35:10

True to his style of writing, Isaiah makes quick shifts in both content and mood from chapter to chapter. Having reached the peak of God's promise in chapter 32, which he introduced with the word "Behold," the prophet plunges back into the depths of God's punishment in chapter 33 with the very first word "Woe" (33:1). The pattern is consistent with the prophetic cycle of Isaiah's writing. An oracle of punishment prompts a word of promise and an oracle of promise prompts a word of judgment. But rather than feeling like a yo-yo at the end of a string, there is a rhythm of reality in Isaiah's writing. As beauty is best known in comparison with ugliness, so God's promise is best known in comparison with God's punishment. The rhythm of Isaiah's writing with its point of promise and counterpoint of punishment, then, is an ingenious instrument for effective communication.

Another pulse in the rhythm of Isaiah's writing is the shift from general to specific prophetic pronouncements. By and large, the more futuristic the prophecy, the more general and poetic the prophet's writing. The closer he comes to current events or imminent happenings, the more specific and prosaic he becomes. Yet, his oracles do not easily divide into one category or another. Chapter 33, for instance, contains an oracle in transition between current and future events, punishment and promise, poetry and prose. Consequently, we can expect to find in the text the full prophetic cycle from historical *provocation*, through prophetic *proclamation*, human *preference*, and divine *punishment*, to redemptive *promise* and ultimate *praise*.

But then we must ask, "What is the special, underlying message that Isaiah wants to communicate?" The pivotal verse of the chapter gives us our answer. As Isaiah has just described the governance of the

312

King who reigns in righteousness (ch. 32), so now he reveals the beauty of the king who acts in judgment (33:17). Isaiah's message is to let us know that beauty and judgment are not contradictory in the character of the Lord of hosts, who is our King. Not only is He even-handed in the means of His judgment, but His end purpose is the beauty of redemption.

The Character of the King (33:1–24)

1 Woe to you who plunder,
   though you have not been plundered;
And you who deal treacherously,
   though they have not dealt
   treacherously with you!
When you cease plundering,
You will be plundered;
And when you make an end
   of dealing treacherously,
They will deal treacherously with you.

2 O Lord, be gracious to us;
We have waited for You.
Be their arm every morning,
Our salvation also in the time of trouble.

3 At the noise of the tumult
   the people shall flee;
When You lift Yourself up,
   the nations shall be scattered;

4 And Your plunder shall be gathered
Like the gathering of the caterpillar;
As the running to and fro of locusts,
He shall run upon them.

5 The Lord is exalted,
   for He dwells on high;
He has filled Zion with justice
   and righteousness.

6 Wisdom and knowledge
   will be the stability of your times,
And the strength of salvation;
The fear of the Lord is His treasure.

7 Surely their valiant ones
   shall cry outside,
The ambassadors of peace

      shall weep bitterly.

8 The highways lie waste,
The wayfaring man ceases.
He has broken the covenant,
He has despised the cities,
He regards no man.

9 The earth mourns and languishes,
Lebanon is shamed and shriveled;
Sharon is like a wilderness,
And Bashan and Carmel
      shake off their fruits.

10 "Now I will rise," says the LORD;
"Now I will be exalted,
Now I will lift Myself up.

11 You shall conceive chaff,
You shall bring forth stubble;
Your breath, as fire, shall devour you.

12 And the people shall be like the burnings of lime;
Like thorns cut up they shall be burned in the fire.

13 Hear, you who are afar off,
      what I have done;
And you who are near,
      acknowledge My might,"

14 The sinners in Zion are afraid;
Fearfulness has seized the hypocrites:
"Who among us shall dwell with the devouring fire?
Who among us shall dwell with everlasting burnings?"

15 He who walks righteously
      and speaks uprightly,
He who despises the gain of oppressions,
Who gestures with his hands,
      refusing bribes,
Who stops his ears from hearing of bloodshed,
And shuts his eyes from seeing evil:

16 He will dwell on high;
His place of defense will be the fortress of rocks;
Bread will be given him,
His water will be sure.

17 Your eyes will see the King in His beauty;
They will see the land that is very far off.

18 Your heart will meditate on terror:
"Where is the scribe?

Where is he who weighs?
Where is he who counts the towers?"
19 You will not see a fierce people,
A people of obscure speech,
beyond perception,
Of a stammering tongue that you
cannot understand.
20 Look upon Zion,
the city of our appointed feasts;
Your eyes will see Jerusalem,
a quiet habitation,
A tabernacle that will not be taken down;
Not one of its stakes will ever be removed,
Nor will any of its cords be broken.
21 But there the majestic Lord
will be for us
A place of broad rivers and streams,
In which no galley with oars will sail,
Nor majestic ships pass by
22 (For the LORD is our Judge,
The LORD is our Lawgiver,
The LORD is Our King;
He will save us);
23 Your tackle is loosed,
They could not strengthen their mast,
They could not spread the sail.
Then the prey of great plunder is divided;
The lame take the prey.
24 And the inhabitant will not say,
"I am sick";
The people who dwell in it will be
forgiven their iniquity.

Isaiah 33:1–24

THE KING SEES OUR DISTRESS (33:1)

"Woe to you who plunder . . . and you who deal treacherously . . ." is
a warning to Assyria and a promise to Zion. Against God's warning,
Hezekiah, king of Judah, had sent a tribute of gold and silver to
Sennacherib, king of Assyria, with the hope of staving off an attack upon
Jerusalem. The morals of Sennacherib, known for overkill (plunder) in

his conquests, permit him to accept the tribute without keeping his word. So, while God was displeased with Hezekiah's decision, He was more displeased with Sennacherib's treachery. Through Isaiah, He sends the pronouncement of punishment against Assyria that will turn the tables of their plundering and treachery. *"You will be plundered"* and *"they will deal treacherously with you"* are fitting judgments for their sins. In a paraphrase of the Scripture, "All who take the sword will perish by the sword" (Matthew 26:52), Isaiah is saying, "Those who live by plunder will die by plunder" and "Those who live by treachery will die by treachery." No punishment is more severe than to become a victim of the same sins by which we destroyed others.

THE KING HEARS OUR PRAYERS OF REPENTANCE (33:2–4)

King Hezekiah learned his lesson. After Sennacherib kept the tribute, but betrayed the truce and marched his troops up to the gates of Jerusalem to lay siege to the city, Hezekiah led his people in a prayer of repentance, "This is a day of trouble, and rebuke, and blasphemy; for the children have come to birth, but there is no strength to bring them forth" (2 Kings 19:3). Isaiah shares that prayer with the king and his people as he pleads, *"O Lord, be gracious to us"* (v. 2). The invocation of God's grace is the surest sign of genuine repentance. To ask for grace is to confess that all human effort has proven futile and no human merit can warrant salvation. From foolish trust in tribute to Assyria, the king and his people put total trust in the Lord of hosts. Like a convicted criminal, they throw themselves on the mercy of the highest court.

Their prayer of repentance also claims the promise that the Assyrians will flee *"at the noise of tumult"* (v. 3). In these words is the confession that they hold no alternative except total dependence on the power of God to save them. Trust then opens their eyes to see the Lord plundering the plunderer and tricking the treacherous into utter confusion and shameful flight. By waiting upon the Lord with penitent spirit, Hezekiah and his people got a confirming glimpse into the vision of God that Isaiah had already seen.

THE KING ACCEPTS OUR PRAISE (33:5–6)

As natural as the dawn following the darkness, praise follows promise in the prayer of Hezekiah and his people. God is exalted in

His majesty, His justice, and His righteousness (v. 5). In direct refutation of the decision to send tribute to Sennacherib, the wisdom of His ways and the knowledge of His Word are acknowledged as the only source of stability and strength for the nation. And as for the future, the *"fear of the LORD"* will be a treasure of hope, not a lodestone of dread. Hezekiah and his people seem to have learned their lesson and Isaiah seems to be vindicated. But like most of us, our faith is strong until we meet the next crisis.

THE KING KEEPS HIS PROMISE (33:7–9)

God's response to Israel's prayer is to reassure the people that He sees and understands the depth of their distress as Sennacherib breaks his promise, surrounds the city, and demands surrender. Victims outside the walls cry for help, ambassadors of peace weep bitterly at their betrayal, all highways to the city are ruined, and no one dares to travel to or from the city (vv. 7–8a). With unmistakable reference to Sennacherib, God indicts him on the evidence of the broken covenant, wasted cities, and total disdain for the value of human life (v. 8b). The consequences can be seen in the environment of the earth—wasted, shamed, desolate, and shaken (v. 9). As if reopening the cosmic court that the Lord convened in the beginning of the prophecy (1:2), heaven and earth are again called as witnesses to the evil motives and wicked deeds of the Assyrian king.

THE KING ACTS ON TIME (33:10–13)

In further response to the prayers of repentance and the voice of praise, God assures Israel that He will act on time. *"Now I will rise,"* *"Now I will be exalted,"* and *"Now I will lift myself up"* leave no doubt about God's intention. His wrath will come down on Sennacherib and his army to blow them away like chaff before the wind and burn them up like stubble under the torch of fire that they had used on others, but now turns against them (v. 11). Like the burnings of sulfurous lime and dry-cut thorns, the mysterious death and unexpected flight of the Assyrians will be proof to Israel that only the all-powerful LORD of hosts could have worked the miracle.

God's timing is always right. If He had kept Sennacherib from marching against Jerusalem, Hezekiah and his people would have thought that their tribute to Sennacherib made the difference. If He had waited until the Assyrian siege took effect, Israel would have lost hope. But at precisely the moment when His redemptive purpose can be advanced, God announces, "Now I will rise."

THE KING TEACHES HIS PEOPLE (33:14–16)

No promise is more difficult to accept than the Lord saying, "For whom the LORD loves He chastens" (Hebrews 12:6). This is a fact with which we all live and suffer. The children of Israel in Isaiah's time knew exactly what the promise meant. After letting the Assyrians breathe their own fire, God warns *"sinners in Zion"* against His judgment upon their enemy. Looking out over the devastating scene of death and destruction that remained after the Assyrians fled, fear struck the hearts of hypocrites who questioned, *"Who among us shall dwell with the devouring fire?"* and *"Who among us shall dwell with everlasting burnings?"* Guilt broke the facade of their hypocrisy and motivated the kind of eternal questions God honors with a patient word of instruction. As repetitious as it may have seemed for Isaiah, God walks sinners who ask honest questions through the steps of the qualities of character, conduct, and consequences that mark the man or woman of God.

Righteousness is an internal quality and an external expression for persons who are redeemed. In both their walk and their talk, they are like Job, "blameless and upright" (Job 1:1). These are the qualities that set them apart from the "sinners in Zion" whose hearts were evil and the *"hypocrites"* whose lips told lies.

Justice in human affairs follows righteousness of heart and uprightness of lips. Again, like Job, the fear of God and the shunning of evil go together. Righteous persons know that they are accountable to God for their actions, not only to pursue good works, but to avoid the temptations to sin. Four specific sins are to be shunned: (1) ill-gotten gains from the oppression of the poor and needy; (2) accepting bribes against the public trust; (3) gloating over the bloodshed of enemies; and (4) enjoying the sight of evil (v. 15). In each case, injustice against others is the consequence of the sin. When it comes to justice, the righteous are hard on themselves and easy on others while the sinful are easy on themselves and hard on others.

Peace is the spiritual consequence of righteousness in character and justice in conduct. *"He will dwell on high; his place of defense will be the fortress of rocks"* (v. 16) is the promise of a peace of mind and heart that is not dependent upon the circumstances. In a very real sense, the man or woman of God lives above the turmoil that swirls and spins in human existence. To *"dwell on high"* does not mean immunity from trouble, but it does mean a perspective of trust that circumstances cannot shake. To dwell in the *"fortress of rocks"* as the place of defense does not mean isolation from the conflict, but it does mean a position of peace that is not shattered by enemy attack. *Shalom* is the Hebrew word that best describes the perspective of trust and the position of peace that God promises to those who dwell in Him.

Strength, both physical and spiritual, is the baseline consequence of righteousness. Bread and water are fundamental for human survival. Water gives life and bread gives strength. While no promise is given that God will supply the *wants* of the righteous, we are assured that our *needs* will be met. For those of us who can readily quench our thirst or fill our stomachs, this promise may lack meaning. We need to put ourselves in the circumstances of the children of Israel. They lived on survival margins in a land where water was in short supply and food depended upon the kindness of the seasons. For them to know that their daily needs for bread and water were assured would certainly lift their spirits and raise their hopes. With these needs met, they could anticipate using their energies in the creative ventures of building community, refining culture, honoring God, and caring for others.

The King Reveals His Beauty (33:17–19)

Righteousness is an eye-opener. While the righteous person *"shuts his eyes from seeing evil"* (v. 15b), they are wide open to see *"the King in His beauty"* (v. 17a). Scholars debate whether the "King" is Hezekiah, the Messiah, or a generalized concept of kingship. Isaiah's train of thought, before and after this key verse, leads us to one conclusion: The King is the Messiah. In His presence, we either see hope in the future or shake in terror at the thought of tomorrow. Terror will grip those who counted upon the tribute money to assuage the evil of Sennacherib as they ask in panic, *"Where is the scribe?"* *"Where is he who weighs?"* and *"Where is he who counts the towers?"* Their misplaced trust in the attorneys who put together the agreement, the auditors who assessed the value of the tribute, and the military strategists who sounded the alarm at the sight of the towers of siege, are all dumbfounded. The Assyrians are gone and in the quiet of the countryside there is the beauty of the LORD of hosts that only the eyes of the righteous can see.

THE KING REIGNS IN PEACE (33:20–23a)

Having looked out upon the beauty of the countryside after the Assyrian retreat, the children of Israel are invited to turn and look at their beloved Zion. Jerusalem, a city at peace, is ready for a feast to celebrate the fulfillment of God's promise to deliver His people by the mystery of His providence. Behold His majesty! The Lord is our judge who champions the cause of justice; the Lord is our lawgiver who speaks the word of truth; the Lord is our king who reigns and rules in righteousness. He and He alone is our Savior. All of Israel's efforts to save themselves are like a ship in a storm when the tackle comes loose, the mast starts to wobble, and the sail cannot be raised (v. 23). Either swamping or shipwreck is ahead. As God stepped in to save Israel from the Assyrians, only trust in the One who rules the wind and knows the storm can ever save them.

THE KING FORGIVES SIN (33:23b–24)

In one last look at the events surrounding the Assyrian withdrawal, Isaiah moves the tense of the text forward with the word *then* to foresee the day when the helpless, the sick, the poor, and the needy will have their share of the bounty of good things left by the Assyrian army. One can imagine the people of Jerusalem pouring over the grounds where the Assyrian army was encamped to help themselves to the food, clothing, and treasures left behind. For those who were lame or sick and could not participate in the party, a choice portion would be reserved for them. Ironic as it might be, they might have come upon the gold and silver of Hezekiah's tribute that Sennacherib forgot to take in the haste of retreat. While these verses are open to conjecture, the meaning is clear. The absence of the Assyrians is the assurance that the prayers of the Israelites are answered. God has *"forgiven their iniquity."*

Day of Vengeance (34:1–17)

1 Come near, you nations, to hear;
   And heed, you people!
   Let the earth hear, and all that is in it,
   The world and all things that come forth from it.

2 For the indignation of the LORD
       is against all nations,
   And His fury against all their armies;
   He has utterly destroyed them,
   He has given them over to the slaughter.

3 Also their slain shall be thrown out;
   Their stench shall rise from their corpses,
   And the mountains shall be melted with their blood.

4 All the host of heaven shall be dissolved,
   And the heavens shall be rolled up like a scroll;
   All their host shall fall down
   As the leaf falls from the vine,
   And as fruit falling from a fig tree.

5 "For My sword shall be bathed in heaven;
   Indeed it shall come down on Edom,
   And on the people of My curse, for judgment.

6 The sword of the LORD is filled with blood,
   It is made overflowing with fatness,
   And with the blood of lambs and goats,
   With the fat of the kidneys of rams.
   For the LORD has a sacrifice in Bozrah,
   And a great slaughter in the land of Edom.

7 The wild oxen shall come down with them,
   And the young bulls with the mighty bulls;
   Their land shall be soaked with blood,
   And their dust saturated with fatness."

8 For it is the day of the LORD's vengeance,
   The year of recompense for the cause of Zion.

9 Its streams shall be turned into pitch,
   And its dust into brimstone;
   Its land shall become burning pitch.

10 It shall not be quenched night or day;
   Its smoke shall ascend forever.
   From generation to generation
       it shall lie waste;
   No one shall pass through it forever and ever.

11 But the pelican and the porcupine
     shall possess it,
Also the owl and the raven
     shall dwell in it.
And He shall stretch out over it
The line of confusion
     and the stones of emptiness.

12 They shall call its nobles to the kingdom,
But none shall be there,
     and all its princes shall be nothing.

13 And thorns shall come up in its palaces,
Nettles and brambles in its fortresses;
It shall be a habitation of jackals,
A courtyard for ostriches.

14 The wild beasts of the desert
     shall also meet with the jackals,
And the wild goat shall bleat
     to its companion;
Also the night creature shall rest there,
And find for herself a place of rest.

15 There the arrow snake shall make her nest and lay eggs
And hatch, and gather them under her shadow;
There also shall the hawks be gathered,
Every one with her mate.

16 "Search from the book of the LORD, and read:
Not one of these shall fail;
Not one shall lack her mate.
For My mouth has commanded it,
     and His Spirit has gathered them.

17 He has cast the lot for them,
And His hand has divided it among them with a
     measuring line,
They shall possess it forever;
From generation to generation they shall dwell in it."

Isaiah 34:1–17

Isaiah's oracles of punishment and promise come to a grand finale in his vision of final judgment on all nations and final restoration of Zion. The prophet's mastery of comparison is never more pronounced than in the changes that he foresees taking place when the LORD of hosts vents His anger against sin and shows His grace for the sinner.

322

One scholar borrowed from Dante the terms "Inferno" and "Paradise" to highlight the contrast. Another chose to entitle chapter 34 as "Final Judgment" and chapter 35 as "Final Salvation." Still others have chosen the titles "Desert" and "Garden" for the two contrasting chapters.

All of these insights are needed to embrace the meaning of the chapters. Even then, after reading and studying, the full force of meaning eludes us because Isaiah's vision has taken us to the edge of eternity with a finality of hope but not a finality of explanation. At best, we can ask the Spirit of God to open our eyes as we read and enlighten our minds as we see. The Spirit will not disappoint us. Each reading will bring new insights of spiritual depth that will increase our desire to be separated from the sins upon which His eternal punishment will fall and draw us toward the grace upon which His eternal promise will be fulfilled.

Chapters 34 and 35 also serve a dual function in the progress of Isaiah's prophecy. They summarize the oracles that focus upon punishment in chapters 12–33 and introduce the oracles of promise in chapters 40–66. An autobiographical bridge of Isaiah's encounters with King Hezekiah is provided in chapters 36–39 as part of the prophet's actual ministry. We stand, then, at a point from which we look back upon the major theological and spiritual themes of Isaiah's prophecy during his lifetime and forward to his foresight in advancing those same themes to the future with the coming of the Messiah.

All of the nations and people of earth have been called into judgment in earlier oracles of Isaiah when he drew his prophecies together in transitional summaries (chs. 12 and 24). Now, like the culmination of a crescendo in a symphony, he strikes the chords of the grand finale with emphasis upon the eternal consequences of God's angry judgment against sin at its source and wickedness in action. *Change* is the key to understanding this prophecy of punishment in comparison with the forthcoming prophecy of promise. Whereas chapter 35 dramatizes the transformation of Zion from a desert into a garden to the glory of God, chapter 34 paints a vivid picture of the glory of nations devastated by God's anger into an eternal wasteland.

DESTRUCTION OF THE NATIONS (34:1–4)

Once again, the cosmic court is called to order when God commands all nations, all people, and all things to stand before Him and hear His word of judgment. He has been indignant against sin before, but now His anger is flamed into fury (v. 2a). Utter destruction of pagan armies has been predicted before, but now the slaughter will be so complete that the number of the dead will not permit their burial (v. 3). Israelites would not mistake the message. For them, no shame exceeded the disgrace of being denied a decent burial. Even though Jesus died as a criminal on the cross, Nicodemus provided a borrowed tomb hoping to save Him from ultimate disgrace. The nations and people of the earth who have opposed God and attacked Israel will not even have a borrowed tomb. Once known for their haughty pride, the stench from their corpses will be the smell of unbounded shame.

To punctuate the totality of devastation wrought from the Lord's fury, Isaiah goes beyond an earlier prophecy when he foresaw the earth reeling like a drunkard and swaying like a hut in the wind (24:20). In the final judgment, the created order of the whole universe will give way to the void and chaos before the Spirit of God hovered over the waters (Genesis 1:1). In a preview of Revelation 6:12, Isaiah forecasts that *"All the host of heaven shall be dissolved, and the heavens shall be rolled up like a scroll"* (v. 4). The interlocking nature of the universe and its Creator cannot be denied. As Adam's sin put a curse upon the earth, so the power of God's unleashed anger can dissolve the galaxies and roll up the skies.

CURSE ON EDOM (34:5–7)

God's anger becomes action in the symbol of His sword. The words *"For My sword shall be bathed in heaven"* gives the impression that it has been poised over the earth for a long and patient period of time. When it falls, all nations will feel its fatal cut. But the brunt of the blow will come upon Edom, archenemy of Judah that parallels Babylon as the symbol of evil. With a history of bad blood among brothers reaching back to the confrontation between Jacob and Esau (Genesis 33), conflict after conflict had widened the chasm between the two nations (Numbers 20:18; Deuteronomy 2:4; Judges 11:17). Despite God's instruction, "Do not abhor an Edomite, for he is your brother" (Deuteronomy 23:7), the hostility continued unabated with Edom in the aggressor's role. Long after Isaiah's time, the Edomites plagued Israel, even to the extent of aiding and abetting the Babylonians when they destroyed Jerusalem in 586 B.C. Isaiah's pronouncement of doom, then, is more than his nationalism gone berserk. God Himself says that His sword *"shall come down on Edom, and on the people of My curse, for judgment"* (v. 5b). Edom is under the curse of God because of its sin against God and its brother nation of Judah.

CONSEQUENCES FOR ALL CREATION (34:8–15)

Two theological concepts come into view with Isaiah's gory description of the sword of the Lord slaughtering animals and drenching the land with blood. Symbolically, Edom becomes the sacrifice required for the forgiveness of sin. The concept will carry over into Isaiah's later picture of the Messiah as the Suffering Servant and into the New Testament image of Jesus as the Lamb of God (John 1:29; 1 Corinthians 5:7; 1 Peter 1:19; and Revelation 5:6). Edom's special punishment, then, is not without cause. "Without shedding of blood there is no remission " (Hebrews 9:22), is a truth that Edom must face if the deep-seated sin of jealousy and hatred is ever to be forgiven.

The second theological concept with which we must struggle as we read of God's pointed wrath against Edom is the eternal finality of which the prophet speaks again and again. The smoke of the blazing pitch will *"ascend forever"*; the nation will lie desolate from *"generation to generation"*; and *"no one shall pass through forever and ever"* (vv. 9–10). If there is forgiveness in the sacrifice, why is the punishment forever? The answer may rest in the ongoing description of the devastation of Edom. In addition to the streams being turned into burning *"pitch"* and the land made so desolate that no one will ever pass through it again, God's judgment will leave the land to desert animals (v. 11a); will wipe out its ruling classes; will overrun her palaces, cities and forts with thorns, nettles and brambles; and will make Edom a haunt for jackals and a home for owls among other desert creatures (vv. 11–15).

Edom, the proud nation known for its good crops, beautiful palaces, strong forts, and innovative government, will suffer the greatest shame of all: *"They shall call its nobles to the kingdom, but none shall be there, and all its princes shall be nothing"* (v.12a). In answer to our question, the kingdom will be sacrificed for the sins of the people. And in that sacrifice is their hope for salvation.

THE WORD OF THE LORD (34:16–17)

Having pronounced His sentence of judgment upon all nations and Edom in particular, God closes the final session of the cosmic courtroom with the invitation for all nations to attest the authority with which He speaks. *"Search from the book of the LORD and read,"* He says (v. 16). You will find that every fact is true and consistent with other facts. What is the scroll or book to which God refers? Some scholars suggest that Isaiah's writing of this prophecy will be the permanent record to which future generations can refer. Others suggest a "Book of Divinity" that the Hebrews held as sacred. Still others see the scroll as the writings of prophecy in general. The first suggestion seems most likely because God had instructed Isaiah to put his prophecies into a book as a permanent record for future generations (30:8). Because Isaiah spoke the Word of the Lord, we can expect that he also wrote the Book of the Lord. God's authority, however, is not limited to a book. The writing comes from the commands of His mouth and interpretation comes from the gathering of Spirit (v. 16b).

DAY OF VICTORY (35:1–10)

1 The wilderness and the wasteland
   shall be glad for them,
And the desert shall rejoice
   and blossom as the rose;
2 It shall blossom abundantly
   and rejoice,
Even with joy and singing,
The glory of Lebanon
   shall be given to it,
The excellence of Carmel and Sharon.
They shall see the glory of the LORD,
The excellency of our God.
3 Strengthen the weak hands,
And make firm the feeble knees.
4 Say to those who are fearful-hearted,
   "Be strong, do not fear!
Behold, your God will come with vengeance,
With the recompense of God;
He will come and save you."

5 Then the eyes of the blind
    shall be opened,
And the ears of the deaf
    shall be unstopped.
6 Then the lame
    shall leap like a deer,
and the tongue of the dumb sing.
For waters shall burst forth in the wilderness,
And streams in the desert.
7 The parched ground
    shall become a pool,
And the thirsty land springs of water;
In the habitation of jackals,
    where each lay,
There shall be grass with reeds and rushes.
8 A highway shall be there, and a road,
And it shall be called
    the Highway of Holiness.
The unclean shall not pass over it,
But it shall be for others.
Whoever walks the road,
    although a fool,
Shall not go astray.
9 No lion shall be there,
Nor shall any ravenous beast
    go up on it;
It shall not be found there.
But the redeemed shall walk there,
10 And the ransomed of the LORD shall return,
And come to Zion with singing,
With everlasting joy on their heads.
They shall obtain joy and gladness,
And sorrow and sighing
shall flee away.

Isaiah 35:1–10

No one can call Isaiah a prophet of doom. At the slightest provocation, He becomes a poet and a songster when he sees what God has in store for His people. Each time he is compelled to prophesy the judgment of God, he follows with a picture of God's redemptive purpose. As his oracles of punishment have deepened in severity, so his oracles of promise have soared to new heights. Therefore, after Isaiah's gory revelation of God's fury against the nations and Edom in chapter 34, we can expect poetry and song unmatched in his earlier prophecies of promise. Isaiah does not disappoint us. In his vision of the future transformation of Zion, all of his creative impulses are released in the text and tone of divine inspiration. One way to capture those impulses is to join Isaiah in the transformations that turn the "wilderness and the wasteland" of Zion into a garden of gladness to which the redeemed come singing the praises of God.

FROM WASTELAND TO GARDEN (35:1–2)

As creation was reversed in the devastation of Edom, so the garden is restored in the transformation of Zion. As a means of communicating with the children of Israel, Isaiah may well be envisioning the desert region known as the Arabah, which runs down through the Dead Sea to the Gulf of Arabah on the Persian Gulf. A deep valley below sea level, the Arabah is the Death Valley of the Middle East—uninhabited, unproductive, and uninviting. To transform that desert into a carpet of crocuses whose beauty gladdens the heart and puts a song on the lips is a miracle indeed. Every person in Judah and Jerusalem who had seen the Arabah would understand the transformation that brought the cedars of Lebanon, the oaks of Carmel, and the roses of Sharon to the wasteland (v. 2). The smell, the strength, and the sight of these wonders of nature would cause every eye to open wide and see the *"glory of the LORD"* and *"the excellency of our God"* (v. 2b).

Moments ago, I drove over the top of Queen Anne Hill in Seattle, Washington, to look out across Puget Sound toward the rugged, snow-capped Olympic Mountains framed against the clear blue sky. Dazzled with a sense of awe, I found myself spontaneously quoting the Psalm 121, "I will lift up my eyes to the hills—from whence comes my help? My help comes from the LORD who made heaven and earth." After dark and drizzly days for which Seattle is known, the striking beauty sets the heart to singing praise to God. For the children of Israel, the contrast would be far more striking. In the transformation of the wasteland into a wonderland, they would see the glory of the Lord and sing His praise.

From Weak to Strong (35:3–4)

The transformation of the environment has a direct effect upon human emotions. Every student in Introductory Psychology remembers learning about the Hawthorne Effect. Low morale among workers at a General Electric plant in the eastern United States affected both their productivity and the quality of their work. Then, when the drab walls were scheduled for repainting, the workers were invited to choose the colors. Inspired by the invitation to participate in the decision, they chose new and bright colors for the walls. Immediately, their spirits were lifted with measurable gains in both quality and productivity.

Three morale problems are addressed in the transformation of attitudes among the children of Israel. *"Weak hands"* is the symbol of powerlessness and the inability to get things done. *"Feeble knees"* suggests the inability to move forward with a sense of direction. As we remember, the drunken leaders of Israel had misled the people so that they no longer trusted their leaders or themselves. The *"fearful-hearted"* are the people who have been traumatized again and again by threats of attack and destruction so that they lived emotionally on the raw edge of frenzy. To live constantly in fear drains the body, mind, and soul of its vitality, creativity, and faith.

Put yourself in the place of a person who has no hope, or confidence, and lives in constant fear. To you the Lord says, *"Be strong, do not fear . . . He will come and save you!"* (v. 4). Your weak hands feel the strength to get things done again, your feeble knees are steadied for a forward step, and your fearful heart is calmed in the confidence that the Lord will dispel your enemies and save you. The change of the environment from a desert to a garden might have been miraculous, but it is nothing compared to the transformation of the human spirit.

From Lame to Leaping (35:5–6a)

Physically disabled persons are close to the heart of God. While we must never treat them as less than whole persons with compensatory gifts for their disability, we know that their healing is a miracle that glorifies God. As Jesus said of the blind man whose disability was explained by the Pharisees as an act of sin on his part or his parents, "Neither this man nor his parents sinned, but [this happened] that the works of God should be revealed in him life" (John 9:3). A similar work is promised in the transformation of the physical disabilities of blind, deaf, lame, and mute people. In a forecast of Jesus' ministry, the blind will see, the deaf will hear, the lame will run *"like a deer,"* and the mute will sing. While Isaiah has used blindness and deafness as metaphors for persons who are spiritually blind and deaf to the Word of God, the fact that he joins them with the disabilities of being lame and mute means that he expects physical as well as spiritual healing. The transformation of Zion and its people would not be complete without physical healing.

FROM DROUGHT TO DELTA (35:6b–7)

Life in the Middle East depends on water. In the desolation of judgment revealed in chapter 34, the sources of water dried up, leaving only dust in its place (vv. 7–9). Old Testament symbolism equates water with life and dust with death. So naturally, in the transformation of Zion, out of the dust of the wilderness, the desert, the parched ground, and the thirsty land burst the artesian wells, streams, pools, and springs of life-giving water. In direct contrast, then, with Edom being turned into a dusty land where only thorns and thistles grow, God's transforming power will turn the "habitation of jackals" (34:13 and 35:7) into a fertile delta of grass, reeds, and rushes. As Egypt had its rich delta created by the waters of the Nile, so Zion would have its deltas created by the miracle of God.

FROM WILDERNESS TO HIGHWAY (35:8–10)

In forthcoming chapters, a *"highway"* is to become one of Isaiah's favorite analogies for envisioning the return of the children of Israel from exile and communicating the meaning of God's way for His people (40:3; 41:17; 43:14; 48:21). The concept is introduced here as part of the transformation of the uncharted wilderness into a super-highway for the redeemed of the Lord. Israel did not have a reputation for its roads. Without the techniques and tools for road building that gained sophistication with the coming of the Roman Empire, the mountains and hills of the Holy Land were traversed with narrow, winding and stony footpaths through wilds where animals lurked in ambush of the unsuspecting traveler. Because of the terrain, major roads for caravans bypassed Jerusalem on the east along the Mediterranean coast and on the west around the Dead Sea. The children of Israel could only dream of a highway through Judah and to Jerusalem that would be broad, straight, and safe for trade and travelers.

Their dream is fulfilled in the glorious future of Zion when God transforms the uncharted wilderness into a superhighway that would be the envy of modern road builders. To qualify as a highway, a path through the mountains will have to be cut and the valleys raised to make the road level and straight. Its name will be the *"Highway of Holiness"* because it is the work and the way of the Holy One of Israel. Yet, as Wolf notes, it is a "limited access highway."[1] Only those who are redeemed from sin can travel there. Not that those with privileged access are perfect in holiness. If so, a resident mansion rather than a highway would have been built. In the book *A Holy Company*, biographical vignettes of saints through the ages show one quality in common. Although not perfect, they never stopped "hobbling toward holiness."[2] All who are "redeemed" are invited to join their Pilgrim's Progress on the Highway of Holiness (v. 9b).

The Highway of Holiness will also be so plainly marked that the simplest soul can travel on it without going astray and so safely protected that the most innocent souls can walk on it without fear of animal ambush (v. 9). All of us know the exhilaration of finishing a long trip by turning on the familiar road that takes us home. For the *"ransomed of the* LORD,*"* the Highway of Holiness leads home. Zion is the destination and the songs of joy and gladness replace the dirge of *"sorrow and sighing"* as the destination comes into view. C. S. Lewis likens the Christian journey to a citizen of London travelling home.[3] The signposts that point to London along the way are not mistaken for the final destination, but the Londoner presses on with gladness because he or she is on the way home. The return of the remnant from Babylonian exile must have been a similar experience for the children of Israel. On the highway from Babylon to Jerusalem, they did not stop short of their goal, but as the signposts showed them coming closer and closer to their home, their singing would have had the sound of heaven.

Pilgrimages to Jerusalem still convey Isaiah's vision. One morning during our visit to the Mount of Olives, we heard in the distance the

measured singing from a company of Christians making the pilgrimage to the Holy City. As the company came around the mountain and
caught their first view of Jerusalem spread in splendor before them,
they burst into a song of triumphant praise, giving the glory to God.

Whether the pilgrimage is a return from exile, a company of Christians visiting the Holy Land, or the homecoming of redeemed into
the presence of God, they will *"come to Zion with singing, with everlasting joy on their heads"* (v. 10).

NOTES

1. H. M. Wolf, *Interpreting Isaiah* (Grand Rapids: Zondervan, 1985),
185.

2. E. Wright, *A Holy Company: Christian Heroes and Heroines* (New
York: MacMillan, 1980), 256.

3. C. S. Lewis, *Surprised by Joy: The Shape of My Early Life* (New York:
Harcourt Brace, 1955), 238.

PART SIX

The Vision Affirmed

Isaiah 36:1–39:8

CHAPTER SIXTEEN

Hezekiah's Crisis

Isaiah 36:1–37:38

In the opening subscript to the book of Isaiah, the prophet indicates that his ministry spanned the reigns of the Judean kings Uzziah, Jotham, Ahaz, and Hezekiah (1:1). Uzziah's death coincided with Isaiah's calling, but Uzziah's son Jotham is not mentioned again in the prophecy. Ahaz, however, is the major player to date in the unfolding history of Judah and Jerusalem in the second half of the eighth century before Christ. Little good can be said of Ahaz. His epitaph is recorded in 2 Kings 16:2, "He did not do what was right in the sight of the LORD his God, as his father David had done." Isaiah became his most severe critic when Ahaz refused to trust God, aggressively entered into a military alliance with Assyria, paid tribute to Tiglath-Pileser, became enamored with the idols of Damascus, and built an altar to the pagan gods in Jerusalem (2 Kings 16:1–19). The historical record of Isaiah's confrontation with Ahaz and the prophecies of judgment, resulting from Ahaz' sin, dominates chapters 1–35.

With the death of Ahaz, Uzziah his son ascended to the throne. Another era of history opens in the record of Isaiah's relationship with Hezekiah when he too is tempted to depend upon a military alliance with Egypt for protection against Assyria and then is threatened with destruction by the Assyrian king Sennacherib if he does not surrender to his forces (ch. 36). Hezekiah's response is exactly the opposite of his son Ahaz. Hearing Isaiah's call for trust in God with the promise of Assyria's defeat, Hezekiah leads his people in a prayer for deliverance and sees the prayer answered by Sennacherib's mysterious retreat and assassination by his own sons as he bowed at the altar of his god Nisroch (ch. 37).

Personal details of Hezekiah's reign follow in the familiar story of his cure from fatal illness by God's healing and the promise of fifteen more years of life (ch. 38). In his final days, however, Hezekiah sets the stage for the Babylonian captivity by giving almost all of his treasures as tribute to the king Merodach-Baladan (ch. 39). With the word from the Lord, Isaiah interpreted his act as a symbol of the forthcoming Babylonian conquest and captivity when "everything will be carried away" and "nothing will be left" (ch. 39).

Hezekiah died in peace, leaving the legacy of a good king who trusted the Lord during his reign but forfeited the future by his final decision. So, as an interlude between prophecies and a prelude to Babylonian captivity, chapters 36–39 record in prose form the relationship between Isaiah the prophet and Hezekiah the king at another turning point in Israel's history.

TACTICS OF A TYRANT (36:1–20)

1 Now it came to pass in the fourteenth year of King Hezekiah that Sennacherib king of Assyria came up against all the fortified cities of Judah and took them.

2 Then the king of Assyria sent the Rabshakeh with a great army from Lachish to King Hezekiah at Jerusalem. And he stood by the aqueduct from the upper pool, on the highway to the Fuller's Field.

3 And Eliakim the son of Hilkiah, who was over the household, Shebna the scribe, and Joah the son of Asaph, the recorder, came out to him.

4 Then the Rabshakeh said to them, "Say now to Hezekiah, 'Thus says the great king, the king of Assyria: "What confidence is this in which you trust?

5 "I say you speak of having counsel and strength for war; but they are vain words. Now in whom do you trust, that you rebel against me?

6 "Look! You are trusting in the staff of this broken reed, Egypt, on which if a man leans, it will go into his hand and pierce it. So is Pharaoh king of Egypt to all who trust in him.

7 "But if you say to me, 'We trust in the LORD our God,' is it not He whose high places and whose altars

Hezekiah has taken away, and said to Judah and Jerusalem, 'You shall worship before this altar'?" '

8 "Now therefore, I urge you, give a pledge to my master the king of Assyria, and I will give you two thousand horses—if you are able on your part to put riders on them!

9 "How then will you repel one captain of the least of my master's servants, and put your trust in Egypt for chariots and horsemen?

10 "Have I now come up without the Lord against this land to destroy it? The Lord said to me, 'Go up against this land, and destroy it.'"

11 Then Eliakim, Shebna, and Joah said to the Rabshakeh, "Please speak to your servants in the Aramaic language, for we understand it; and do not speak to us in Hebrew in the hearing of the people who are on the wall."

12 But the Rabshakeh said, "Has my master sent me to your master and to you to speak these words, and not to the men who sit on the wall, who will eat and drink their own waste with you?"

13 Then the Rabshakeh stood and called out with a loud voice in Hebrew, and said, "Hear the words of the great king, the king of Assyria!

14 "Thus says the king: 'Do not let Hezekiah deceive you, for he will not be able to deliver you;

15 'nor let Hezekiah make you trust in the Lord, saying, "The Lord will surely deliver us; this city will not be given into the hand of the king of Assyria."'

16 "Do not listen to Hezekiah; for thus says the king of Assyria: 'Make peace with me by a present and come out to me; and every one of you eat from his own vine and every one from his own fig tree, and every one of you drink the waters of his own cistern;

17 'until I come and take you away to a land like your own land, a land of grain and new wine, a land of bread and vineyards.

18 'Beware lest Hezekiah persuade you, saying, "The Lord will deliver us." Has any one of the gods of the nations delivered its land from the hand of the king of Assyria?

> 19 'Where are the gods of Hamath and Arpad?
> Where are the gods of Sepharvaim? Indeed, have they
> delivered Samaria from my hand?
> 20 'Who among all the gods of these lands have
> delivered their countries from my hand, that the LORD
> should deliver Jerusalem from my hand?'"
>
> *Isaiah 36:1–20*

MAKE A GENEROUS OFFER (36:1–3)

Isaiah's account of Sennacherib's campaign in Judah parallels the record of 2 Kings 18:13–16. The specific incident described in both accounts rises out of a background in which Sennacherib put down revolts against Assyrian occupation that spread from Babylon to Syria and to Palestine. Sennacherib swept from north to south either crushing the rebels or receiving their surrender. After devastating Samaria, he marched into Judah and, according to his own annals, captured forty-six fortified cities and 200,140 people.

Fearful of an attack upon Jerusalem, Hezekiah paid three hundred talents of silver and thirty talents of gold to Sennacherib (2 Kings 18:14). After accepting the tribute, however, the treacherous king still sent his Rabshakeh, or commander-in-chief, along with a large army to Hezekiah and demanded surrender of the city. The Rabshakeh, however, does not come with the ultimatum, "Surrender or die." Although he is backed up by superior firepower, he comes with the tactics of a negotiator trying to reach a compromise that benefits both parties. Evidently Sennacherib did not want to tie down his forces with a long siege of Jerusalem when he had other worlds to conquer. Lachish, a fortress city of Judah from which he sent the Rabshakeh to Jerusalem, was still under siege and the Egyptians continued to be a threat in the south. Yet, in his annals, Sennacherib bragged that he had Hezekiah shut up like a bird in a cage. Perhaps with the confidence of his superiority, he could afford to sound generous. In any case, the Rabshakeh was met at the aqueduct of the upper pool by three representatives of Hezekiah: Eliakim, the palace administrator; Shebna, the palace administrator demoted to secretary as Isaiah had prophesied; and Joah, the recorder (v. 3).

Significance is attached to the place of the meeting. Isaiah had confronted Ahaz at the "end of the aqueduct of the upper pool" in a futile effort urging him to put his trust in God rather than Assyria for deliverance from the two "stubs of smoking firebrands," Syria and Ephraim (7:4). Thirty years later, Ahaz's son, Uzziah, faced a similar decision. While Ahaz had taken the initiative in seeking an alliance with the Assyrians, Hezekiah must decide how he will respond to the Rabshakeh's offer.

The art or science of negotiation is one of the most popular subjects in books on business and management. Roger Fisher and William Ury have written a bestseller in the field under the title *Getting To Yes*. Their formula is simple and sound. Four steps are recommended for the process of reaching a negotiated settlement:

1. Separate people from the problem
2. Focus on interests, not position
3. Invent options for mutual gain
4. Insist on using objective criteria[1]

Although these steps are supported by contemporary research, they are also the results of intuition and experience. Obviously, the Rabshakeh never read the book *Getting to Yes*, yet his skills in seeking a negotiated agreement with Hezekiah follow each of these steps. Even though he failed, we can learn from him.

SEPARATE PEOPLE FROM THE PROBLEM (36:4–7)

From the utterance of his first word, we know that the Rabshakeh had no respect for King Hezekiah or his people, the children of Israel. Addressing the delegation led by Eliakim, he said, *"Say now to Hezekiah, 'Thus says the great king, the king of Assyria'"*(v. 4). Hezekiah is not addressed with his royal title while Sennacherib is touted by title and greatness. His disdain, however, is not evident in the subtlety of his approach. Separating the people, Hezekiah and Sennacherib, from the problem, he asks the disarming question, *"What confidence is this in which you trust?"* His military intelligence had to be excellent. How else would he know that this is a question with which King Hezekiah struggled? Moreover, the Rabshakeh knew the two answers over which the people were divided. Either they could put their trust in a military alliance with Egypt or they could say, *"We trust in the LORD our God"* (v. 7). With the brilliance of a debater undermining an opponent's case by stating it for him or her, the Rabshakeh uncovered their fears by the reminder that Egypt had been reduced to a *"broken reed . . . on which if a man leans, it will go into his hand and pierce it"* (v. 6). The Jerusalemites knew that he was right. Sennacherib had already scored a major victory over the Egyptian army at Eltekeh so that any nation that aligned itself with Pharoah took the risk of Assyrian vengeance.

On the other hand, if Hezekiah and his people answered, *"We trust in the LORD our God,"* the Rabshakeh anticipated their response by playing on their doubts. Hezekiah had instituted a religious reform by ordering the destruction of all high places and altars of worship at the local level and commanding the people to worship only at the temple and altar in Jerusalem. As with all arbitrary decrees, even when they are right, controversy brewed among the people who had not been consulted and whose habits of worship were affected. Hezekiah could not declare, "We will trust in God," in the face of grave danger without deepening those doubts. With the finesse of a master at manipulating human emotions, the Rabshakeh knew that he had touched the raw nerves of fear and doubt with the beleaguered people of Jerusalem without directly attacking them, their king, or their prophet.

FOCUS ON INTERESTS, NOT ON POSITION (36:8–15)

To his credit, the Rabshakeh knows the primary and conflicting interests of the children of Israel. They want the assurance of military protection at the same time that they want the favor of God. So, rather than taking a position demanding their surrender, he sounds like God the Father appealing to his wayward children in Isaiah 1:18, *"Now therefore, I urge you, give a pledge to my master the king of Assyria"* (v. 8a). Then to satisfy their interest in military protection, the Rabshakeh offers two thousand cavalry horses. But his fatherly facade slips when he blurts out sarcastically, *"If you are able on your part to put riders on them!"* Judah lacked not only horses, but trained riders. The Rabshakeh's slip of the tongue should have alerted his listeners to the fact that their mountainous country neutralized the effectiveness of cavalry in warfare. Still, he played on the idea that Judah would never have military prestige without a crack corps of horsemen and chariots. If Assyria launched an attack, Judah could not protect itself and Egypt had already shown its vulnerability at Eltekeh. Only a pledge to the king of Assyria could satisfy that interest.

How can Judah put its trust in Assyria and still curry the favor of God? The Rabshakeh has a ready answer. With unmatched arrogance, he puts himself into direct opposition with Isaiah by claiming to be a prophet to whom the Lord has spoken. Again, with a solicitous tone, he asks his listeners, *"Have I now come up without the LORD against this land to destroy it?"* (v. 10). The inferred answer is, "Of course not, you can trust me." His lie is spoken with unabashed blasphemy, *"The LORD said to me, "Go up against this land, and destroy it"*" (v. 10b). From some source he had heard Isaiah's prophecy of judgment upon Judah and twisted it in hope of bringing Jerusalem to its knees. By pretending to be religious, he appealed to the religious interests of the people.

Hezekiah's ambassadors panic when they realize the Rabshakeh's ruse. He is speaking in Aramaic, not Hebrew, to the people on the walls in order to rally public opinion in favor of his offer and incite rebellion if Hezekiah refuses his offer. The Rabshakeh's tactics, devilish as they are, have to be admired. He knows that in the game of power, whether a monarchy or democracy, the people can veto the decisions of leadership by refusing to comply, frustrating the system, or engaging in outright rebellion.

According to the rules of negotiation, Hezekiah's delegation should have asked for a break in the talks in order to reduce the panic and plan a response. Instead, they revealed their fears and the weakness of their position by meekly asking the Rabshakeh to speak in the diplomatic language of Hebrew rather than the common language of Aramaic. Like a hound cornering a wounded fox, the Rabshakeh went right to the heart of the interests of the people on the wall— human survival! Dropping his facade of diplomacy, he revealed his true mission in the grossest of terms when he told the delegation that he came to speak both to them and to the men on the wall because in the siege they would eat their own feces and drink their own urine together. Having made his point so forcefully, the Rabshakeh then stood and shouted out the ultimatum from Sennacherib, his king. Mimicking the preaching of the prophet by calling *"Hear the words of the great king, the king of Assyria"* (v. 13), he charges Hezekiah with deception in assessing their military strength and foolishness for trusting in the Lord to save them from Sennacherib. But like Isaiah who prophesied of punishment, he also has a promise.

INVENT OPTIONS FOR MUTUAL GAIN (36:16–17)

Sennacherib needs peace with Jerusalem in order to turn his attention to other conquests. The people of Jerusalem need peace to avoid annihilation. So, playing on the common element for mutual gain, the Rabshakeh offers an attractive option. If they will make a peace offering to Sennacherib, he will guarantee them the food and drink they urgently need and a prosperous future in a rich agricultural land not unlike their own. Behind the invented option is the assumption that the children of Israel would rather be fed than dead. The offer, however, is laced with arsenic. Along with the promise of peace and prosperity comes the shame of deportation to a foreign land. At this point, the Rabshakeh's began to misread the motives of the Israelites. Their fierce nationalism based upon ethnic identity and religious history went deeper than their love for life.

INSIST ON USING OBJECTIVE CRITERIA (36:18–20)

The Rabshakeh now goes for the jugular vein in his negotiating scheme. After putting out the carrot of a promise to the people, he hits them with the stick of facts that are common knowledge. Again, attacking Hezekiah's credibility and his faith in God, the commander-in-chief of the Assyrian army cites the record of conquest over the nations of Hamath, Arpad, Sepharvaim, and Samaria whose gods failed to save them from the hand of Sennacherib. Historians note that the Rabshakeh falsified the facts by crediting Sennacherib with victories over Hamath and Arpad, which were in reality conquered by his predecessor Sargon II.

Arrogance knows no bounds and propaganda feeds on falsified facts and half-truths. In the Rabshakeh's case, the facts became his undoing. His source of information about the Jews failed to warn him against insulting the God of Judah by relegating Him to the level of any other god. Fierce nationalism came from the history of the children of Israel, but inherent monotheism came from their heart. The

Rabshakeh has gone too far. If he had stopped with the veiled threat of military destruction, he might have won the day. But when he presumed upon the religious identity and the spiritual history of the Jews, he lit the fires of resistance for which Israel is known to this day.

THE ADVANTAGE OF SILENCE (36:21–22)

21 But they held their peace and answered him not a word; for the king's commandment was, "Do not answer him."
22 Then Eliakim the son of Hilkiah, who was over the household, Shebna the scribe, and Joah the son of Asaph, the recorder, came to Hezekiah with their clothes torn, and told him the words of the Rabshakeh.

Isaiah 36:21–22

Errors resulting from the Rabshakeh's arrogance gave the advantage back to the Jews. In negotiating terms, he had prematurely exposed his BATNA—or the Best Alternative To a Negotiated Agreement,[2] namely, total surrender and deportation for the people of Jerusalem. Wisdom, however, dictated Hezekiah's instructions to his delegation. By obeying the king's commandment, *"Do not answer him,"* they gained the advantage of time and reflection before making their decision and revealing their BATNA, which was to trust in God for their deliverance from Sennacherib. Fisher and Ury identify this tactic as "Going to the Balcony" from which perspective can be gained.[3] Still, the advantage of time for reflection did not overcome the threat of destruction. In deep despair, Hezekiah's representatives tore their clothes as a sign of mourning and reported the Rabshakeh's words to the king. Behind the threat lurked the question the Rabshakeh asked and Hezekiah had to answer, "In whom will I trust, the LORD of hosts or the king of Assyria?" Jerusalem's destiny hangs in the balance.

THE PRAYER OF FEAR (37:1–4)

1 And so it was, when King Hezekiah heard it, that he tore his clothes, covered himself with sackcloth, and went into the house of the LORD.

2 Then he sent Eliakim, who was over the
household, Shebna the scribe, and the elders of the
priests, covered with sackcloth, to Isaiah the prophet,
the son of Amoz.

3 And they said to him, "Thus says Hezekiah:
'This day is a day of trouble and rebuke and
blasphemy; for the children have come to birth, but
there is no strength to bring them forth.

4 'It may be that the LORD your God will hear the
words of the Rabshakeh, whom his master the king of
Assyria has sent to reproach the living God, and will
reprove the words which the LORD your God has
heard. Therefore lift up your prayer for the remnant
that is left.'"

Isaiah 37:1–4

Isaiah's historical record continues without a break in the action as
King Hezekiah receives the report from a delegation clothed in the
rags of mourning. A series of events follow that lead to Sennacherib's
mysterious retreat from the gates of Jerusalem and his assassination
by his own sons twenty years later. While the history is fascinating
and the literature is worthy of study, the character of God is so mag-
nificently defined in this chapter that our minds come alive and our
hearts respond when we seek to understand Isaiah's message of theology behind the history. Hezekiah's prayers and God's responses
are central to Isaiah's message.

THE PREPARATION FOR PRAYER (37:1–2)

King Hezekiah's immediate response to the Sennacherib's threat of
annihilation or deportation for his people is a lesson for us in a time
of fear. His wise command that the delegation remain silent rather
than responding to the Rabshakeh gives him time to reflect upon his
decision. An air of desperation must have pervaded the palace as
Hezekiah took the lead for his people by covering himself with sackcloth, the symbol of repentance before God.

When leaders sin, their people suffer; however, when leaders repent, their people follow. Elton Trueblood, the esteemed Christian
philosopher and Quaker statesman, wrote a book entitled *Abraham
Lincoln: Theologian of American Anguish*. In it, he recounts the story of

a Quaker woman who gained a brief audience with President Lincoln as he weighed the decision of whether or not to sign the Emancipation Proclamation. Knowing the consequences for good and evil, Lincoln's deep anguish was accompanied by what he called "the black dog of depression." The Quaker woman entered the Oval Office without a word and sat in prayerful silence before her president. At the end of her time, she arose and left without a word being spoken. From that moment, Lincoln became a man of resolve. He opted for freedom over slavery and signed the Emancipation Proclamation.[4]

When Richard Nixon anguished over his decision of whether or not to tell the truth about Watergate, Elton Trueblood requested a similar audience with his president. He intended to repeat the history of Lincoln and the Quaker woman by praying in silence with Richard Nixon. The request was rejected, repentance never came, and tragedy followed. To this day, Elton Trueblood and others contend that if Richard Nixon would have repented and asked the forgiveness of his people, he would have remained in office as one of our greatest presidents.

King Hezekiah not only put on the sackcloth of repentance in the privacy of his chambers but he went publicly to the house of the Lord to pray. All of his people knew that he repented of his failure to trust in the Lord and sought forgiveness through sacrifice in the temple. When he arose, he humbly sent his chief emissary Eliakim, Shebna the scribe, and the *"elders of the priests,"* all in sackcloth, as a delegation to Isaiah. For once in his life, the much-maligned prophet is dignified by a delegation of state appearing at his door wearing the symbol of repentance for which Isaiah had called. Having repented of his sins and offered his sacrifice for forgiveness, Hezekiah demonstrates the vulnerability of genuine repentance by opening himself to the counsel of the prophet of God.

THE PROMPTING FOR PRAYER (37:3)

Hezekiah's appeal to Isaiah echoes his prayer to God. Honest with his fears, the king begins by describing the current situation as a *"day of trouble and rebuke and blasphemy"* (v. 3). Sennacherib is the cause of "trouble" for his people, "rebuke" for his kingship, and "blasphemy" against God. One might argue that Hezekiah turns to God only as a last resort to save his own skin, but that argument is lost in his confession that he is responsible for the trouble, rebuke, and blasphemy of the day. His leadership has produced children in the womb who come to the time of birth in a breech position and cannot be delivered without either death or supernatural intervention.

THE PROMISE OF PRAYER (37:4a)

Prayer is claiming the promises of God with full confidence. Hezekiah is handicapped by fear and guilt as he asks the prophet to pray for him. With hesitation, based upon the fear that God will not accept his repentance, Hezekiah lays the groundwork for his petition by meekly suggesting *"It may be that"* the Lord will hear the words of the Rabshakeh and will reprove them. Hezekiah's guilt is still in control of his prayer. He dare not even address the Lord as "his" God, but asks Isaiah if *"your"* God will hear and reprove the Assyrian. Even though he has repented in sackcloth and sought forgiveness through sacrifice, he has not forgiven himself for violating the word of God that came through the prophet. To return, then, to Isaiah and ask for the word of God to be spoken against the blasphemy of Sennacherib makes Hezekiah understandably sheepish. Unconsciously, he probably fears what God will say to him.

THE PETITION OF PRAYER (37:4b)

Hoping against hope, Hezekiah asks Isaiah to pray that God will preserve a remnant of his people. The *"remnant"* may refer to the population of Judah that has already been decimated by Sennacherib's conquest of forty-six fortress cities and all of Judah except Jerusalem. Or Hezekiah's fear and guilt may lead him to believe that Sennacherib's siege is inevitable and so he wants Isaiah to pray that his people will not be totally annihilated. In either case, the king seems to have no hope for relief from the current crisis and little hope for the future.

GOD'S FIRST ANSWER TO HEZEKIAH (37:5–7)

5 So the servants of King Hezekiah came to Isaiah.

6 And Isaiah said to them, "Thus shall you say to your master, 'Thus says the LORD: "Do not be afraid of the words which you have heard, with which the servants of the king of Assyria have blasphemed Me.

7 "Surely I will send a spirit upon him, and he
shall hear a rumor and return to his own land; and I
will cause him to fall by the sword in his own land."' "
Isaiah 37:5–7

God responds to Hezekiah's most immediate needs of relief from his fear and his guilt. Telling him the same thing He told his father Ahaz when he feared Assyrian conquest, God says *"Do not be afraid"* (v. 6). God backs up these words of comfort by letting the king know that He has heard the words of blasphemy spoken by the *"servants"* or lackeys of the king of Assyria. Hezekiah's guilt must also have been relieved by the absence of any word of retribution from God against him for failing to trust Him. God always honors genuine repentance with full forgiveness.

Hezekiah also learns that God is a doer as well as a hearer. Matching the tactics of Sennacherib in psychological warfare that had struck paralyzing fear into the heart of His people, God counters with the sure promise of putting such fear into Sennacherib's heart that a rumor will cause him to retreat to his own land where he will die by the sword (v. 7). Propagandists are their own worst enemy. To be effective in the manipulation of truth, propaganda must be totally one-sided. The slightest breach caused by truth will bring down the whole system.

The tyrant, Sennacherib, is especially vulnerable to the truth. He is far away from his home in Nineveh because of rebellion throughout his far-flung empire. Without his presence at home, there is always the threat of a palace revolt. So the slightest rumor can unnerve him. All God needs to do is *"send a spirit"* of fear upon him and even a rumor will cause him to panic. Solomon wrote, "The wicked flee when no one pursues" (Proverbs 28:1). God does not tell Hezekiah exactly what He will do, but asks the king to have faith that Sennacherib will *"return to his own land"* and will *"fall by the sword."* Be not afraid and trust in Me. Simple to say, but hard to do.

THE RABSHAKEH'S FATAL ERROR (37:8–13)

8 So the Rabshakeh returned, and found the king
of Assyria warring against Libnah, for he had heard
that he had departed from Lachish.

9 And the king heard concerning Tirhakah king
of Ethiopia, "He has come out to make war with
you." So when he heard it, he sent messengers to
Hezekiah, saying,

10 "Thus you shall speak to Hezekiah king of
Judah, saying: 'Do not let your God in whom you
trust deceive you, saying, "Jerusalem will not be
given into the hand of the king of Assyria."

11 'Look! You have heard what the kings of
Assyria have done to all lands by utterly destroying
them; and will you be delivered?

12 'Have the gods of the nations delivered those
whom my fathers have destroyed, Gozan and Haran and
Rezeph, and the people of Eden who were in Telassar?

13 'Where is the king of Hamath, the king of
Arpad, and the king of the city of Sepharvaim, Hena,
and Ivah?'"

Isaiah 37:8–13

Meanwhile, the Rabshakeh returned to give his report to Sennacherib. For some reason, the king had lifted his siege against
Lachish and moved ten miles north to do battle against Libnah, another fortress city. The tactical move may have been made in
response to word that Tirhakah, king-to-be of Ethiopia, had rallied
his army to march in rebellion against Sennacherib. If Libnah fell,
Tirhakah would savor the taste of victory and Sennacherib would
lose the advantage of choosing the place of battle. At the same time,
Sennacherib could not afford to leave his flank exposed by the uncon-
quered forces at Jerusalem. So he put in writing the ultimatum that
the Rabshakeh had verbally delivered to Hezekiah.

Although the demand for total surrender is the same, the reasons
for the ultimatum are escalated by an air of desperation. The *"spirit"*
that God put on Sennacherib and the *"rumor"* that Sennacherib heard
may already be taking effect on the king as he escalates the ultimatum to
a new level of blasphemy and bombast. Through the Rabshakeh he
had told the people, "Do not let Hezekiah deceive you" (36:14). Now
he says to Hezekiah, *"Do not let your God . . . deceive you"* (v. 10).
With this charge, Sennacherib entered into contest with the LORD of
hosts. "Who will you trust?" is still the question. Integrity and sovereignty are the stakes.

To his blasphemy, Sennacherib adds bombast. The Rabshakeh had overstated the cities and nations that the Assyrian had conquered without opposition from their gods. At least Sennacherib gives credit to his ancestral kings for conquering *"Gozan and Haran and Rezeph and . . . Telassar"* (v. 12). Then, he brings history up to date with a list of recent conquests for which he takes credit—Hamath, Arpad, Sepharvaim, Hena, and Ivah (37:13). The continuity of dynasty is impressive, but when used to claim divinity, it is blasphemy. Sennacherib has made the fatal error. God's honor is on the line and His sovereignty has been challenged. Hezekiah must decide in whom he will trust and God must decide how He will respond.

THE PRAYER OF TRUST (37:14–20)

14 And Hezekiah received the letter from the hand of the messengers, and read it; and Hezekiah went up to the house of the LORD, and spread it before the LORD.
15 Then Hezekiah prayed to the LORD, saying:
16 "O LORD of hosts, God of Israel, the One who dwells between the cherubim, You are God, You alone, of all the kingdoms of the earth. You have made heaven and earth.
17 "Incline Your ear, O LORD, and hear; open Your eyes, O LORD, and see; and hear all the words of Sennacherib, who has sent to reproach the living God.
18 "Truly, LORD, the kings of Assyria have laid waste all the nations and their lands,
19 "and have cast their gods into the fire; for they were not gods, but the work of men's hands—wood and stone. Therefore they have destroyed them.
20 "Now therefore, O LORD our God, save us from his hand, that all the kingdoms of the earth may know that You are the LORD, You alone."

Isaiah 37:14–20

When Hezekiah reads Sennacherib's letter, he is quick to perceive the challenge against the integrity and sovereignty of God. As if the Lord needs to read the letter for Himself, Hezekiah spreads it out before Him as he bows in prayer. The king is not to be criticized. Many times I have taken a threatening letter or an attractive proposal and spread it out before the Lord as I have knelt in prayer. For me, the action symbolizes my need for the counsel of God and my willingness to do His will. Hezekiah's prayer confirms the same motives as he spreads Sennacherib's letter before the Lord. In contrast with his first prayer of fear, the king now bows in the presence of God with a trust that gives us a model for prayer.

EXALTING THE CHARACTER OF GOD (37:14–16)

A full course in theology is contained in Hezekiah's opening exaltation of the character of God (v. 16). No contrast in Isaiah's prophecy is more pronounced than the difference between Hezekiah's earlier prayer of fear and his present prayer of trust. In his prayer of fear, he began with the trouble of his people, the rebuke of his kingship, and blasphemy against his God (37:3). None of this is mentioned in the opening of his prayer of trust. The center of attention has shifted from his problems to God's character. *"O LORD of hosts"* is the exaltation of God in His omnipotence over all the earth. *"God of Israel"* is the gratitude for the special relationship of God the Father with his chosen family of Israel. *"The One who dwells between (or over) the cherubim"* acknowledges His transcendence over all creatures in heaven and earth. *"You are God, You alone, of all the kingdoms of the earth"* recognizes that He is the sovereign Lord of human history and in control of all human events, including Sennacherib and his ultimatum. *"You have made heaven and earth"* covers any contingency of time and space, person and history. He and He alone is eternal. "All things were made through Him and without Him nothing was made that was made." (John 1:3).

Hezekiah teaches us the first principle of effective prayer—we begin with God's character, not our need. Elihu, the brash young critic of Job in his suffering, set this principle when he said, "But no one says, 'Where is God my Maker, Who gives songs in the night'" (Job 35:10). When Jesus gave us the model for prayer, He applied the same principle. "Our Father in heaven, Hallowed be Your Name" brings us into His presence as worshipers before we are petitioners. God may honor our desperate cry for help as He did in response to Hezekiah's prayer of fear. But emergency aid has no longterm benefits for our relationship with God or for the development of our faith.

Expressing Confidence in God (37:17)

Marked contrast between Hezekiah's prayers continues as he expresses his complete confidence in God's omniscient power to hear and see *"all of the words of Sennacherib, who has sent to reproach the living God"* (v. 17). A second principle of prayer follows naturally from exalting the character of God. Because of His character, we have complete confidence to ask Him to hear and see the cause and the conditions of our plight. But wait. Hezekiah is now more concerned about God's honor than about his own plight. Maturity in prayer has come quickly to the king. Having exalted the character of God in whom he puts his trust, he will not stand by to see His God blasphemed.

Skeptics, of course, will say that self-interest is still Hezekiah's primary motivation and his appeal is to God's self-esteem. Because human motives in prayer are often mixed and seldom pure, it is the priority that counts. Obviously, Hezekiah still has deliverance from Sennacherib in mind, but God's honor now comes first. Jesus struggled with His motives in the Garden of Gethsemane just as we do. His will to live caused Him to ask His Father, "Let this cup pass from Me". But the struggle ended when He set the priority for His prayer in the purpose of God, "Nevertheless, not as I will but as you will" (Matthew 26:39). Give Hezekiah credit for the same commitment. God's honor took precedence over his deliverance. At the same time, his deliverance depended upon God's honor. The two motives are not in conflict.

Objectifying the Dilemma (37:18–19)

Open disclosure of our dilemma is a third principle of effective prayer. God does not object to an honest statement of the facts that confound us. In fact, as Jesus gives us the model in His garden prayer, God the Father invites us to verbalize the issue before Him and confess that we do not have a ready answer. In his earlier prayer, Hezekiah could not speak his fear of the facts that the Rabshakeh had recited about Sennacherib's conquests of other nations and their gods. Now the king acknowledges the truth that the Assyrian kings had literally conquered the world and had *"laid waste all the nations"* (v. 18). But there his fear stops. The gods of those nations are the work of men's hands, made of wood and stone, and subject to destruction. Hezekiah, however, has declared his faith in the "living God," who can neither be created nor destroyed. The facts of history remain, but the greater fact is found in the God of history. In Him—the living God—Hezekiah will put his trust.

MAKING BOLD PETITION (37:20)

Hezekiah's *"Now therefore, O LORD our God"* (v. 20) brings his prayer of trust to its timely and logical conclusion. On the basis of the sovereignty, sensitivity, and supremacy of His God, Hezekiah boldly asks for deliverance from the hand of Sennacherib. Deliverance, however, is not an end in itself. It is a means to the greater end of the glory of God. In that glory, Hezekiah sees the ultimate purpose of God's redemptive plan—*"that all the kingdoms of the earth may know that You are the LORD, You alone"* (v. 20b). All of our petitions in prayer must be framed in the same context and directed toward the same purpose. No petition can be an end in itself. If its answer only satisfies our self-interest and does not bring glory to His name, our prayer is misdirected and our petition is faulty.

So Hezekiah's prayer ends where it began. With the final confession, *"You are the LORD, You alone,"* Hezekiah leaves us with a model of effective prayer based upon trust not fear, and centered in the character of God not upon the crisis of our needs.

GOD'S SECOND ANSWER TO HEZEKIAH (37:21–29)

21 Then Isaiah the son of Amoz sent to Hezekiah, saying, "Thus says the LORD God of Israel,'Because you have prayed to Me against Sennacherib king of Assyria,
22 'this is the word which the LORD has spoken concerning him:

> "The virgin, the daughter of Zion,
> Has despised you,
>> laughed you to scorn;
> The daughter of Jerusalem has shaken her head behind
>> your back!

23 "Whom have you reproached and blasphemed?
Against whom have you raised your voice,

352

And lifted up your eyes on high?
Against the Holy One of Israel.
24 By your servants you have reproached the LORD,
And said, 'By the multitude of my chariots
I have come up to the height of the mountains,
To the limits of Lebanon;
I will cut down its tall cedars
And its choice cypress trees;
I will enter its farthest height,
To its fruitful forest.
25 I have dug and drunk water,
And with the soles of my feet
    I have dried up
All the brooks of defense.'
26 "Did you not hear long ago
How I made it,
From ancient times that I formed it?
Now I have brought it to pass,
That you should be
For crushing fortified cities into heaps of ruins.
27 Therefore their inhabitants had little power;
They were dismayed and confounded;
They were as the grass of the field
And as the green herb,
As the grass on the housetops
And as grain blighted before it is grown.
28 "But I know your dwelling place,
Your going out and your coming in,
And your rage against Me.
29 Because your rage against Me
    and your tumult
Have come up to My ears,
Therefore I will put My hook
    in your nose
And My bridle in your lips,
And I will turn you back
By the way which you came.'"

Isaiah 37:21–29

While Hezekiah prayed, God spoke to Isaiah. Whereas Hezekiah put the crisis with Sennacherib last in his prayer of trust, God puts him first in his answer. The response is so pointed and intense that Isaiah forsakes the prose of the historical record for the poetry of the divine Word. To counter the bombast of Sennacherib's boasting, God sings His own taunting song. Jerusalem is like a virgin who defies a rapist, laughs him to scorn, and wags her head in pity as he slinks away. Sennacherib could not mistake the message. God had taken his challenge and refuted his threat of attack on Jerusalem.

I Heard You (37:21–24a)

God is still in a belligerent mood as He counters Sennacherib's blasphemy with the inferred questions. "Who do you think you are?" and "Who do you think I am?" In reponse, He says, "I know how you have reproached Me, blasphemed My Name, raised your voice against Me, and exalted yourself as God. Your lackeys brought the message."

In addition to blasphemy, Sennacherib is guilty of boasting as if he were God. Demonstrating His omniscience, God goes on to say, "I also know about your boast of superior power in chariots, advanced technology in lumbering, inventiveness in finding water in the desert, and the overwhelming numbers of your ground forces whose feet tramped dry the protective waters of Egypt. If this is the basis for your challenge of Me, I'll meet you on your own ground."

I Made You (37:24b–27)

God meets the arrogance of Sennacherib's blasphemy and boasting in the same way that He confronted the arrogance of Job. As He asked Job the question, "Where were you when I laid the foundations of the earth?" (Job 38:4), so He asks Sennacherib the question, *"Did you not hear long ago, how I made it, from ancient times that I formed it?"* (v. 26). Although Sennacherib demonstrated the arrogance of the wicked and Job the arrogance of the righteous, both had to answer the same question. Standing speechless before their Creator, they had to face the corollary truth: What God creates, He controls. To Job, He put the question, "Can you bind the influence of Pleiades?" and to Sennacherib, the declaration, *"Now I have brought it to pass that you should be . . ."* (v. 26).

The Lord of history has spoken. All of Sennacherib's claims of sovereign power, in crushing cities and conquering nations, become idle boasts before the fact that his power is not inferred by a divine nature, but derived from the sovereign God. As in Romans 13, the power of rulers is ordained by God to wield the sword upon evildoers. All persons in authority, then, must humbly acknowledge the source of their power, the limits of their authority, and the Person to whom they are accountable. Servant-leadership, as modeled by Jesus, follows. But if the person in authority becomes so arrogant as to assume that he or she is the source of power without limits of authority and accountable to no one, the ruler is playing God.

Sennacherib's sin is as old as human history and as new as today's headlines. Arrogance caused Adam and Eve to succumb to Satan's tempting promise to become as wise as God. A senator who uses the power of his position to pad his checkbook, or a priest who uses the authority of his office is molest young boys, is no less guilty. As power increases, arrogance becomes the temptation leading to abuse. Norman Cousins asked Charles Beard to sum up in a sentence what he learned in a lifetime of studying American history. The prominent scholar answered, "Whom the gods would destroy, they first make mad with power." With a drunken sense of power, Sennacherib had sown the seeds of his own destruction.

A fine line divides God's control over human history, including the utilization of pagan instruments of wrath to bring judgment upon sin, and the question of God's participation in evil. "How can God permit evil and still be good?" is the universal question that Job asked in ancient times and Rabbi Kushner asks in modern times in his book *When Bad Things Happen to Good People*.[5] Cynicism answers by limiting the power of God or forgiving Him for evil; faith answers by confessing the paradox of eternal truth and the limited perspective of God's redemptive purpose while declaring with Job, "Though He slay me, yet will I trust Him" (Job 13:15). Isaiah took the course of faith as he dealt with the dilemma. His vision of God included prophecies of punishment for sin upon Judah and the nations of the world, but for the purpose of purging the sin in order to fulfill His promise of redemption with the coming of the Messiah.

I KNOW YOU (37:28)

Having resolved the issue of omnipotence, God puts in another barb that Sennacherib cannot counter. Exercising His omniscience, God tells the pretender to His throne, *"I know your dwelling place, your going out and your coming in, and your rage against Me"* (v. 28). People of faith find great comfort in the promise of the Psalm, "The LORD shall preserve your going out and your coming in from this time forth, and even forevermore" (Psalm 121:8). Sinners have just the opposite reaction. Terror must have struck Sennacherib to learn that God knew precisely where he was, watched every movement, and heard every word he spoke. Furthermore, in current vernacular, God tells him that "He is fed up to the ears with the garbage He has heard." God has had enough!

I CONTROL YOU (37:29)

To back up His Word, God acts. Turning the tables on Sennacherib, He employs language that the tyrant must have spoken often with a sneer on his lips as he plotted his conquests. God says, *"I will put My hook in your nose and My bridle in your lips, and I will turn you back by the way which you came"* (v. 29). When conquered people were deported by forced march to Assyria, hooks were put in their noses and bridles in their lips like the ball and chain or leg irons that are put on convicts in a labor camp. Easily controlled by their captors and permanently marked as slaves, the hook and bridle symbolized their disgrace. Sennacherib's retreat from Jerusalem will be equally forceful. He who prided himself in controlling conquered people as if they were animals is due for the same treatment. His destiny is not in his hands. All of his grandiose plans will fail, and he will be powerless to resist being turned by the hook in his nose and the bit in his lips. To this day, a "hook in the nose" and "a bit in the teeth" are negative collo-quialisms connoting control and submission. No doubt remains. Sennacherib's challenge of God's integrity and sovereignty has come to its conclusion. There is no contest.

GOD'S ANSWER TO HIS PEOPLE (37:30–38)

30 "This shall be a sign to you:
   You shall eat this year such as grows of itself,
   And the second year what springs from the same;
   Also in the third year sow and reap,
   Plant vineyards,
      and eat the fruit of them.

31 And the remnant who have escaped
        of the house of Judah
    Shall again take root downward,
    And bear fruit upward.
32 For out of Jerusalem shall go a remnant,
    And those who escape from Mount Zion.
    The zeal of the LORD of hosts will do this.
33 "Therefore thus says the LORD concerning the king of
        Assyria:
    'He shall not come into this city,
    Nor shoot an arrow there,
    Nor come before it with shield,
    Nor build a siege mound against it.
34 By the way that he came,
    By the same shall he return;
    And he shall not come into this city,'
    Says the LORD.
35 'For I will defend this city, to save it
    For My own sake
        and for My servant David's sake.'"
36 Then the angel of the LORD went out, and killed
in the camp of the Assyrians one hundred and eighty-
five thousand; and when people arose early in the
morning, there were the corpses—all dead.
37 So Sennacherib king of Assyria departed and
went away, returned home, and remained at Nineveh.
38 Now it came to pass, as he was worshiping in
the house of Nisroch his god, that Adrammelech and
Sharezer his sons struck him down with the sword;
and they escaped into the land of Ararat. Then
Esarhaddon his son reigned in his place.

Isaiah 37:30–38

Having addressed the immediate threat of Sennacherib against
Jerusalem, God turns His attention to His people whose morale needs to
be bolstered by an affirmative sign. God chooses a sign that will be
readily understood by the people and will be relevant to their needs.

THE PROMISE OF PEACE (37:30)

Agriculture was the backbone of the economy for the children of

Israel in Judah and Jerusalem. With Sennacherib's army marching across the land, they lost their livelihood and with his army camped at the gates of Jerusalem, their food supply diminished. The Rabshakeh had seen their plight and promised them the peace that would permit them to eat their own fruit and drink their own water if they would surrender to Sennacherib. He also promised them a fertile land of bread and wine just like their own in Assyrian exile. God counters these false promises with a promise of His own for hungry and thirsty people of an agricultural nation. His promise is to give them the peace that will permit them to return to normal life. During wartime, the agricultural cycle of sowing and reaping is broken because sowers in fields located outside the city walls are vulnerable to attack by marauding armies and reapers are in danger of losing their harvest to enemy forces. Peace is needed first, produce will follow.

God promises less to His people than Sennacherib. Realistically, He says that His sign of peace carries with it the promise of a return to the normal cycle of sowing and planting over a period of three years or planting seasons. In the first year, the people will eat only the fruit that seeds itself either naturally or from past sowings. The second year will be a bit better, but still limited to the harvest from the process of self-seeding according to the laws of nature. Not until the third year will the normal cycle of sowing and reaping, planting and eating, be restored. In other words, God promises His children the miracle of peace, but not the miracle of planting. As a test of their continuing trust in Him, the people of Jerusalem will have to let nature take its course in the recovery of their productive land.

Signs from God are often a mixture of supernatural intervention, natural processes, and human faith. In the promise of sign, God says, "I'll do My share and you do yours. Trust Me." In truth, the conditions of such a promise show His faith in us and His respect for our human dignity. If He covered every contingency by supernatural intervention, continuing faith would not be needed and there would be nothing for us to do. But we can be assured, God will give us what we need most, even if it takes a miracle. For the people of Jerusalem, their primary need was peace and God took care of that.

The Promise of Posterity (37:31–32)

Along with the promise of peace, God also reaffirms His promise that, whatever the circumstances, there will always be a remnant from Jerusalem to *"take root downward, and bear fruit upward"* (v. 31). In these words, the people of Jerusalem would again hear God speaking to their forefather, Abraham, ". . . in blessing I will bless you, and in multiplying I will multiply your descendants as the stars of the heaven and as the sand which is on the seashore; and your descendants shall possess the gate of their enemies. In your seed all the nations of the earth shall be blessed, because you have obeyed My voice" (Genesis 22:17–18). To the promise of peace is added the promise of posterity.

The Promise of Deliverance (37:33–35)

Coming full cycle in His promises, God assures the people of Jerusalem that they will be delivered from Sennacherib. He had already told the king that He would put a hook in his nose and a bit in his lip to turn him away from the city and head him back home. Now, to His children God details the miraculous promise. With a special touch of love, God says, *"He shall not come into this city"* (v. 33). In fact, he will not shoot one arrow, posture with one shield, or build one mound for his siege machines. Instead, by his retreat and return to Assyria, *"I will defend this city, to save it for My own sake and for My servant David's sake"* (v. 35). Notably, God does not directly say that He will defend and save Jerusalem for the sake of its people. Nothing they have done merits their defense or deliverance. But for the sake of God's redemptive purpose and for the sake of the lineage of David through whom the Messiah will come, the people will be the beneficiaries of His grace. In the capsule of a single sentence, we see our own salvation.

The Proof of the Promise (37:36–38)

Isaiah returns to writing in prose as he reports the results of a historical happening. Some scholars dispute the historical accuracy of the way in which the Assyrians were killed and the number of the casualties. Some account for the slaughter by the fast-moving bubonic plague known to have been a problem of those times. Others refer to Herodotus, the ancient historian, who reported that an army of mice who were carriers of the bubonic plague also ate the gut of the bowstrings of the Assyrians and left them either dead or unarmed (2 Kings 19:35–37). However, it is almost an exact word-for-word confirmation of Isaiah's report. Scholars then debate whether Isaiah and the author of Kings had a common source or if one preceded the other. We leave those questions for critical commentaries and accept the fact that Scriptures, the writings of Herodotus, and the annals of Sennacherib confirm the essential elements of Isaiah's report—the mysterious retreat of Sennacherib from the gates of Jerusalem, never to mount another attack against the city, and death in disgrace at the hands of his own sons. From a hook in the nose to a sword in the back, Sennacherib serves as fair warning to all pretenders for the power of God and all competitors for His name.

NOTES

1. R. Fisher and W. Ury, with B. Patton, ed., *Getting to Yes* (New York: Penguin Books, 1983), 17 ff.

2. Ibid., 97 ff.

3. Ibid.

4. E. Trueblood, *Abraham Lincoln: Theologian of American Anguish* (New York: Harper & Row, 1973), 43–44.

5. H. S. Kushner, *When Bad Things Happen to Good People* (New York: Schocken Books, 1971).

CHAPTER SEVENTEEN

Hezekiah's Tombstone Test

Isaiah 38–39

Isaiah's historical interlude continues with the story of Hezekiah's fatal illness and miraculous healing. "In those days" implies a sequence of time either during the confrontation with Sennacherib or after his retreat from the gates of Jerusalem. Biblical scholars find it difficult to put exact dates on the events, especially in relationship to the length of Hezekiah's reign, the addition of fifteen years to his life, and the time of Sennacherib's threat against Jerusalem. "In those days" may mean that Hezekiah's healing took place around the same time, within the same time, or after the same time, as the events of the previous chapter. Our choice is to place Hezekiah's healing during the time of his confrontation with Sennacherib because God's response to Hezekiah's prayer includes His promise that He will deliver Jerusalem from the king of Assyria and defend the city (38:6). Even then, the message of Isaiah cannot be lost in historical details. Whatever the prophet writes has a purpose. Our task is to discover his purpose and communicate his vision as the Spirit of God may lead us.

HEZEKIAH'S HEALING (38:1–8)

1 In those days Hezekiah was sick and near death. And Isaiah the prophet, the son of Amoz, went to him and said to him, "Thus says the LORD: 'Set your house in order, for you shall die and not live.'"

2 Then Hezekiah turned his face toward the wall, and prayed to the LORD,

3 and said, "Remember now, O LORD, I pray,

how I have walked before You in truth and with a loyal heart, and have done what is good in Your sight." And Hezekiah wept bitterly.

4 Then the word of the LORD came to Isaiah, saying,

5 "Go and say to Hezekiah, 'Thus says the LORD, the God of David your father: "I have heard your prayer, I have seen your tears; and I will add to your days fifteen years.

6 "I will deliver you and this city from the hand of the king of Assyria, and I will defend this city."'

7 "And this is the sign to you from the LORD, that the LORD will do this thing which He has spoken:

8 "Behold, I will bring the shadow on the sundial, which has gone down with the sun on the sundial of Ahaz, ten degrees backward." So the sun returned ten degrees on the dial by which it had gone down.

Isaiah 38:1–8

A SICKNESS UNTO DEATH (38:1)

God continues to communicate with Hezekiah through Isaiah. To date, all of the communication has been positive and promising. But truth also has its negative side. Isaiah must have been reluctant to carry God's latest message to the king when he needed a word of comfort and hope. *"Set your house in order, for you shall die and not live"* is a brutal approach for a pastoral visit to a dying parishioner. On the other hand, it is a fair approach because it permits the person to prepare for death by taking care of unfinished business—both temporal and eternal. As the king of Judah without a son to assume the throne, Hezekiah had special responsibilities. "Set your house in order" may also be translated "Give your last orders" with the thought of transition in mind. At the age of thirty-nine, Hezekiah basked in the prime of life. As with us at that age, he looked forward to a family and a future. Little thought had been given to the consequences of an early death for either himself or his kingdom. Isaiah's message must have come like a doctor's sobering word, "You have only a few days to live, do whatever you need to do."

A Prayer of Bitterness (38:2–3)

Hezekiah reacted to Isaiah's message as we would react. Facing death, he turned away from people to be alone with his God and to pray. As Kubler-Ross discovered in her study of *Death and Dying*, Hezekiah reacted with a mingling of bargaining and anger.[1] With the hope of saving his life, he bargained with God on his character, his motives and his deeds. Without bragging about his character, Hezekiah could say *"I have walked before You in truth."* Asking God to remember their relationship, he added to the quality of his walk in life, *"a loyal heart."* Daring, then, to stand accountable for his deeds as king, Hezekiah reminded God that he had *"done what is good in Your sight."* In one short sentence prayer, we see Hezekiah as the model of righteousness, obedience, and justice—the qualities of leadership that Isaiah preached. Moreover, in the spiritual lineage of David, we see him as "a man after God's own heart."

Few of us could ask God to remember our righteousness, our obedience, and our good works. More likely, we would want to invoke the words on a motel sign in Indianapolis, Indiana, which read, "For some of us, a clear conscience is a short memory." At the time of death, we want God to forget our character, our motives, and our deeds. We also know that the word of imminent death "wonderfully clears the mind." As our past life passes in front of our eyes, the hindsight is 20-20. We see what we failed to do and remember what we tried to forget. So when Hezekiah turned his face to the wall, saw his relatively short life pass before his eyes, and still asked God to remember his righteousness, loyalty, and goodness, we see why one translation describes him as "perfect in heart." As far as he knew, no shadow of sin separated him from his God. Like Job shouting his questions to the wind from atop the ashheap, Hezekiah's honest and open relationship with God permitted him the inferred questions, Why me? Why this? Why now?

With equal honesty, Hezekiah *"wept bitterly."* Tears of anger are as natural to our humanity as the terms of bargaining when we face death. At the prime of life with a desire to live, the king vents his anger through bitter tears and against the vicissitudes of life that reveal his mortality and cut short his life. Each of us who has had the scare of terminal disease knows how Hezekiah felt. A false signal on a blood test caused the doctor to call me and speak in morbid tones, "I need to see you in my office." An escalated PSA count indicated prostate cancer. With the ominous sound of the doctor's voice echoing through my mind, I went home to sleepless nights and troubled days awaiting a biopsy. Questions of life and death obsessed me. With Hezekiah, I found solitude and prayer to be the vehicles through which I asked God the question *why* and shed tears of grief and anger. Also, like Hezekiah, I dared not ask for life. Peace came only after the weeping stopped and the question *why* received the answer, "Not my will, but Thine be done." Whatever the results of the biopsy, I was ready.

Hezekiah's brief prayer and bitter tears went straight to the heart of God. Before Isaiah even leaves the palace (2 Kings 20:4), the Lord comes to him with instructions to return to Hezekiah with the word of answered prayer. Although Hezekiah asks nothing of the Lord, he receives a fivefold answer. God says,

> I have heard your prayer,
> I have seen your tears;
> I will add to your days fifteen years.
> And I will deliver you and this city from
> the hand of the king of Assyria,
> And I will defend this city.
>
> *Isaiah 38:5–6*

God's generous response is characteristic of His grace. Ruth Graham once told me about her study of the Psalms. She took a sheet and drew a line down the middle. In the left-hand column she wrote down all of the things that God expects of us in each of the Psalms she analyzed. In the right-hand column she listed all of the things that we can expect from God according to the same Psalm. When she finished, she said that she could hardly believe her eyes. A very short list in the left-hand column was matched by a very long list in the right-hand column. Ruth said, "I saw how little God expects of us and how much we can expect of Him."

Hezekiah not only got far more from God than he expected, but the Lord gave him a miraculous sign to affirm His word. Not by coincidence, God directed him to look out his window at the sundial of Ahaz and, according to 2 Kings 20:9, gave him the alternative of seeing the shadow go forward ten degrees or backward ten degrees. Hezekiah answered, "It is an easy thing for the shadow to go down ten degrees; no, but let the shadow go backward ten degrees" (2 Kings 20:10). When Isaiah brought the king's choice to the Lord, He did just as He promised: the shadow moved backward ten degrees (Isaiah 38:8 and 2 Kings 20:11).

How this happened is a matter of never-ending conjecture and debate for both biblical scholars and physical scientists. As with all events of supernatural intervention, the miracle cannot be explained by natural law. Isaiah would find more meaningful discussion in the symbol of Ahaz' sundial. Years earlier, God had offered Ahaz a sign of trust that the king rejected because he had already decided to enter into an alliance with Assyria. Still, God gave him the sign of Immanuel—God with us—as the only hope for deliverance from future bondage to Assyria, the consequence of his sin (7:14–17). As we know, following that event, Ahaz travelled to Damascus to court the favor of the king of Assyria. While there, he became enamored with the idolatry of Assyria and brought back the plans for remodeling the temple in Jerusalem to accommodate altars and sacrifices to false gods. The sundial too, a recent invention unique to Assyria, might well have been among his souvenirs in the palace courtyard. If so, God's choice of Ahaz' sundial to give a sign to Hezekiah is another direct refutation of Sennacherib's power and Assyrian idolatry. As proof of His promise, the Lord who created and controls all things in the universe, marched the shadow of the obelisk ten degrees backwards on the dial (v. 8).

The Song of Healing (38:9–20)

9 This is the writing of Hezekiah king of Judah, when he had been sick and had recovered from his sickness:
10 I said,
In the prime of my life
I shall go to the gates of Sheol;
I am deprived of the remainder of my years."
11 I said,

"I shall not see YAH,
The LORD in the land of the living;
I shall observe man no more among the inhabitants of
    the world.

12 My life span is gone,
Taken from me like a shepherd's tent;
I have cut off my life like a weaver.
He cuts me off from the loom;
From day until night
    You make an end of me.

13 I have considered until morning—
Like a lion,
So He breaks all my bones;
From day until night
    You make an end of me.

14 Like a crane or a swallow,
    so I chattered;
I mourned like a dove;
My eyes fail from looking upward.
O LORD, I am oppressed;
Undertake for me!

15 "What shall I say?
He has both spoken to me,
And He Himself has done it.
I shall walk carefully all my years
In the bitterness of my soul.

16 O LORD, by these things men live;
And in all these things is the life of my spirit;
So You will restore me
    and make me live.

17 Indeed it was for my own peace
That I had great bitterness;
But You have lovingly delivered my
    soul from the pit of corruption,
For You have cast all my sins behind Your back.

18 For Sheol cannot thank You,
Death cannot praise You;
Those who go down to the pit cannot hope for Your
    truth.

19 The living, the living man,
    he shall praise You,
As I do this day;

> The father shall make known Your truth to the chil-
> dren.
> 20 "The LORD was ready to save me;
> Therefore we will sing my songs with stringed instru-
> ments
> All the days of our life,
> in the house of the LORD."
>
> *Isaiah 38:9–20*

Our admiration for Hezekiah grows as we learn of his gifts as well as his goodness. To express his gratitude to God for his healing, the king writes a psalm and composes a song. We should not be surprised. At the beginning of his reign when he cleansed the temple of idols and restored true worship to the sanctuary, he brought the sound of music:

> And when the burnt offering began, the song of the LORD also began, with the trumpets and the instruments of David, king of Israel. So all the congregation worshiped, the singers sang, and the trumpeters sounded; all this continued until the burnt offering was finished.
>
> *2 Chronicles 29:27–28*

Not only was Hezekiah a lover of song; he was a collector of poetry. Proverbs 25:1 reads, "These also are the proverbs of Solomon which the men of Hezekiah king of Judah copied." Critics who argue that Hezekiah could not have been the author of the song or that it is misplaced in Isaiah's writing are woefully wrong. The writing is consistent with the interest of the king and necessary to his complete healing.

Hezekiah suffered from physical illness and emotional bitterness. Both of these ailments needed the healing touch of God. Hospital chaplains know the need for total healing among patients who are physically sick. More often than not, emotional healing precedes and completes physical healing. Once the patient resolves the feelings of bitterness, the body relaxes and responds to medical treatment. As a former hospital chaplain, then, I read Hezekiah's psalm as an essential part of his healing. By verbalizing the thoughts and feelings behind his bitter weeping, he objectifies the experience and gains the perspective that leads to his song of praise.

Recalling his initial reaction to the news of his imminent death, Hezekiah asked the honest question, *why*. We identify with him when he asks, "Why, in the prime of my life, should I be destined to die, consigned to the shadows of Sheol, and lose the remainder of my productive years?" His bitterness has a base. All who love God and people will also understand his second question, "Why should I be condemned to die and lose my relationship with YAH (the LORD) and my fellowship with other human beings?" God's revelation had not yet progressed to the concept of heaven with its promise of continuing fellowship with God and other human beings. Sheol lurked in Hezekiah's mind as a place, not of punishment or bliss but as a land of shadowy creatures and ambiguous relationships. Only in the land of the living did he have the assurance of communion with God and other people.

HEZEKIAH'S FEELINGS (38:12)

Equal honesty prompts Hezekiah to describe his feelings after Isaiah had told him to "Set your house in order, for you shall die and not live" (38:1). His poetic gift comes forward in the metaphors of the shepherd's tent and the weaver's loom, vehicles of communication with which all of his hearers would understand as thoroughly and feel as deeply as he did. Obviously, the brevity of his life span is the major cause of his bitterness. Not only would death take away from him the productive years of his kingship and the fruitful results of his religious reforms, but he would be deprived of the opportunity to bear a son to succeed him. For a king in the lineage of David, all other accomplishments paled before the desire to continue the seed of Jesse through a son who would also be a forefather to the Messiah.

The temporary nature of a shepherd's tent, then, conveys Hezekiah's feelings about the brevity and uncertainty of his life. As the tent is staked down for a night or two and then pulled up to move on, Hezekiah feels as if his life is equally temporal and uncertain. Matching the shepherd's tent is the weaver's loom. In weaving a cloth on a loom, the weaver has sole discretion for the decision to stop the process and cut the cloth. Hezekiah feels as if God, the weaver, has cut him off from life without warning and before the design is complete.

All who suffer ask the same question of God. "Why now?" is the corollary to "Why me?" when we face death. Whether young or old, death is never timely. Young people feel as if the weaver has cut the cloth too early, and many old people do not understand why the cloth is still being woven after the design seems to be knotted and snarled.

HEZEKIAH'S REACTIONS (38:13–14a)

Honesty continues to characterize Hezekiah's psalm as he reaches deep within his soul to recall his reaction to God's message that he would die from his illness in the prime of life. Three analogies come to mind as he recalls working through his bitterness: the roar of a lion, the chattering of a crane or swallow, and the mourning of a dove. The analogies match three steps in the grieving process. A lion's roar is the voice of anger that is the first natural reaction to the word of death. Behind the question "Why me?" there is the implied cry, "This is unfair!" The cry may be directed outwardly toward God, turned inwardly upon ourselves, or shouted to the winds. Hezekiah describes the pain behind his roar as the feeling of having his bones crushed by God. He and Job could have compared notes. From the depth of his suffering, Job cried out, "I was at ease, but He has shattered me; He also has taken me by the neck, and shaken me to pieces" (Job 16:12). In this case, God becomes the lion rather than the victim, but the thought is the same. Hezekiah too sees the God before whom he is righteous as the oppressor who has crushed the life out of him.

After the initial roar of anger, Hezekiah says that he chattered like a bird. Most likely, his chatter represented his attempt to negotiate a compromise with God. Who has not bargained with God when we get into trouble? Out of our pain we chatter, "God, if you will just give me one more chance, I'll do whatever You want." While we do not know the content of Hezekiah's chatter, his confession tells us how his honesty with God helped him toward healing.

After the roar of bitter anger and the chattering of useless bargaining, Hezekiah accepts the news of imminent death like the mourning of a dove. His honesty and realism impress us again. No matter how accepting we become of our suffering, there is still grief in the soul. In the cooing of a dove, we hear peace and pathos mingled in one

369

sound. Anyone who has a lain on a bed of pain for a long period of time and reached the point where only moaning can express the depths of suffering, knows how Hezekiah felt and why he responded as he did.

HEZEKIAH'S PRAYER (38:14b)

While not blaming God as the cause of his early death, Hezekiah knows that his Creator and his Lord has control over his destiny. Again, like Job, he demonstrates the maturity of his faith by praying for help to the One who oppresses him. All of the confidence of a long-term relationship between Job and God is expressed in the words, "But He knows the way that I take; when He has tested me, I shall come forth as gold" (Job 23:10). Hezekiah conveys the same confidence when he prays, *"O LORD, I am oppressed; Undertake for me!"* At one and the same time, it is a prayer of desperation and faith.

HOW THEN SHALL I LIVE? (38:15–20)

Pain is one of our most effective teachers. Yet many people fail to learn the lessons that pain teaches. Firm resolutions, made during the height of pain, quickly disappear with healing. As a hospital chaplain on the surgery floor of a university medical center, I learned why the senior chaplain rather skeptically told me that every surgery patient wants to become a Christian on the day after their operation. The aftershock of surgery on the body is so great that the patient is convinced that he or she is doomed to die. On the third day, however, the pain subsides as the body adjusts. The desire to live replaces the desire to die and the patient forgets the deathbed vows made the day before.

Hezekiah's spiritual maturity is again credited by his question, "What shall I say?" or, in paraphrase, "What have I learned?" His mental and physical suffering is not forgotten as he goes through the lessons he learned from the experience of suffering. In effect, he answers his own questions, Why me?, Why this?, and Why now?

I will Walk Carefully in Your Sight (38:15)

A new perspective of life is implied in Hezekiah's statement, *"I shall walk carefully all my years in the bitterness of my soul."* He is not saying that he continues to be bitter and in anguish. Rather, he says that the experience has taught him to see life from the perspective of its pain as well as its prosperity. Recognizing that life is brief, Hezekiah has learned the same lesson that Paul taught to the Ephesians: "Walk circumspectly, not as fools but as wise" (Ephesians 5:15). He means that a wise person walks with full awareness of the surroundings and stays on course toward the destination. Hezekiah has learned that lesson from his brush with death. From now on, he will weigh the consequences of his conduct against the framework of his mortality and his accountability to God. At thirty-nine, he had learned a lesson that many do not learn until their later years.

Hezekiah's words can also be translated, "I will walk slowly all my years." He must have been a Type A personality whom pain had slowed down. After his retirement, my father sent me a copy of the prayer that he thought I needed. Appropriately, it is entitled "Slow Me Down, Lord."

> Slow me down, Lord. Ease the pounding of my heart by the quieting of my mind.
> Steady my hurried pace with the vision of the eternal reach of time.
> Give me amid the confusion of the day the calmness of the everlasting hills.
> Break the tensions of my nerves and muscles with the soothing music of the singing streams that live in my memory,
> Help me to know the magical restoring power of sleep.
> Teach me the art of taking minute vacations, of slowing down to look at a flower, to chat with a friend, to pat a dog, to read a few lines from a good book.
> Slow me down, Lord, and inspire me to send my roots deep into the soil of life's enduring values that I may grow toward the stars of my greater destiny.
>
> *Kris Tone*

Living life in the perspective of our mortality sharpens us up and slows us down.

I will Live Dependent upon Your Power (38:16)

Healthy and prosperous people, especially kings, find it easy to take life for granted. Hezekiah realized that he had fallen into this trap. But now, he knows that he is dependent upon the power of God as the source of life for each breath he takes. In a very real sense, he has learned the lesson of living on borrowed time. His power as a king does not include control over the length of his life or the time of his death. As with all other humans, he is dependent upon God for the power that restored him to life and sustains him in life. Never again will Hezekiah take his life for granted.

I will Live Forgiven by Your Grace (38:17)

Hezekiah's learning experiences include the insight that he had gone through the shock of a death sentence for his own good. *"Indeed it was for my peace that I had great bitterness."* While parents often tell their children when they punish them, "I'm doing this for your own good," none of us likes to admit that pain has benefits. Even when the Word says, "whom the LORD loves he chastens" (Hebrews 12:6), our human nature resists the thought. Hezekiah, however, has learned that behind his bitter experience there was the love of God for his own good. He admits that the experience stopped him in his tracks and delivered his soul from the pit of corruption. Without knowing the circumstances, we can guess that the temptations to corruption that come to a king may have reached the point where Hezekiah could have been overwhelmed.

Besides being delivered from the pit of corruption, Hezekiah sees the love of God at work through the bitter experience to cast all of his sins behind the back of God (38:17b). With advanced insight into the meaning of grace, Hezekiah confesses that he is not as righteous as he first professed (38:3) and has learned the meaning of forgiveness through his bitter experience. The maturity of his thought is evident in his recognition that the forgiveness of sins is an act of God and, once forgiven, they are cast behind His back, out of sight, and gone forever.

I will Sing Always in Your Presence (38:18–20)

Still within his limited concept of life after death, Hezekiah sees his added fifteen years as a gift of time to praise God, an opportunity that he would have lost if he had died and gone to Sheol. With the psalmist he will sing, "This is the day which the LORD has made; we will rejoice and be glad in it" (Psalm 118:24). Moreover, he will pass on his spirit of praise to the children of future generations as he teaches them the truth. Hidden in these words is the hope that he will still be able to beget a son to succeed him as king and carry on the lineage of David.

Hezekiah's personal joy in song will be complemented by his leadership for his people. As the one who brought back musical instruments and joyful song to worship in the temple, the king now adds the fact that he will compose songs of praise to God that he will sing with his people *all the days of our life, in the house of the LORD*" (v. 20).

As a person whose religious heritage is in the Wesleyan tradition, I find Hezekiah's commitment to lead his people in joyful songs especially meaningful. For him to become a songwriter, however, is even more important. Paul Amos, Chairman of the Board of American Family Life Insurance Company in Columbus, Georgia, presided at a Christian Leadership Conference where I spoke. After welcoming the three hundred or more guests to a gala banquet that keynoted the Conference, he said, "I have a song I want to sing. It is my song." Although Paul does not have a trained voice, a hush settled over the hall as he sang, "I am satisfied with Jesus. Is He is satisfied with me?" Later on, an accomplished soloist sang and I spoke. But if you ask any person who attended the banquet that evening, he or she would not remember her songs or my speech. The unforgettable moment came when Paul Amos sang his song. Since that time I have asked people, "What is your song?" Invariably, they will have an answer that sums up their own spiritual experience and gives praise to God. To sing "All the days of our life, in the house of the LORD," is a beautiful lesson that we can share with Hezekiah, especially if we have written our own song out of our suffering.

On the note of song, the spirit of Hezekiah is healed. Isaiah now inserts a word on the final step in his healing. Ordering Hezekiah's aides to take a lump of figs, and apply it as poultice on the boil, the prophet pronounces his recovery and Hezekiah asks for the sign of his recovery so that he can fulfill his vow to make his sacrifice and sing his song in the house of the LORD. Second Kings 20:5 puts these events in the sequence preceding the backward movement of the shadow on Ahaz' sundial.

Isaiah may have had another reason for inserting this event at the end of his report on Hezekiah's healing. The poultice on the boil is the final sign of physical recovery and follows the healing of mind and spirit of which Hezekiah sang. Wherever the verses should be placed in sequence, the message is the same: Hezekiah's death sentence brought him face to face with his own mortality, his healing involved body, mind and spirit, and his experience taught him the joy of living by the grace of God.

HEZEKIAH'S LEGACY TO THE FUTURE (39:1–8)

1 At that time Merodach-Baladan the son of Baladan, king of Babylon, sent letters and a present to Hezekiah, for he heard that he had been sick and had recovered.

2 And Hezekiah was pleased with them, and showed them the house of his treasures—the silver and gold, the spices and precious ointment, and all his armory—all that was found among his treasures. There was nothing in his house or in all his dominion that Hezekiah did not show them.

3 Then Isaiah the prophet went to King Hezekiah, and said to him, "What did these men say, and from where did they come to you?" And Hezekiah said, "They came to me from a far country, from Babylon."

4 And he said, "What have they seen in your house?" So Hezekiah answered, "They have seen all that is in my house; there is nothing among my treasures that I have not shown them."

5 Then Isaiah said to Hezekiah, "Hear the word of the LORD of hosts:

6 'Behold, the days are coming when all that is in your house, and what your fathers have accumulated until this day, shall be carried to Babylon; nothing shall be left,' says the LORD.

7 'And they shall take away some of your sons who will descend from you, whom you will beget; and they shall be eunuchs in the palace of the king of Babylon.'"

> 8 Then Hezekiah said to Isaiah, "The word of the
> LORD which you have spoken is good!" For he said,
> "At least there will be peace and truth in my days."
>
> *Isaiah 39:1–2*

To this point in time, everything we know about Hezekiah is highly commendable. As soon as he became king, he instituted sweeping religious reforms. Tearing down the pagan idols and altars of his father Ahaz, Hezekiah restored spiritual worship to the Holy One of Israel. When he faced the crisis of the Assyrian threat against Jerusalem, he defied Sennacherib and trusted God for deliverance. By his own testimony, he walked in truth before the Lord, followed him with a loyal heart, and did good deeds in God's sight. His highest commendation, however, came from God Himself. When Hezekiah suffered under the sentence of death from a fatal illness, God heard his prayer, saw his tears, and extended his life fifteen years. For those who listened to Isaiah's prophecies and waited for the Messiah, Hezekiah might have been a candidate.

Isaiah had another lesson to teach the children of Israel. Just as he warned them against putting their trust in any power other than God, he now warns them not to put their trust in any person other than God. The reasons are clearly spelled out for us in chapters 38 and 39. Hezekiah's encounter with death, coupled with the reprieve from God, introduced us to his mortality (ch. 38). Now his seduction by the Babylonians shows us his fallibility.

HEZEKIAH'S RESPONSE TO FLATTERY (39:1–2)

What Assyria's threat could not do, Babylon's temptation did. Flattery proved to be the flaw in Hezekiah's moral makeup. Following Hezekiah's miraculous healing from mortal illness, the wily king of Babylon, Merodach-Baladan, sent him a letter and a present under the pretense of congratulating him on his recovery. Hezekiah should have known that the king of the rising kingdom of Babylon would not pay attention to his small nation without an ulterior motive. Most likely Merodach-Baladan had heard of Sennacherib's retreat from Jerusalem and wished to form an alliance with Hezekiah in rebellion against the Assyrians. Perhaps he had also heard how Sennacherib's letter of threat failed, so he chose the tactic of a letter of greeting and a gift to soften up Hezekiah. It worked. Like a poor boy coming to riches, the king of little Judah succumbed to the flattery given him by the king of mighty Babylon.

Once Hezekiah's weakness for recognition had been exposed, the minor flaw became a major fault. With naiveté bordering on stupidity, he opened all of the wealth of his treasure house, his armory, and his storehouses and showcased them for Merodach-Baladan's delegation. Without a doubt, the lustful eyes of the Babylonians saw only the potential for conquest.

The seduction of Hezekiah by flattery prefigures the temptations that Jesus faced. In the wilderness, Satan offered him the wealth, power, and glory of all the kingdoms of the world if Jesus would bow down and worship him. Later, the masses came after him with a robe and crown to make him king. Still later the Greeks, representing the intellectual elite of the world, curried His favor with the request for an audience. In each of these attempts to trap Jesus by flattery, He refused to take the bait.

We applaud Jesus, and yet we can identify with Hezekiah. As redeemed people earnestly seeking to live in obedience to God's will, we are constantly under Satan's attack. When he roars like a lion, we can fight back, but when he coos like a dove, our guard goes down. Flattery is Satan's most effective weapon. As with Hezekiah, we are particularly vulnerable to the adulation of the world. During our time, we have witnessed evangelical Christianity move from a beleaguered religious minority to a visible political power. Not long ago, a few evangelical Christians made the guest list for a White House visit. Today, whether the President is a Democrat or a Republican, evangelical Christians must be recognized as a political force. Rather than gloating in newfound glory, evangelicals should read Hezekiah's story and be warned. Trust in God can be undermined by flattery as quickly as it can be overwhelmed by threat.

ISAIAH'S QUESTIONS (39:3–4)

A notable change took place in Hezekiah's mood after he succumbed to Merodach-Baladan's seductive ploy. Under Sennacherib's threat, he sought a word from the Lord through the counsel of Isaiah. But when tempted by Babylon, he acted upon his own. In this moment, he fell into the same pattern of sin that caused the downfall of his father

Ahaz. When they wanted to do their own will, they rejected the Word of the LORD. The lesson is obvious. Whether under threat or flattery, when we want to our own will, the Word of God is the first to go.

Although Isaiah is not summoned by Hezekiah for counsel, he comes to him with three questions, "*What did these men say?*" "*From where did they come?*" and "*What have they seen in your house?*" Hezekiah is not innocent. By ignoring the first question, "What did these men say?" he knows that Isaiah will scold him for letting flattery turn his head from total trust in God. Hoping against hope that he can dazzle Isaiah with his newfound prominence, Hezekiah openly tells him that the men came from Babylon and he showed them "*all that is in my house*" (v. 4).

GOD'S ANSWER (39:5–7)

One of Isaiah's themes throughout his prophecies is to warn that sin carries within itself the seeds of its own destruction. Sennacherib, for instance, has the reputation for deporting the people of conquered nations on a forced march with a hook in their nose and a bit in their lips. God says that He will figuratively do the same to Sennacherib when He turns him back from the gates of Jerusalem and sends him back to Assyria by the way he came (37:29). The same truth is spoken to Hezekiah by Isaiah. Having bragged about his wealth by showing the Babylonians all of his treasures, God informs him that "*all that is in your house, and what your fathers have accumulated until this day, shall be carried to Babylon; nothing shall be left*" (v. 6).

His sin also has consequences for future generations. With the extension of his life, Hezekiah will have the desire of his heart and bear a son, but that son, Manasseh, will not only be wicked and undo the spiritual heritage of his father, but his sons and grandsons will be among the emasculated exiles serving in the courts of Babylon. Isaiah has also repeated his oft-spoken warning given as part of the second commandment in the Law of Moses, "For I, the LORD your God, am a jealous God, visiting the iniquity of the fathers on the children to the third and fourth generations of those who hate Me" (Exodus 20:5). Like the faultline that widens into an earthquake, the flaw of sin in the father will become a fissure of judgment upon his children, grandchildren, and great-grandchildren.

HEZEKIAH'S EPITAPH (39:8)

Scholars are divided over the interpretation of Hezekiah's final words. Does he accept the Word of God as good because it is true? Or does he say it is good because it promises "peace and truth" throughout the remainder of his reign? Although the inflection in Hezekiah's response to God's Word cannot be read in print, it is almost impossible to mistake the sigh of relief in the king when he says, "At least there will be peace and truth in my days." As he forfeited the future of his heirs by showing the Babylonians all of his treasures, so he remained consistent with that short-sighted view by sighing with relief when he learned that he would escape captivity.

By his words, Hezekiah defaulted on greatness. Leaders who leave their problems to the future may be successes in their own time, but failures against the judgment of history. In leadership language, they fail the "Tombstone Test." As sad as it seems, Hezekiah's final words tend to undo a lifetime of good deeds. Like Eliakim, whom Isaiah described as "a peg in a sure place," upon whom all of the glory of the house of Judah and the lineage of David hung, Hezekiah is also remembered as a secure peg that became overloaded by flattery and fell. We would prefer to etch on his tombstone the words "He walked in truth with a loyal heart and did good in the sight of God" (38:3). Personally, we will not take that commendation away from him, but history is a more objective judge. The "Tombstone Test" would have his epitaph read, "At least there will be peace and truth in my days."

As we stand at the end of the historical bridge between Isaiah 1–39 and 40–66, we look back to see Isaiah's vision as oracles of judgment upon Judah and the nations with intermittent promises of deliverance through the coming Messiah. As the final step on that historical bridge, Isaiah has shown us that even the best of kings in the line of David is not good enough. Hezekiah, as good as he was, learned hard lessons about his mortality and his fallibility. With another example of his genius for communicating with his readers by creating a sense of anticipation for things to come, Isaiah leaves us with Hezekiah's forfeiture of Judah's future into Babylonian hands. The prophet's message is not complete. The children of Israel have not yet learned to trust in God. Exile is inevitable and the Messiah is essential. So, for historical sequence and theological integrity, Isaiah must still write his prophecy of hope for the future.

NOTES

1. Elizabeth Kubler-Ross, *On Death and Dying* (London: Tavistock Publications, 1969).

Bibliography

Allis, O. T. *The Unity of Isaiah: A Study in Prophecy*. Philadelphia: Presbyterian and Reformed, 1950.

Alexander, J. A. *Commentary on the Prophecies of Isaiah*. New York: Scribner's, 1846.

Barnes, A. *Notes on Isaiah*. Volume 1. Grand Rapids: Baker, 1980.

Boutflower, C. *The Book of Isaiah Chapters I–XXXIX in Light of the Assyrian Monuments*. London: SPCK, 1930.

Cambridge Ancient History, The. Volume 3. Cambridge: Cambridge University Press, 1929.

Clements, R. E. *Isaiah 1–39*. New Century Bible Commentary. London: Marshall, Morgan & Scott; Grand Rapids, Eerdmans, 1980.

Delitzsch, F. *Biblical Commentary on the Prophecies of Isaiah*. Volume 1. Edinburgh: T. & T. Clark, 1874–1875.

Eissfeldt, O. *The Old Testament, An Introduction*. Tr. P. Ackroyd. New York: Harper & Row, 1965.

Engnell, I. *The Call of Isaiah: An Exegetical and Comparative Study*. UUA 4. Uppsala: Lundequistska, 1949.

Gardiner, A. *Egypt of the Pharaohs: An Introduction*. Oxford: Clarendon Press, 1961.

Gray, G. B. *A Critical and Exegetical Commentary on the Book of Isaiah, I–XXXIX*. Edinburgh: T. & T. Clark, 1912.

Harrison, R. K. *Introduction to the Old Testament*. Grand Rapids: Eerdmans, 1969.

————. *Old Testament Times*. Grand Rapids: Eerdmans, 1970.

Heschel, A. J. *The Prophets*. New York: Harper, 1962.

Jennings, F. C. *Studies in Isaiah*. Neptune, New Jersey: Loizeaux, 1935.

Kaiser, O. *Isaiah 1–12: A Commentary*. Old Testament Library. 2nd ed. Tr. J. Bowden. Philadelphia: Westminster, 1983.

Kaufmann, Y. *The Babylonian Captivity and Deutero-Isaiah*. Tr. C. W. Efroymson. New York: Union of American Hebrew Congregations, 1970.

Kennett, R. H. *The Composition of the Book of Isaiah in the Light of History and Archaeology*. London: Published for the British Academy by H. Frowde, 1910.

Kissane, E. J. *The Book of Isaiah*. Volume 1. Rev. ed. Dublin: Browne & Nolan, Ltd., 1960.

Koch, K. *The Prophets.* Volume 1. Philadelphia: Fortress Press, 1984.

Leupold, H. C. *Exposition of Isaiah*. 2 vols. Grand Rapids: Baker, 1963–1971.

Margalioth, R. *The Indivisible Isaiah: Evidence for the Single Authorship of the Prophetic Book*. New York: Yeshiva University, 1964.

Oswalt, J. *The Book of Isaiah, Chapters 1–39*. The New International Commentary on the Old Testament. Grand Rapids: Eerdmans, 1986.

Saggs, H. W. F. *The Greatness That Was Babylon*. London: Sidgwick & Jackson, 1962.

Scott, R. B. Y. "Introduction and Exegesis of the Book of Isaiah, Chapters 1–39," *The Interpreters Bible*. Volume 3:149–381. V. ed. G. Buttrick, et al. Nashville: Abingdon, 1956.

Seitz, C. R., ed. *Reading and Preaching the Book of Isaiah*. Philadelphia: Fortress Press, 1988.

Skinner, J. *The Book of the Prophet Isaiah*. Volume 1. Rev. ed. Cambridge: Cambridge University Press, 1925.

Smith, G. A. *The Book of Isaiah*. Volume 1. Rev. ed. Expositor's Bible. London: Hadden and Stoughton, 1927.

VanGemeren, W. A. *Interpreting the Prophetic Word*. Grand Rapids: Academie Books, 1990.

Ward, J. M. *Amos and Isaiah: Prophets of the Word of God*. Nashville: Abingdon, 1969.

Watts, J. D. W. *Isaiah 1–33*. Volume 24. Word Biblical Commentary. Waco, Texas: Word Books, 1985.

Young, E. J. *The Book of Isaiah*. Volume 1 and 2. Grand Rapids: Eerdmans, 1964–1972.

————. *Who Wrote Isaiah?* Grand Rapids: Eerdmans, 1958.

DATE DUE

DEMCO, INC. 38-3012